THE MOB

THE HISTORY

OF IRISH GANGSTERS

IN AMERICA

Front cover Design and Maps
James Durney & Brian Durney.

Also by James Durney
Far From The Short Grass.
The Story of Kildare Men in Two World Wars.

Published by James Durney.
Printed by Leinster Leader Ltd. Naas.

Dedicated to the memory of
Kathleen Durney
1940-1989

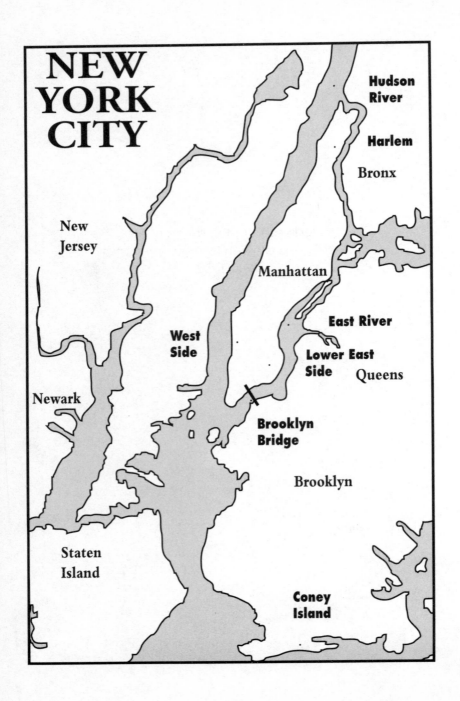

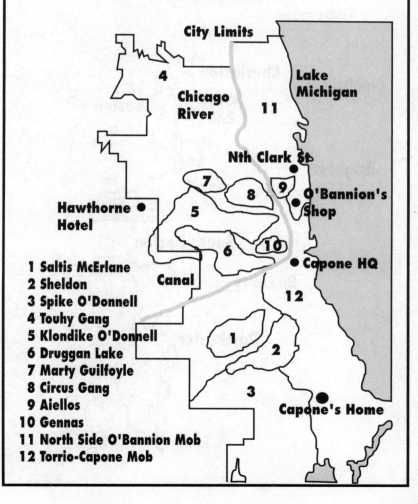

CHICAGO GANGLAND 1920's

City Limits

Lake Michigan

Chicago River

4

11

Nth Clark St

7

8

9

O'Bannion's Shop

Hawthorne Hotel

5

6

10

Capone HQ

Canal

12

1 Saltis McErlane
2 Sheldon
3 Spike O'Donnell
4 Touhy Gang
5 Klondike O'Donnell
6 Druggan Lake
7 Marty Guilfoyle
8 Circus Gang
9 Aiellos
10 Gennas
11 North Side O'Bannion Mob
12 Torrio-Capone Mob

1

2

3

Capone's Home

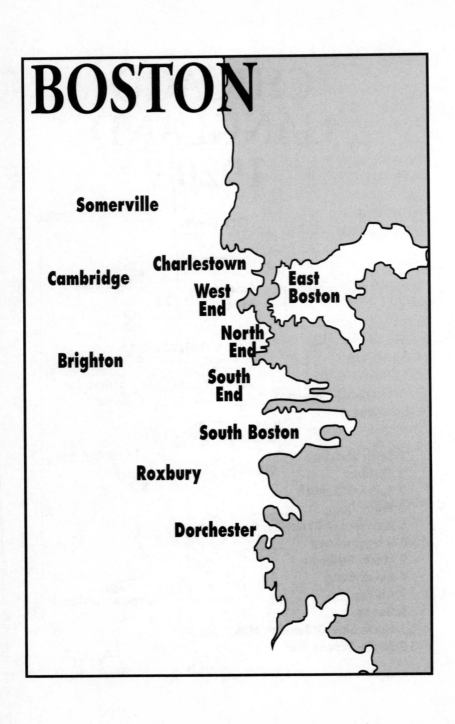

ACKNOWLEDGMENTS

The author wishes to acknowledge all who helped or contributed to this book. Special thanks to Seamus Finn, Declan Furlong, Paul Leeson, Michael McInerney, Tony Ryan, John Lally, Stan Hickey and especially Philip Higgins. Thanks also to Corbis, Hulton/Getty and Associated Press for the kind use of their photographs. Last, but not least, my heartfelt thanks to my wife Caroline and my children Brian and Tara for their love and support which made this possible.

I am also indebted to these highly regarded books:

The Mafia File. The A-Z of Organised Crime in America. Carl Sifakis. New York. 1987.

The World Encyclopedia of Organised Crime. Jay Robert Nash. London. 1992.

The Westies. Inside the Irish Mob. T. J. English. New York. 1990.

Crime Incorporated. The Inside Story of the Mafia's First 100 Years. William Balsamo and George Carpozi Jr. New York. 1988.

Mobster. The Astonishing Rise and Fall of a Mafia Supremo and his Gang. John Cummings and Ernest Volkman. New York. 1990.

How the Irish became White. Robert Ignatiev. New York. 1995.

Mr. Capone. The Real and Complete Story of Al Capone. Robert J. Schoenberg. New York. 1992.

Crime Inc. The Story of Organised Crime. Martin Short. London. 1984.

Contract Killer. William Hoffman and Lake Headley. New York. 1984.

The History of Organised Crime. Howard Abadinsky. New York. 1990.

My Life in the Mafia. Vincent Teresa and Thomas C. Renner. New York. 1972.

Gangland International. The Mafia and Other Mobs. James Morton. London. 1998.

Mad Dog Coll. An Irish Gangster. Brendan Delap. Cork. 1999.

The Bootleggers. The Story of Chicago's Prohibition Era. Kenneth Allsop. London. 1961.

Public Enemies. America's Criminal Past. 1919-1940. William Helmer with Rick Mattix. New York. 1998.

Capone. John Kobler. New York. 1971.

The Boston Irish. A Political History. William H. O'Connor. Boston. 1995.

Tough Guy. Eddie Maloney and William Hoffman. New York. 1995.

Low Life. Lures and Snares of Old New York. Luc Sante. New York. 1991.

The Enemy Within. The McClellan Committee's Crusade Against Jimmy Hoffa and Corrupt Labour Unions. Robert F. Kennedy. New York. 1960.

Mafia Dynasty. The Rise and Fall of the Gambino Crime Family. John H. Davis. New York. 1993.

CONTENTS

FOREWORD

For those who are just vaguely familiar with the American gangster scene (maybe through films, television documentaries or general information on some of the well-known gangsters) James Durney's book will be a revelation.

He leads one through over a century and a half of gangsterism with a particular emphasis on the Irish involvement from just after the famine in Ireland when hundreds of thousands of Irish left for America. Through the American civil war, draft warfare and general rackeetering in the big cities of America many Irish emigrants who had not made it up the social ladder became involved in all the rackets with as much violence as any of the other ethnic gangs to protect their patch. The violence perpetrated by gangs upon one another was quite merciless and left nothing to the imagination.

In a fast-moving narrative the author leads us through all the years in the various cities, naming names and alluding to all the various protection rackets, prostitution, voting irregularities, narcotics, bootlegging during prohibition, union pressure and many others in which the pay-offs were huge sums of money.

Although not many of the gangsters died in their beds, neither did many die in jail – as many witnesses to crimes were unable to attend court for various reasons! By a curious phenomenon of American law some of the gangsters were jailed for not paying taxes on their income which was, of course, obtained from their various criminal activities.

For over a century now we in Ireland have basked in the glory of our American cousins and the struggles of those who "made it" and sent home the money to their relations. However, James Durney's exposé of the other world of the Irish-American gangsters and their exploits will send a chill down the spine of those who were not quite aware of how deeply involved the Irish were in the murky world of violent gangland crime in the major cities of America.

Stan Hickey.

CHAPTER 1

COMING TO AMERICA
IRISH EMIGRATION AND
AMERICAN NATIVISM

Irish emigrants had been coming to America since the discovery of the continent by Christopher Columbus, but it was not until the 19th century that this trickle of emigrants became a flood. Failure of the potato crop - the mainstay of the rural peasant population - led to a severe food shortage. Tens of thousands starved to death and many chose emigration as a way of survival. Between 1840 and 1844 nearly a quarter-of-a-million emigrated to America. Within the next ten years, 1845 to 1855, another one-and-a-half-million Irish emigrants entered the country. They constituted the first large-scale emigration of English speaking non-Protestants to arrive in America. Before their arrival the population was overwhelmingly British and Protestant in heritage and the arrival of large numbers of Irish Catholics filled them with alarm. The Irish were closely followed by large numbers of German emigrants. The Germans were Catholics as well and while they remained in farming the majority of Irish emigrants settled in urban areas.

As it was not customary to have a trade in Ireland the Irish emigrant had no technical skill to offer. They arrived largely ignorant and unskilled to supply a mass of cheap labour for the necessities of urban America; construction workers, street cleaners, police and firemen and service workers of all kinds. They were ready to be exploited by employers, who offered them the cheapest rates. Low pay meant low income housing: cheap, unsanitary hovels with no running water, no air or light. These were appalling conditions, unacceptable to Americans, but these conditions had been endured for generations by the poor in Ireland and were accepted and tolerated by the Irish emigrants. To house the new emigrants new large wooden houses, several stories high, known as "emigrant barracks", were thrown up by speculators and rented out room by room. Old warehouses and cellars were also rented as dwellings. Such habitations not only swarmed with human beings but had within them stores and shops where fruit, vegetables and refreshments - usually spirits - were sold. Unlicensed groggeries and dram shops flourished in these areas and were breeding grounds for crime.

The high hopes of the Irish emigrant were dashed by the terrible reality of the immigrant slums of America. These slums held no comfort for the poor and unfortunate and the Irish drowned their despair in drink and found compensation for their helplessness in violence. United by clannishness and isolated by clannishness from American life the Irish emigrant found expression in street gangs, volunteer fire companies, political clubs centred in grog shops and mob action against non-Irish competitors. Street gangs sprang up in every neighbourhood, reminiscent of secret societies at home; gangs like the Dead Rabbits and Bloody Tubs. They plied their trade - murder, mayhem, extortion and thieving - in the slums and ghettos, every Paddytown in every eastern American city. Their victims were often their own people, or anyone foolish to wander into their territory. The "Irish menace" was the biggest fear of the middle and upper classes - fear of being mugged or murdered or having one's relative dug up by "resurrectionists" and held for ransom.

The poverty, religion and cultural alienation of the Irish emigrant made him an outsider to the older stock of Americans. During the 1830s and 1840s anti-Catholic and ethnic riots occurred in several north-eastern cities with large Irish populations. The worst erupted in 1844 in Philadelphia where battles between "nativists", Irish emigrants and the militia left sixteen dead, scores injured and dozens of buildings, including two churches, burnt down.

"Nativist" political parties had sprung up across the country with the aims of lengthening the period of naturalisation before immigrants could become citizens and vote and restricting public office-holding to native born. This nativism was actually more anti-Catholic than anti-immigrant. Indeed earlier immigrants - especially from the north of Ireland - were among the most violent "Nativist". They brought their anti-Catholic bigotry with them to the New World and were in the vanguard of anti-Catholic riots. (Between 1720 and 1820 a half-million Ulster Presbyterians had arrived in America when the English-speaking population was two-and-a-half-million. They had a lot of influence in the framing of the American Constitution. Once in America they referred to themselves as Irish, that is until the 1840s when the Catholic Irish arrived, when they opted for the name "Scotch-Irish", wishing to disassociate themselves from the unwanted Catholic Irish). As immigration increased so did nativism. Crime and welfare costs soared and nativists attributed these to recent immigrants, especially the Irish, whose arrest rate and share of relief funds were several times their percentage of the population. By 1851 a quarter of the population of New York, Boston, Philadelphia and Baltimore were Irish. Between 1846 and 1853 Cincinnati's crime rate tripled and its murder rate increased seven fold. Boston's expenditures for poor relief rose threefold during the same period. The rise of drunkenness, brawling and crime helped turn temperance reform - again the domain of white Anglo-Saxon Protestants - into a coercive movement aimed at the Irish and German immigrant population where taverns and saloons were centres of social and political life.

Nativist riots and political violence figured more prominently in southern cities than in the north. In Baltimore various gangs, such as the Plug Uglies and Bloody Tubs, became notorious enforcers of Know Nothings dominance at the ballot box. Ethnic political riots were responsible for the deaths of four people in New Orleans, ten in St. Louis, seventeen in Baltimore and twenty-two in Louisville during the 1850s. The early underworld gangs were often more fraternal than criminal and up until the later nineteenth century there was enough of a native-born element to constitute a significant nativist presence.

With the presence of large numbers of enforcers and gangsters working for the various political candidates, America had some of the most violent elections in the world. On June 1 1857 the orderly process of elections in Washington, D.C. was threatened by the arrival from Baltimore of a large number of Plug Uglies and Bloody Tubs, who were determined to seize and control the polling places. Baltimore was a hotbed of subversion and election rigging with local gangs the enforcers of Know Nothings political dominance. (On October 7 1849 the celebrated author, Edgar Alan Poe, died. An alcohol and drug abuser, he was found drunk and delirious outside a saloon in Baltimore. He had been waylaid four days earlier by thugs in the employ of a candidate for local office, plied with liquor and forced to vote repeatedly in the municipal elections.) When

Washington's police were frightened off by the heavily armed mob, the mayor sent out an emergency call for assistance from U.S. Marines stationed at their Headquarters. The two groups confronted one another near 5th and K Streets. Undeterred by the presence of the military the gangsters aimed a cannon at the line of Marines.

At that moment a white-whiskered man in civilian clothes and carrying a gold-headed cane stepped from the onlooking crowd and walked up to the line of thugs. The man was the seventy-four year old Marine Commandant, Brigadier General Archibold Henderson. He stood in front of the cannon's muzzle and spoke calmly to the mob; "Men, you had better think twice before you fire this piece at the Marines."

A thug thrust a pistol at Henderson two feet from his face. The Commandant seized the man and hauled him away to be placed under arrest. A volley of shots aimed at the Marines rang out, and the leathernecks returned a withering hail of answering fire. Dozens of the gangsters were killed and injured in the well aimed Marine reply. Within a few seconds the rioters fell back, then took to their heels and fled.

In the late 1850s nativism abated before the gathering storm of the Civil War and in 1861 middle-class Irish-Americans tried to persuade themselves that the advent of the war had banished bigotry and united Irish and native-born. But, it was not so. Anti-Irish prejudice remained blatant, manifesting itself in the inequitable application in the military draft to working-class Irish wards and the unnecessary, if not intentional, waste of Irish regiments in hopeless combat situations. The draft riots of 1863 destroyed any myth that the Irish and the native-born were on an equal footing. It would be a long time before the Irish would be allowed to forget their part in America's worst ever riot.

Beset by hostility and discrimination the Irishman discovered that he possessed at least one commodity that someone wanted: his vote. Local ward bosses were quick to register the immigrant, get him accommodation and a job and therefore gain his trust and loyalty. In return the immigrant only had to vote for him in every election. Tammany Hall, which had become synonymous with New York's Democratic Party, had a reputation for dispensing favours and social services and quickly gained the loyalty of the Irish immigrant.

Despite nativist and anti-Catholic prejudice in Tammany, the Irish quickly rose to leadership positions and by the turn of the century dominated 'the Hall'. The rough and ready Irishman was a 'natural' for street politics. So too were the street gangs. On election day they were used as 'repeaters' and 'sluggers' who attacked rival campaign workers and intimidated voters. The gangs became the enforcement arm of Tammany, and from the 1850s and into the next century gang activity and political activity were well co-ordinated. In most cities, particularly New York, Chicago, Boston, Philadelphia, St. Louis and Pittsburgh, as the political machine performed services for legitimate business it also did the same for illegal ventures. Boston was frequently characterised in the national press and by nativists as the prime example of a city controlled by a 'political machine', especially when it was under the control of James Michael Curley, who served four terms as mayor and was jailed for mail fraud. For half-a-century, the scandals of 'Curleyism' and 'Fitzgeraldism' (John F. "Honey Fitz" Fitzgerald, father of Rose Fitzgerald Kennedy and maternal grandfather of President John F. Kennedy, was a North End ward boss who became the first Boston-born Irish Catholic to become mayor of the city), had established an image of Boston as a city whose political leaders, almost to a man, were corrupt, criminal and untrustworthy. Some Irish political victories were won by bribery, extortion, blackmail and physical intimidation. In the 1905 mayoral campaign Fitzgerald's opponent, Martin Lomasney, the legendary boss of the West End Ward 8, and his brother Joseph, were shot and wounded. When Honey Fitz won the election there were jobs for all his loyal followers, including Tim Crowley, recently acquitted of the Joe Lomasney shooting, who was appointed Deputy Sealer of Weights and Measures and James Doyle as Superintendent of Streets, a gold mine of patronage for thousands of construction jobs - Doyle had been expelled from the state legislature a year earlier for election fraud. The Irish would dominate Boston politics for over a century right up to the 1990s.

While the Irish dominated the Democratic party the nativists had swung to the Republicans. Reform was usually led by rural Protestant Republican interests. The most successful campaign waged by rural reformers was the banning of alcohol. It was the triumph of the small town over the crime and foreign-born filled city. But the repercussions of this nativist triumph would be felt for a long time as the Volstead Act changed the whole face of organised crime and gave it the strength and stranglehold it still maintains in America today.

CHAPTER 2

TALES OF OLD NEW YORK

New York City, America's biggest and busiest city, was a centre of immense wealth and home to the wealthiest of Americans, like the Vanderbilts and Rockefellers. Nevertheless, it retained some of the features of a frontier town with wooden houses, muddy streets and wild pigs and cattle roaming the city. During the 1840s and early 1850s huge numbers of poor Irish emigrants arrived in the city. By 1850 twenty-six per cent of the population - 133,000 out of 513,000 - had been born in Ireland. These new emigrants settled mainly on the Lower East Side and around the Brooklyn Bridge area. The street gangs of New York had emerged as early as 1825 in the once prosperous, but decaying, Five Points area. This tenement jammed slum spread from Broadway to Canal Street, from the Bowery to Park Row. At its centre was the dreaded Five Points which came together at a wide intersection of Cross, Anthony, Little Water, Orange and Mulberry Streets. Originally built on swampy land the area had become so unhealthy its only residents were poor Irish immigrants and freed black slaves. (Within two decades the black population had been ousted by the

Irish. They moved to Greenwich Village where they were displaced by the Italians. The black community then shifted to the West Side where they were again ousted by the Irish and eventually settled in Harlem.)

With its abundance of saloons, grog shops, dance halls and brothels it was fertile ground for crime. Many gangs sprang up with their own territories - usually centred around a grocery store which doubled as a backroom saloon. Here thugs gathered to plan their next venture. These grog shops produced violent gangs, most of them Irish, with colourful names like the Hibernians, Chichesters, Roach Guards, Forty Thieves, Kerryonians, Plug Uglies and Dead Rabbits. The Plug Uglies and Dead Rabbits were the most vicious of the Five Points gangs. The Plug Uglies were all huge Irishmen (reputedly from Connemara and with a height requirement of six foot) who took their names from high plug hats stuffed with leather and wool which they wore as helmets in street battles. They wore hob-nailed boots and carried clubs, knives, pistols and axes, often stained with the blood of previous victims. In the America of the time the name Plug Ugly became synonymous with thuggery.

The Dead Rabbits were an off-shoot of the original Roach Guards, formed by a disgruntled Roach named "Shang" Allen. The Roach Guards were named after Ted Roach, a liquor dealer who backed them. In the 1830s the Roaches suffered a factional dispute and during the argument a rabbit carcass was thrown into the assemblage of the disgruntled faction. The rabbit was hoisted on a stick and henceforth it became their banner. They were proud of their new name as in the criminal language of the day 'dead' meant best and 'rabbit' a tough guy. When they went into battle they carried a dead rabbit stuck on a pike. Further distancing themselves from their parent body, the Dead Rabbits wore a red stripe down their pants leg while the Roach Guards sported a blue stripe. The Dead Rabbits turned out numerous owners of dives like Shang Allen, Kit Burns and Tommy Hadden and such notable enforcers as Hell-Cat Maggie, who filed her front teeth and wore artificial brass fingernails for tearing and gouging and went on to make an independent career of saloon brawling.

Although the Five Points gangs fought each other regularly they often merged as common allies in pitched battles with the gangs of the nearby Bowery. The equally rough Bowery - it came from the Dutch word *bourie,* which means wide boulevard - spawned its own gangs; Bowery Boys, Atlantic Guards, O'Connell Guards and True Blue Americans. Again mostly Irish, they fought each other but could find common ground in their opposition to all things English. The gangs of the Bowery and Five Points would unite to denounce the British Empire and exploit civil disturbances. Fiercely patriotic, and extremely racist, these gangs showed no reluctance to riot against anything British.

On May 10 1849 long simmering anti-British sentiments flared into a riot outside New York's Astor Palace Opera House. Over 10,000 people, many of them from Irish gangs, surrounded the theatre presenting the British tragedian, William Charles Macready, who was feuding with Edwin Forrest, the popular American actor, appearing at a nearby theatre. The Astor Palace mob turned uglier as the night wore on, chanting "Down with the English hog", hurling stones and charging the militia, who eventually opened fire, killing at least 20 people and wounding about 100.

At the forefront of the Astor Palace mob were the Kerryonians, a Five Points gang formed in 1825 and composed of natives of County Kerry. They preyed exclusively on Englishmen, or those thought to be English, i.e. rich men. Their headquarters was in a grog shop on Centre Street, near

Anthony. While the gangs of the 'Bloody Ould Sixth Ward', which encompassed Five Points, were mostly Irish the Bowery gangs were mixed between Irish and nativist. The Bowery Boys, American Guards and Atlantic Guards were nativist, while the O'Connell Guards and even the True Blue Americans were Irish. While as a matter of course these gangs fought each other it was the use of the gangs by the political parties of the day that made them mortal enemies. The Irish rallied to Tammany Hall and the nativists to the Nativist Party or Know-Nothings.

The Bowery Boys and the Dead Rabbits were the major rivals of the day and clashed regularly on a rise between Mott Street and Broadway known as Bunker Hill. Battles could last for days at a time with the gangs massed along military lines behind piled carts with a steady supply of paving stones, rocks, brick-bats, knives, pistols and sometimes even a cannon. More than once the city had to call out the National Guard or the 27th Militia Regiment to break up the fighting, at which times the gangs would unite to fight a common enemy.

Gang wars between the other gangs were as common. In June 1835 the O'Connell Guards fought for two days against the Atlantic Guards with the fray starting at Grand and Crosby Street and spreading eastward into the Sixth Ward, where the Five Points gangs joined in, fighting impartially against both sides. Both the Irish and nativist gangs sided together in common disputes like the Abolitionist riots of 1833, the general looting after the fire of 1835 and the Astor Palace Riot of 1849. Yet the nativist gangs would assure the co-operation of their neighbours by spreading rumours of an Irish invasion while the Irish could do the same by spreading rumours that the nativists were assisting the Republicans or Orangemen.

Gang violence was frequent and bloody. In 1857 what became known as the 'Dead Rabbits Riot' occurred. The Dead Rabbits, with a membership of as many as five-hundred, were

Five Points biggest and most vicious gang. They controlled most of the Five Points area, waging bloody battles with their main rivals the Plug Uglies and Roach Guards. Despite this they often united with their enemies to fight the gangs of the Bowery and the Fourth Ward. While the two police forces in the city, the Municipal police and the Metropolitan police were at logger-heads about who was to patrol the streets, the Dead Rabbits decided to take advantage of the dispute and attack their mortal enemies.

On July 4 1857, a day of celebration for many Americans, scores of Dead Rabbits and Roach Guards invaded a saloon at 42 Bowery. They were met by dozens of Bowery Boys and Atlantic Guards. Using brickbats, clubs and paving stones the mobs battled one another for several hours until the Five Pointers retreated. In the afternoon they returned and the bat-tle started again. The newly established Metropolitan police tried to quell the riots but were attacked by both mobs and had to make a hasty retreat. The Municipal police, not yet amalgamated into the new state run force, refused to help the Metropolitans stating that the riots were not their affair.

The Dead Rabbits and Roach Guards returned to Five Points but the battle was not over. The next day saw the largest num-ber of gangsters ever assembled in one place at one time in America. More than 5,000 thugs armed with every type of weapon, belonging to all the Five Points gangs marched into the Bowery. Dozens of Roach Guards stormed into the Green Dragon, a Bowery Boy hang-out, tearing up the floorboards, smashing the furniture and drinking all the liquor on the premises. The Five Pointers then marched to Bayard Street, where an estimated 5,000 Bowery thugs awaited them, the Atlantic Guards in the forefront.

There was a tremendous roar as the two crowds clashed. The two mobs tore into each other mercilessly. The police were again summoned, but when they tried to baton a wedge between the battling thugs, the gangs instantly united against them. Hundreds of police reinforcements arrived and the lines of combatants battled back and forth for several hours along Worth and Centre Streets. Eventually the gangs backed off after several prominent Dead Rabbits were shot. The police, too, retreated, taking their prisoners with them; two gangsters whom they had managed to knock out!

Seeing the police retreat the gangs swarmed back on to Bayard and Bowery Streets. Scores of thugs entered the buildings and drove the residents onto the street, throwing some unfortunates out of the upper storey windows. The thugs climbed up on top of the buildings and hurled bricks and other missiles down on top of the battling gangsters and the retreating police.

The police appealed to the ageing gangster and political boss Isaiah Rynders, who pleaded with the mobs to end the fighting. They jeered him and sent him scurrying away. Rynders made his way to the Police Commissioner and demanded that he call out the military. Three National Guard Regiments arrived late in the evening and took up their positions, their muskets at the ready. The mobs took a long look at the troops and perhaps looking for an excuse to end the battle or remembering the carnage inflicted at the Astor Palace Riot, turned tail and fled.

Although eight men were reported killed and one-hundred injured, it was commonly believed that as many as one-hundred were killed in the two-day battle, for dozens of new graves appeared in the Bowery and Five Points. The police concluded that the gangs had dragged off their dead to bury them secretly, to keep their casualties unknown.

While the mobs of New York spent much of their time feuding with one another they also had time for their other activities; mugging, robbery, pickpocketing and running armies of prostitutes - though this was an activity the Irish took very little part in. The gangs were undisciplined and badly organised and stooped to the lowest form of crime to survive. While prostitution was considered too lowly for Irish gangsters they had no qualms about digging up the bodies of the recently buried wealthy and holding them for ransom or supplying recently arrived fellow-countrymen and their families, at so much a head, to boarding houses of ill-repute, where the unfortunate emigrants were fleeced of all money and valuables and then thrown out into the street.

For entertainment the gangsters staged dog fights, slicing off the dogs ears to prevent them from being chewed off in combat. Ratting was also popular at the time. Rats were let loose in a pit against a starved dog. Bets were placed on how many rats the dog would kill in a given period. Illegal drinking and gambling dens flourished and some gangsters made a fortune. Two Roach Guards, Tommy Hadden and Kit Burns, became millionaires after investing the spoils of their activities into gambling and drinking dens in the Fourth Ward.

Bordering the Bowery, the Fourth Ward was another Irish slum and housed the Sportsman's Hall, which provided entertainment to some of the city's most notorious thugs. Owned by Kit Burns and frequented by the roughest gangs in the area - the Whyos, Daybreak Boys, Border Gang, Patsy Conroys, Shirt Tails, Swamp Angels and Slaughter Housers - the Sportsman's Hall was an entire three-story building in which every vice was pursued and regarded by the blood-thirsty clientele as sporting events, though none so famously as the one which gave it its common name, the Rat Pit. Ratting was the premier sport of the nineteenth century and a big money maker. Entry to these illegal prize fights started at fifty cents and could cost up to $5 - huge sums in those days. From 1845 to 1870, until it was torn down as part of a redevelopment program, the Sportsman's

Hall was the scene of various atrocities. Murders were common there and seven people were killed on the premises in a two month period in 1845.

The Fourth Ward, like the Bowery and Five Points, was a breeding ground for criminal gangs. Most of the gangs concentrated on mugging and looting East River shipping traffic. Police action curtailed much of this activity around the time of the Civil War and most of the gangs faded away. However, around this time the Whyos appeared on the scene. They were the first of the really organised criminal gangs in New York. Formed in the late 1860s they were the first of the modern gangs; the first full-time criminals; thieves, protection racketeers, shakedown artists and contract killers. The Whyos were the first to "offer protection" to street traders and stuss parlours. (Stuss was a variation on faro, and a game where a player had an even chance of winning.) They evolved from the earlier Chichesters, dominating the Fourth Ward, but claiming the whole of Manhattan as their territory. Their headquarters was in the back of a grimy Bowery saloon named the Morgue, the scene of at least one-hundred murders over the years. Gang fights and shoot-outs were a regular occurrence there. Later they moved to Big Tim Sullivan's Dry Dollar saloon on Chrystie Street.

Among the most notorious members of the Whyos were Red Rocks Farrell, Slops Connolly, Big Josh Hines, Hoggy Walsh, Bull Hurley, Piker Ryan, Mike McGloin, Dorsey Doyle and Dandy John Dolan. Mike McGloin was the Whyos leader in the early 1880s. He established membership requirement of at least one murder to gain admission to the gang. "A guy ain't tough until he has knocked his man out!" McGloin was quoted as saying in 1883. McGloin, an avid practitioner of his own word, was hanged in the Tombs prison on March 8 1883 for the murder of a saloon-keeper.

Danny Lyons and Danny Driscoll took over leadership of the Whyos and jointly ruled the gang until they were both hanged in 1888. Driscoll was hanged on January 23 for the killing of a prostitute named Breezy Garrity. Breezy was not the intended target, but she happened to stop the bullet meant for John McCarthy and Driscoll was convicted of murder. Danny Lyons followed his fellow boss to the gallows several months later, on August 21, when he was hanged for the murder of Joseph Quinn, who was shot to death over the favours of another prostitute, Pretty Kitty McGowan.

Another Whyo thug of some note was Dandy John Dolan, whose claim to fame was his invention of a copper eye-gouger worn on the thumb which was capable of plucking out a victims eyeball in one swift move. (He no doubt copied this device from Hell-Cat Maggie's earlier invention.) Dolan also used the Plug Uglies technique of imbedding sharp axe blades in the soles of his boots for stomping a fallen victim. In 1876 a shopkeeper confronted Dolan in the course of a robbery and was beaten over the head with a crowbar. The murderous Dolan gouged out his victims eyes with his invention, proudly showing off his souvenirs to his fellow hoodlums. When the police arrested Dolan he still had them in his possession. He was convicted of murder and went to the gallows on April 21 1876.

In 1884 police arrested Piker Ryan and found in his pocket a now infamous checklist of 'services' offered and the corresponding fees.

Punching	$2.
Both eyes blacked	$4.
Nose and jaw broke	$10.
Jacked out (knocked out with a blackjack)	$15.
Ear chawed off	$15.
Leg or arm broke	$19.

Shot in leg. . . . .$25.
Stab . . . .$25.
Doing the big job (murder) . . . .$100 and up.

Lacking political protection, and falling prey to that most addictive of Irish drugs - alcohol - the Whyos continued as the most feared mob in New York City until the turn of the century when they were absorbed by the Five Pointers, a fifteen-hundred strong mob, led by an ex-boxer, Paolo Vaccarelli, who had fought under the name of Paul Kelly. With his Irish moniker he found it easier to move in the fighting circles, then dominated by the Irish. On retiring from the ring Kelly found his Irish name opened doors in the political and criminal world. The Five Pointers were mainly Italian hoodlums, while their biggest rivals were the Jewish, two-thousand strong, Monk Eastman mob.

The rise of Italian and Jewish gangs in New York - and in the rest of the country - was a reflection in the city's racial balance. Irish dominance of street crime began to be challenged by the arrival of newer waves of European immigrants. (The new criminals even aped the Irish gangster dialect saying 'youse', 'dese' and 'dem'.) Between 1880 and 1914 two-million Eastern European Jews arrived in America, 1,250,000 of them settling in New York, mainly on the Lower East Side, pushing out the resident Irish. They were joined by half-a-million Italian and Sicilian immigrants, who settled on the Lower East Side, Harlem and the Brooklyn Bridge area, all neighbourhoods which until then were mainly Irish. The Italian and Sicilian immigrants brought with them their Mafia, Black Hand and Camorra secret societies and criminal fraternities.

The Irish immigrants, (who were still arriving at an average of fifty-thousand a year) began to move out of some of the worst slums and gain a level of acceptance. But, some still had no choice and stayed in the urban hell-holes, slums like Hell's

Kitchen on Manhattan's West Side, where the tenements were the most overcrowded in the world and disease and infant mortality were rife. The area stretched from 34th Street in the south to 59th Street in the north and spread as far west as 8th Avenue. The name allegedly came from a rookie Irish policeman looking at his new environment and remarking "Surely, this is Hell's Kitchen."

Gangs roamed the streets of Hell's Kitchen fighting to control the waterfront and the local rackets. The most powerful gang were the Gophers - usually pronounced "Goofers" - so named because they usually met in the cellars and basements of abandoned buildings. Formed in the 1890s they were by 1907 five-hundred strong and so formidable a force that even Monk Eastman's awesome gang avoided them. At this time the gang was ruled by a committee, which included Marty Brennan, Stumpy Melarkey and Newburg Gallagher. They usually met to plan their activities in a saloon named Battle Row, owned by Mallet Murphy, who was named for the type of weapon he used to settle disputes.

One of the most notorious of Gophers was One-Lung Curran, a huge muscle-bound thug who loved to attack rookie policemen and steal their long blue coats. He would be seen strutting around Hell's Kitchen, in the police coat, daring the cops to come and try to take it back. When they did try, they came in force. Curran eventually died of tuberculosis, when his one good lung packed in, but, while he lived he was a terror to both police and criminals.

Like the Dead Rabbits and the Whyos before them, the Gophers fostered a juvenile branch, the Baby Gophers, who were taught the art of stealing and fighting at an early age by their elders. There was also a female branch, called the Lady Gophers. They met in the Battle Row saloon and officially referred to themselves as the Battle Row Ladies Social and

Athletic Club. A huge and fearless woman, named Battle Annie, led the Lady Gophers, often as reserves for the Gophers in pitched battles with invading gangs.

With the passing of such stalwarts as One-Lung Curran and the imprisonment of most of the other leaders the Gophers began to decline in numbers and power. In 1910 the New York Central Railroad organised a special force to take action against the marauding gangs that were playing havoc with their trade. Many of the special force were ex-policemen, who had taken beatings from the Gophers and had a score to settle. The Railroad staged an attack on the Gophers, beating and intimidating the gangsters until the railroad yards on 30th and 60th Streets became a no-go area for hoods. Further weakened the Gophers fell prey to their old rivals, the Hudson Dusters, who became the dominant gang in the area.

The Hudson Dusters had been formed in the 1890s and took their name from their headquarters, a second-floor, two-room apartment on Hudson Street. They controlled the West Side below 13th Street and east to Broadway. They fought many battles with smaller gangs, namely the Pearl Buttons and the Marginals, for the lucrative Hudson River waterfront rackets. The Dusters usually won these encounters, as they could muster upwards of two-hundred thugs. As they grew in size and importance, leaders such as Mike Costello, Red Farrell and Rubber Shaw, became election "specialists", thus earning the political protection of Tammany Hall.

Reporters frequenting the popular taverns of Greenwich Village gave the Dusters great press. A frequent haunt of the gang was the Golden Swan Bar, which once stood on the corner of 6th Avenue and 4th Street, and was known as the Hell Hole, the Bucket of Blood and other enticing nicknames. The saloon was frequented by journalists and the playwright Eugene O'Neill, who was good friends with the Dusters and drew many of his characters from the personalities in the tavern.

However, one thing many of the reporters did not write about was the Dusters addiction to narcotics. Most of the leaders and the ordinary members were cocaine addicts and it was part of their downfall. Around the time of WW1 most of the leaders had died of drug overdoses or had been imprisoned. Their old rivals the Marginals, led by Tanner Smith, had grown stronger and finished off the remains of the Hudson Dusters. However, the Gophers reappeared under the leadership of Owney Madden, who wasted little time in taking over the rest of the West Side, swallowing the Village, and absorbing the Marginals, after the death of Tanner Smith in 1919.

In 1913 there were more gangs in New York than at any time in the city's history. They terrorised the city and no street was safe. Reformers demanded action and within a few years the police had put away two-hundred of the city's top gangsters, including Owney Madden. The ones who could not be convicted were clubbed or harassed off the streets, until all the major gangs were smashed. By the end of WW1 this drastic police action had severely curtailed gang activity in New York and most of the big gangs, including the Five Pointers and the Eastmans were broken. It would take the Volstead Act of 1919, banning the sale of alcohol to the public, to bring the gangs of New York back from the brink of obscurity.

CHAPTER 3

CHICAGO
THAT WICKEDEST CITY

Chicago, Illinois, became a city in 1837 and witnessed a boom when the Lake Michigan-Illinois canal - built largely by Irish immigrants - opened in 1848. By 1855 the city was the greatest meat packing centre and biggest grain port in the country. The city's boom naturally attracted many newly arrived immigrants - Irish, German and Polish - along with many undesirables - pimps, prostitutes, pickpockets, burglars and gunmen - to give Chicago the title of the "wickedest city in the United States." In 1855 riots halted an attempt to close the 'low-class dives' by imposing a local prohibition law. Two years later it had a district of brothels, grog shops, bare-knuckle prize-fighting booths and gambling dens.

In the mayoral election of 1873 Michael "King Mike" McDonald, a gambler-gangster, who led an Irish immigrant bloc which financed the Democratic party, backed Harvey D. Colvin as his candidate. Colvin won and from then until his death, in 1907, "McDonald had Chicago in his back pocket." He controlled mayors, congressmen and senators and forged alliances with the street gangs. With his backing "Bath-House" John Coughlin and Michael "Hinky-Dink" Kenna became "Lords of the Levee" - the First Ward, which contained the city's central business district and the thriving glittering brothels that lined the riverfront, where there was no recognisable law and order. John Coughlin, born in 1869, in the Irish district between Monroe and Adams, earned his nickname by working in a Clark Street bath-house, scrubbing the backs of politicians and eventually earning enough money to open two bath-houses of his own. He entered politics under the guidance of Oyster Joe Macklin. Michael Kenna, a small, dour man - his nickname came from a local pool he swam in as a kid - owned a saloon and worked well with Coughlin. The two were masters of the fix and had the police of the ward and the Quincey Street Boys, who included some of the most ferocious hoodlums of the First Ward, to do their bidding. The use of street gangs in Chicago politics became widespread. The majority of the gangs were Irish and were at the beck and call of the ward bosses.

By 1902 the Irish Market Street Gang had become a strong force and even had a juvenile division - the Little Hellions, which sported an up and coming young thug, Dion O'Bannion, as its leader. Another Irish mob, the Valley Gang, controlled the Bloody Maxwell Street section. On the South Side, around the stockyards, Ragen's Colts ruled the roost. In 1915 Republican William Hale Thompson became mayor of Chicago. He delivered the city from the saloon owning politicians and handed it over to the new breed of gangsters like Dion O'Bannion and Big Jim Colosimo. Labour unions, too, were dominated by Irish violence. Maurice "Mossy" Enright was one of Chicago's first labour racketeers, who specialised in bombing and beating jobs on behalf of organised labour. His chief enforcer was Walter Stevens, born in 1867, a gracious, quiet man who for twenty years cared devotedly for an invalid wife and adopted three children giving them good educations. Stevens was of high morals, did not drink and censored the classics before allowing them into his home. As an Enright lieutenant he was known as the "dean of Chicago hitmen." He was widely believed to be the triggerman in at least half-a-dozen murders, including that of Peter Gentleman, a policeman's son turned gunman. Stevens' price scale ran from $20 for cracking open a skull to $50 and up for murder. Mossy Enright was murdered on February 3 1920 in front of his home by Sunny Jim Cosmano as a favour to Big Tim Murphy, a rival labour racketeer. The murder was attributed to the fight for control of the Street Cleaners Union.

The involvement of Cosmano in the Enright murder was a consequence of Italian and Sicilian encroachment on Irish dominated Chicago crime. Thousands of Italian and Sicilian immigrants had arrived in the city in the later half of the 19th century, settling in the worst of Chicago's ghettos. By 1916 the Italian immigrants held the majority of votes in the West Side 19th Ward - or as it was known "The Bloody Ward." Once a completely Irish area, the 19th Ward still had an Irish alderman. Shut out of political influence by the Irish power structure, the Italians rallied around Tony D'Andrea, a disgraced former priest. He ran for office on several occasions against Johnny "The Pow" Powers, the Irish boss of the ward since 1888, but continually lost.

With the onset of Prohibition in 1920 the Genna brothers, the main Sicilian gangsters in Little Italy - which was in the heart of the 19th Ward - felt they needed their own man in power to guarantee their bootleg operations. They shot dead Frank Lombardo, a ward boss for Powers in a Taylor Street saloon. It was the beginning of an all-out campaign against Powers. Both sides believed they could influence the balloting by murder. In a bizarre twist both sides took to posting the name of their next intended victim on a certain poplar tree in Loomis Street, in

Little Italy. It became known as the "Dead Man's Tree." Virtually all of the thirty men killed in the "Alderman's War" had their names posted on the tree, including Tony D'Andrea, who after another defeat, announced his retirement from politics, only to be killed on May 11 1921. In the end the Gennas discovered all the killing had been in vain. Chicago was the city of the fix. They found that all the men they could not vote, or shoot, out of office could be bought. On May 11 1920 Big Jim Colosimo was murdered on the orders of his second-in-command, Johnny Torrio. Big Jim arrived in America in 1895 and settled in Chicago's Levee district. He became a bagman for Bathhouse John Coughlin and Hinky-Dink Kenna. Soon he became one of the most successful crime lords in Chicago. Unfortunately, he had not got the foresight to see the millions that could be made from Prohibition. He dismissed Torrio's advice, concentrating on his brothels and his new wife, a young cafe singer. It was a fatal mistake. The ambitious Torrio had Big Jim murdered and with a young killer, named Al Capone, at his side he took over the reins of Colosimo's empire. Torrio was a man of vision and began to approach all the major mobs in Chicago for co-operation. He foresaw the dangers of rivalry between gangs and he realised that with proper organisation there was enough for everyone to make huge profits. Chicago was carved up into sections, each to be a territory of a different gang. The gangs would have political and police protection. Bootleg booze was given a set price and no one was to undercut that price.

Torrio was diplomat. He brought all the major gangs together; the North Side was controlled by Dion O'Bannion; on the West Side were the O'Donnell gang; between Little Italy and Cicero were another Irish mob, the Valley Gang; Little Italy on the South Side was in the hands of the Gennas, six murderous Sicilian brothers; on the far South Side were Ragen's Colts, the

Saltis-McErlane mob and another mob of O'Donnells - no relation to the West Side O'Donnells; Torrio was based on the South
Side, expanding as far as Cicero; Screwey John Moore led the
Circus Gang on the Northwest Side, while the Terrible Touhy's
ran the far North Side. For three years everything ran smoothly
until the South Side O'Donnells began running beer in the "Back
of the Yards", home of the Saltis-McErlanes. This sparked off the
beginning of the Chicago Beer Wars and a lawless decade
that would leave upwards of five-hundred dead and give
Chicago its infamous name.

After Torrio retired from Chicago's rackets, in 1925, Al
Capone took over, building a formidable and sophisticated
empire. Under Capone the Chicago mob became the most
sophisticated criminal organisation in America. It was then, and
still is to this day, the most formidable mob in American criminal
history. Under Capone's leadership the Outfit eliminated all their
main rivals, branched into legitimate businesses and became
multi-ethnic. There was a place for everyone, Italians, Sicilians,
Irish, Jews, Poles, Greeks, Germans and Anglo-Saxons. Capone
did not discriminate. Much of the Outfit's strength today is
based on the strategic use of non-Italians on its board of
directors. Capone even taught his successors well. Owing to his
mistakes his successors are careful not to court publicity and
are prompt in paying their taxes.

After the North Side O'Bannion mob was eliminated many
of the smaller gangs came under the umbrella of the Capone
organisation. One of these was the Valley Gang. The Valley
Gang, an Irish street gang, was formed in the 1890s, around 15th
Street in the Bloody Maxwell section of the city's West Side. They
took their name from "the Valley", a flat wasteland of squat
brick tenements southwest of the Loop. Around the turn of the
century the Valleys graduated from burglaries and pick-pock-
eting to leg-breaking and contract murders. Around the time of

WW1 the gang was under the leadership of Paddy "The Bear" Ryan - a giant of a man, who ran the gang's activities from a saloon he ran on South Halstead Street. In 1920 Paddy the Bear was murdered by a rival gangster, Walter Quinlan.

Leadership of the Valley Gang passed to Terry Druggan and Frankie Lake, two shrewd business-like gangsters. The Valley's became known as the Druggan-Lake Gang. Druggan was the nominal leader, a small man who lisped when excited. Lake, the junior partner, a burly ex-fireman, aped Druggan in every manner, wearing a fedora and expensive suits. Both men wore glasses, which gave them the appearance of mild-mannered businessmen. They were far from it. They were ruthless thugs who murdered and hijacked their way to become millionaires. Like O'Bannion and his boys, both Druggan and Lake were devout Catholics. Once after hijacking a truckload of bootleg from Herschie Miller's Jewish mob, Druggan waved his pistol at his captives and sending them marching down the street, pointed at a nearby church, warning them, "Hats off, you Jews, when you're passing the House of God, or I'll shoot them off!"

Druggan and Lake led the gang to great prosperity. They were the most flamboyant gang in Chicago, and had interests in several breweries. Yet for the first two years of Prohibition the two leaders continued as if they were still back in the Valley Gang; Druggan was arrested for a $11,000 jewellery robbery, while Lake was arrested for shooting former policeman Timmy Mulvihill. While on bail both were again arrested for hi-jacking a truckload of bootleg. All this occurred while the they had their own breweries and were raking in millions!

In 1924 Druggan and Lake were jailed for a year for contempt in disobeying an injunction against one of their breweries. But jail was to be of little inconvenience to them. Morris Eller, boss of the 20th Ward, told Sheriff Pete Hoffman, "Treat the boys right." And he did. Twenty-thousand dollars in bribes to Warden Wesley Westbrook, and other officers, at Cook County Jail ensured the "boys" could do as they wished. A reporter went to the jail to interview the two was told, "Mr. Druggan is not in today." He then asked for Frankie Lake and was told, "Mr. Lake also had an appointment downtown. They'll be back after dinner."

As a result of this conversation, the *Chicago American* launched a major investigation into the Cook County Jail. It turned out the pair ran their affairs as normal as ever. Druggan's chauffeur-driven limousine picked him up so he could spend most of his evenings with his wife at his Gold Coast apartment. Lake spent most of his time at his mistresses North State Parkway home. The two gangsters also enjoyed dining out, golfing, shopping and going out to the theatre!

For their part in the scandal Sheriff Hoffman and Warden Westbrook ended up in the dock. Westbrook received a four-month jail term, while Hoffman was fined $2,500 and given a thirty-day sentence. On their release Druggan and Lake continued their flamboyant lifestyle, buying a string of breweries and flashy cars for their underlings. Al Capone, the most powerful gang leader at the time, was impressed with their style and the gangs became allies.

On June 1 1930 three Druggan affiliated gangsters and their friends were machine-gunned to death and two wounded in the "Fox Lake Massacre" at Manning's, a small resort hotel on Piskatee Lake. The five were sitting drinking on the glass screened terrace when a tommy gun mowed them down. They were George Druggan, a brother of Terry, Joseph Bertsche, a brother of North Side mobster Barney Bertsche, Michael Quirk, labour racketeer and beer runner, Sam Pellar, who had previously escaped death when his boss, Hymie Weiss, was killed and Mrs. Vivian Ponic McGinnis, the wife of a Chicago lawyer. Pellar,

Quirk and Bertsche died. George Druggan and Mrs. McGinnis were wounded. Verne Miller allegedly carried out the attack in revenge for the killing of Eugene "Red" McLaughlin, who had been taken for a ride by the Druggans.

In November 1931 police raided Terry Druggan's home and discovered how flamboyant the Valley gangster really was. His name was engraved in gold on his dinner service, on the furniture, his silver toilet set and on his sixteen pairs of shoes. Sets of Shakespeare, Dickens and Thackeray were bound in tooled Levant morocco. Oriental rugs covered the floors, while the rooms were panelled in walnut. Behind one wall police found an arsenal of machine guns, bombs and ammunition and incriminating letters. The following year both Druggan and Lake were convicted of income tax evasion and sent to Leavenworth. Their gang was absorbed by the Capones and when they were released they found there was a place for them in the Outfit.

Soon after Druggan and Lake quarrelled over something minor at a party and split up. Druggan spent the rest of his life in and out of hospitals, suffering from ulcers, asthma and heart disease. He died friendless and in poverty in 1954. Lake moved to Detroit, lived in an exclusive suburb, became president of a coal and ice company, while his wife was given to society-page good works. He died in 1947, in his fifties and unlike many of his contemporaries, of natural causes and very wealthy.

Many other Prohibition-era gangs were Irish, among them the Circus Gang, the Guilfoyle Gang and Ragen's Colts. Screwey John Moore, a.k.a. Claude Maddox, headed up the Circus Gang on Chicago's Northwest Side. Their headquarters was in Moore's Circus Cafe, on West North Avenue, hence the name. The gang became allies of Al Capone in the mid-1920s sending Capone a percentage of their bootleg profits in exchange for political and police protection arranged by Big

Al. Moore also provided the Capone mob with specialists in all criminal pursuits, be it gunmen, safe-crackers or otherwise. Moore was a prime suspect in the St. Valentine's Day Massacre, as one of the machine-gunners. (He was originally a member of the St. Louis gang, Egan's Rats, who also allegedly provided the rest of the hit squad.) The police car used in the killing was found in a garage on North Wood Street. The man that had rented the garage gave a false name, but a real address: 1859 West North Avenue. Police raided the address but found it empty. It was the second time in a month they had raided it. On the first occasion they had found Claude Maddox, who had given his real name John E. Moore. He was found hunkered down in a corner of a room, bare of all furnishings except a fully loaded hundred round machine gun drum, and a dozen over-coats, one with an automatic in its pocket. It was this sort of thing that gave Moore his nickname "Screwey." 1859 was also next door to the Circus Cafe. Still there was not enough evidence to charge Moore with anything.

With the repeal of Prohibition, Moore and his Circus Gang were absorbed into the Outfit. Moore became one of the Outfit's top men, and a prime suspect in many murders, including that of Matt Kolb in 1931, Machine-Gun Jack McGurn in 1936 and Danny Stanton in 1943. Moore happened to be standing beside Stanton when the latter was hit by a shotgun blast fired through the door of a Chicago tavern. Screwey John Moore died in June 1958. By then he was a millionaire several times over.

Another Irish ally of Capone was the Guilfoyle Gang. Based on the near Northwest Side the gang was led by Marty Guilfoyle. Like Moore, Guilfoyle was west of the river and impor-tant to Capone in his battle with the O'Bannions. As allies of Capone the gang distributed liquor throughout the West Side. Guilfoyle's top aide was an ex-Chicago police lieutenant, Al

Winge. Political protection came from Matt Kolb, who had important connections in City Hall. The near Northwest Side was a profitable little fiefdom - worth $2 million a year by 1928. With a small gang of 'salesmen' and 'persuaders' Guilfoyle had put the squeeze on the local bootleggers, Louis and Max Summerfield, who seeing their profits dwindling away, began to hit back. After a minor little war a dynamite bomb sorted the Summerfield's out and Guilfoyle emerged the undisputed power in the area. In 1931 the gang was absorbed by the Outfit.

On the South Side, around the stockyards was another Irish gang, Ragen's Colts. Like many other street gangs Ragen's Colts started out as a baseball team. It was formed by Frank and Mike Ragen and was officially called Ragen's Athletic and Benevolent Association. Frank Ragen was the star pitcher, but was also the political operative of the club and soon proved invaluable to the city's Democratic Party, offering muscle in election campaigns. Many members of the city council and state legislature owed their election to the Colts, prompting one Colt to boast, "When we dropped into a polling place, everyone else dropped out." The Colts hired themselves out for political intimidation, assault, kidnapping and murder. They specialised in supplying muscle for labour disputes, selling themselves to the highest bidder.

By 1902 the gang numbered 160 and six years later it adopted the motto, "Hit me and you hit two-thousand." It was only a slight exaggeration. Many of the neighbourhoods social events, picnics and dances were centred around the gang's activities. In 1917 the clubs New Year's Eve party was attended by more than 5,000 people. The Colts prided themselves on their patriotism and five-hundred members went into the armed forces in WW1. They were at the height of their power in the first two decades of the century. Over the years the list grew of aldermen, councillors, sheriffs and other officeholders who owed their election to the club. Besides providing political muscle and running a number of rackets the Colts were notable racists and started the 1919 Race Riot that left thirty-eight dead and hundreds injured. With the onset of Prohibition the Colts turned their attention to bootlegging. Many Colts joined opposing bootleg gangs and its membership dwindled. On August 4 1927 the twelve remaining members met and voted to disband the club. Frank Ragen had become a respected public figure, taking a job as a Cook County Commissioner. He had long announced his separation from the Colts.

James Ragen, a younger brother of Frank and Mike, was also active with the Colts and went on to become a force in nation-wide gambling. A veteran of the Chicago newspaper wars, he graduated to bootlegging and labour slugging. In the 1930s he supervised office operations for Moses Annenberg's General News Bureau, providers of racetrack information. The racing wire was a highly profitable business and the Chicago Outfit badly wanted to control it. Pressurised by the Outfit on one side and income-tax investigators on the other side Annenberg sold it to Jim Ragen on November 15 1939. Ragen changed the name to the Nation-Wide News Service. He, too, came under pressure from the mob, who established a wire service of their own, calling it Trans-American Publishing and charging bookies $100 a day to subscribe to it. The mob still coveted Ragen's wire service and when he resisted all offers to sell, or take a silent partner, he was wounded in an assassination attempt as he drove his car along State Street. While in hospital, recovering from his wounds, Ragen was poisoned and died on August 15 1946 leaving the way open for the mob to take over his wire service.

Roger Touhy was another opponent of Capone and the Outfit. Touhy was a prominent bootlegger who operated with a small gang in the northern suburbs of Chicago, with his headquarters in Des Plaines. Born in 1896, the son of a policeman, Roger Touhy's childhood was normal and crime free. After a stint in the navy, during the war, he went into the trucking business. It was only when he started transporting bootleg beer that he began to make any money. With his brothers, Tommy and Eddie, he began distributing bootleg booze in Chicago's Northwestern suburbs. The Touhy's formed an alliance with Matt Kolb, who provided them with political protection. Together they produced what was considered the best Prohibition beer in the Midwest, at a cost of less than $5 a barrel, which they sold for $55 a barrel. Touhy paid off the police in the suburbs with barrels of his premium beer, or cases of bottled beer from his own bottling plant.

Al Capone began ordering hundreds of barrels of the famous brew and once tried to short Touhy of $1,900 saying there were leaks in some of the barrels - a favourite ploy of his. Touhy had a reputation as a fearsome gangster and fixed Capone with his famed hard stare. "Don't chisel me, Al," he said. Capone paid. Touhy's fearsome reputation was much a creation of good public relations, largely of his own doing. As far as the rest of the underworld, and the press were concerned, Touhy - the press dubbed him Roger "The Terrible" - and his brothers ran the most vicious mob in the Midwest. Whenever rivals, including the Capones, made noise about moving in Touhy invited them to his headquarters, The Arch, a roadhouse in Schiller Park. Here visiting hoods saw tommy guns lining the wall. Every few minutes men would come in and take a weapon from the stockpile and mutter something about a gun-battle somewhere. Touhy would wave them out as if this was an everyday occurrence. When Touhy's visitors left they reported that it would be insane to go to war with the gang. What they did not know was that the weapons were provided by friendly cops, who more than likely were the same men that came in talking of gunbattles and killings. Touhy was a middle-class bootlegger and used no more force than was necessary to sell his beer.

The Outfit tried to put the squeeze on Touhy to share his profits, but Touhy would not back down. Even when Matt Kolb was kidnapped he paid the ransom, but still refused to sell-out. Kolb was then murdered and with the local police behind him Touhy struck back. When all else failed the Outfit had Touhy framed on a kidnapping charge for which he was given a 199 year sentence, leaving the way open for the Outfit to take over the North-western suburbs. Chicago was now the complete domain of the Outfit. After a lengthy campaign to prove his innocence, Roger Touhy was finally freed in 1959, only to be gunned down several days later as he left his sister's apartment. As he lay dying on the pavement he said "The bastards, they never forget."

CHAPTER 4

ARMIES OF THE STREETS
THE DRAFT RIOTS

As the American Civil War dragged into 1863 without any sign of victory for either side the Republican government of the North introduced conscription to fill the ranks of the army so badly depleted in the savage fighting of the last two years. Three-hundred thousand men were needed and all males between twenty and forty-five were enrolled. All men inducted were to serve three years. The draftees were called up by lottery in each district. Opportunities for corruption were everywhere. Unscrupulous doctors granted unwarranted deferments for a price and any man who could come up with three-hundred dollars as a "commutation fee" or could find a substitute willing to serve in his place, was exempt. This led to calls of the war being a "rich man's war and a poor man's fight", as no working-class man could possibly come up with $300.

None were more resentful of the system's inequities than the Irish working-class, who feared the blacks with whom they competed for the lowest paying jobs and for whose freedom they were unwilling to fight and die. A militia draft in several states the previous year had met violent resistance in some areas, including Irish neighbourhoods in the coalfields of eastern Pennsylvania where mobs attacked enrolment officers and troops had to be sent in to keep order and carry out the draft. In several cities anti-black rioting broke out during the summer of 1862. Some of the worst violence occurred in Cincinnati, where blacks replaced striking Irish dockworkers. Black neighbourhoods were attacked by mobs which included many gang members. In Brooklyn an Irish mob tried to burn down a tobacco factory where two dozen black women and children were working.

The Democratic Party exploited the race issue and the civil war for all its worth. Democrat newspapers preached that the draft would force white working men to fight for the freedom of blacks who would come north and take away their jobs. "Shall the working class be equalised with the Negro," one headline screamed. The Democratic Party was fiercely anti-Negro and had preached that the Republican government was willing to sacrifice the interests of 20 million whites for that of 3 million blacks. In the cities of the north the Democrats support came from workers who resented the de-skilling of artisan labour and from Irish immigrants who took offence at Republican Protestant efforts to reform their drinking habits or force their children into public schools. In a Fourth of July speech to Democrats in New York, Governor Seymour warned Republicans, "Remember this - that the bloody and treasonable doctrine of public necessity can be proclaimed by a mob as well as by a government." Such rhetoric inflamed an already tense atmosphere.

As the deadline for the draft drew near anti-black violence erupted again and several enrolment officers were murdered by mobs. Nowhere was.the tension greater than in New York City with its large Irish population and powerful Democratic machine. Crowded into filthy tenements in a city with the worst disease mortality and highest crime rate in the Western world, working in low skilled jobs for minimum rate, fearful of black competition, hostile towards the Protestant middle and upper class the Irish were ripe for revolt against this "rich man's war." Wage increases had lagged twenty per cent behind price increases since 1861. Numerous strikes had left a legacy of bitterness, none more than a longshoreman's walkout over a raise to twenty-five cents for a nine hour day in June 1863 when blacks under police protection took the place of striking Irishmen.

Into this powder-keg arrived draft officers to begin the drawing of names on Saturday, July 11. The first day's drawing went quietly enough and the names appeared in the next day's newspapers alongside long lists of those who had fallen at the recent battle of Gettysburg. There were many Irish names on both the draft list and the casualty list. Hundreds of angry men congregated in bars, and egged on by unscrupulous lower ranked politicians and gang leaders vowed to attack the draft offices the next day. Sunday passed without incident as gangsters stockpiled bricks, stones and clubs for the next draft selection. That night huge bonfires lit up the slums.

On Monday morning, July 13, as more names were drawn a massive parade, numbering 10,000, carrying banners and placards proclaiming "No Draft" marched up 6th Avenue to Central Park, recruiting from factories along the way. The crowd were angry and in a violent mood. Many were armed and waved sticks and cudgels. The majority of the crowd were working class and an estimated two thirds were Irish. (One-third of the crowd were women.) Scattered among the massive crowd were gangs from every part of the city; Plug Uglies, Bowery Boys, Dead Rabbits, Shirt Tails, Hibernians, they were all there. It was an army of the streets, an army of the poor and wretched. And they were thirsting for blood.

The speakers at the rally had whipped their bloodlust into a frenzy. As the rally broke up the great crowd divided into smaller ones. Four thousand of them, mostly Irish labourers, marched to the draft offices at Broadway and 29th Street. They attacked the offices, destroying the files and torching the building. The draft officers were lucky to be absent. The mob kept fire apparatus from the building and flames shortly spread to the entire block. Attempts by the police and a small detachment of U.S. Marines to disperse the rioters provoked the mob to intensified violence. The rioters, joined by additional thousands of sympathisers, roamed freely through the city, destroying property and committing other outrages.

The mob fanned out across the city indulging in indiscriminate looting and destruction and seizing guns from the State Armoury at 21st Street and 2nd Avenue. A detachment of troops fought off the rioters until the Armoury was torched. The troops then abandoned the armoury escaping out through a rear exit. With the fires out of control the top floors collapsed killing an unknown number of looters. As in most riots, the mobs singled out targets that were related to the underlying causes of their problems. Federal property was razed; the rich mansions on Lexington Avenue were ransacked and blacks were attacked and beaten up and several were strung up on lamp posts and set on fire. Negro homes were attacked and the Coloured Orphan Asylum on 5th Avenue was burned to the ground - the children had been evacuated by locals just moments before the fires were lit. Businesses that employed blacks were burned or wrecked. Several Republican newspaper buildings were attacked. The ground floor of the pro-war *Tribune* was burnt out and the mob beaten back by rifle-firing employees. The *Times* was defended by three recently invented Gatling guns. The mobs had swollen to thousands and they attacked the homes of several prominent abolitionists and anti-labour employers even destroying street-sweeping machines and grain-loading elevators that had automated the jobs of the unskilled workers who made up the majority of the mob. Several Protestant churches and missions were also razed by the mobs.

The city fathers turned out the Invalid Corps for the emergency to help the hard pressed police. (All available troops in the New York City area had been rushed to counter the Confederate invasion of Pennsylvania.) Two disabled veterans were killed, the chief of police was beaten unconscious and an unarmed officer home on leave was stoned to death. The rioting subsided late Monday night but was resumed with even greater violence on Tuesday. Police, aided by small detachments of troops stationed in and near the city, made vain attempts to disperse the mobs. More blacks were murdered, black neighbourhoods were burned, and general looting took place.

For three days the East Side of Manhattan belonged to the mobs, who numbered seventy-thousand, swept up in the spiralling "carnival of violence", as one observer called it. They broke into the homes of the wealthy and looted scores of shops, stores and saloons. The Plug Uglies and their like had a field day. They flocked out to "wreck vengeance on the symbols of property, propriety and Protestantism."

A black pall of smoke, from burning buildings, hung over the city. Every time the fire fighters arrived they were pelted mercilessly by the mobs. The police and soldiers, untrained in riot control, courageously battled rioters back and forth through the streets, in and out of buildings and across rooftops. That night, heavy rain put out most of the fires throughout the city. Many of the firemen who were volunteers and eligible for the draft had joined the mobs leaving the stretched police and military to tackle the dozens of blazes. Were it not for this piece of meteorological luck the better part of the city could have burnt down.

On July 15 temporary suspension of the draft was announced and that same evening five regiments of sun-burned troops fresh from the front in Pennsylvania arrived to help impose order. The next morning the troops were in their positions. A breastwork of overturned carts, hacks and wagons stretched across Broadway from curb to curb just below 43rd Street. Field cannons had been placed around City Hall and Police Headquarters on Mulberry Street. The mob storming the breastwork were met by volley after volley of musket fire from the veterans of Gettysburg. It had the same deadly effect on the rioters as it had on the Confederates at the recent decisive battle of Gettysburg. Again and again the troops met the mobs and blasted them off the streets. By nightfall law and order had been restored. The next day an uneasy peace returned to the shattered city.

The power of the mobs was broken. They retreated back to their hovels and shanties fearful now of the wrath of the law for the authorities were thirsting for revenge. Dozens were arrested. The police and military seized 11,000 firearms and recovered most of the property stolen by the mobs.

Determined to carry out the draft in New York - if it was a fail-ure there it would fail everywhere - the government built up troop strength around the city to 43 regiments totalling twenty-thousand soldiers, who enforced calm during the resumption of drafting on August 19. Altogether about 120 people were believed to have died in the riots; eighteen of those were black victims of the mob, eight were soldiers, two National Guardsmen and three were policemen; the rest were rioters and innocent civilians. Thousands were injured and hundreds of blacks were forced from their homes. (Some accounts give the dead as high as 2,000.) The riots are still the worst in American history. Nothing before or since have been as bad. The Draft Riots are considered a major embarrassment to the city of New York and are very rarely mentioned. There are no monuments or plaques to mark the sites of the great battles. New Yorkers would rather forget that an insurrection so vast took place in their city. Apart from the casualties more than fifty large buildings were destroyed by fire. Property damage was estimated at $2 million, a huge sum at that time.

For a long time after nativists pointed to the Draft Riots as proof of Irish immigrants disloyalty. The riots also took much off the well publicised achievements of Irish soldiers and units like the Irish Brigade. The former colonel of the Fighting 69th, a renowned Irish regiment, Robert Nugent, was acting as provost marshal, in effect the head of the Military Police, in the city at the time and his house was burned down. Yet after the war the Irish acquired a new status. The "No Irish need apply" mentality was modified as the Irish basking in the afterglow of their contribution to the Union and the Confederate armies, began to be gradually accepted.

There were disturbances in other Irish areas, the most serious in the coalfields of Pennsylvania, where protests were led by violent secret societies like the Molly Maguires.

Trouble also broke out in Boston on July 14, only a day after the outbreak of New York's Draft Riots. A group of irate women in the largely Irish North End attacked two provost marshals who had come to serve conscription papers. A number of men joined in, beating local policemen attempting to rescue the marshals. The melee escalated and developed into a full-scale riot between angry residents and the police. Three companies of militia, backed up by regular troops were called in as night fell and six people were shot dead in skirmishes. Unlike the New York riot there was no looting of shops, or destruction of property and no attacks on the black community. By the next morning it was all over. Although tension remained high for several days the Boston Irish settled back in a spirit of resentment against Lincoln and the Republican government.

CHAPTER 5

PROHIBITION
AND THE EVOLUTION
OF ORGANISED CRIME

On January 16 1920 the National Prohibition Act became law. This law prohibited the sale of "intoxicating liquors", although it made concessions for liquors sold for medicinal, sacramental, and industrial purposes, and for fruit or grape beverages prepared for personal use in homes. Temperance organisations blamed alcohol consumption for the rising incidence of crime, poverty and violence. Temperance reform had began as early as 1808. The American population increased rapidly after the Civil War, and soon there were more than 100,000 saloons in the country. These saloons became increasingly competitive for the drinker's money.

Thus, many of them permitted gambling, prostitution, sales to minors, public drunkenness and violence. By 1900 millions of Americans regarded the saloon as the most dangerous social institution then threatening the family. By 1916 no less than twenty-three of the forty-eight states had adopted anti-saloon laws, which in those states closed the saloons and prohibited the manufacture of any alcoholic beverages. The national elections of that year returned a U.S. Congress in which the dry members (those who supported Prohibition) outnumbered the wet members (those who were against Prohibition) by more than two to one. On December 22 1917 with majorities well in excess of the two-thirds requirement, Congress submitted to the states the 18th Amendment to the Constitution, which prohibited "the manufacture, sale or transportation of intoxicating liquors". By January 1919 ratification was complete, with 80 per cent of the members of forty-six state legislatures recorded in approval.

Prohibition, instead of curing America's social ailments actually created more. By the mid-1910s the great street gangs were on the brink of extinction. Their chief racket - enforcers for the political machines - was no longer viable. Reformers were everywhere. The American public would no longer tolerate gang violence in their elections. Many gang leaders ended up behind bars, their gangs falling apart in violent in-fighting. Even the old reliable, prostitution, was badly hit. It appeared that the era of the great gangs was over. Then with Prohibition the gangs were back. Across the country 200,000 illegal "speakeasies" sprang up to meet the demand. Large bootlegging gangs were required to supply them. There were massive fortunes to be made and to make sure they stayed in business gangsters paid out millions in bribes. America became a country on the take. Politicians, police and Prohibition agents were bribed to keep everything running smoothly. Bootleggers and rum runners imported liquor from abroad, brought it across the Canadian border or "home-brewed" it. Disrespect for the law grew as ordinary citizens visited speakeasies or served bootleg liquor in their homes. The bootlegger, the gangster and the speakeasy became popular institutions and the profits available to criminals from illegal liquor corrupted almost every level of government.

One of the first to see the enormous potential of Prohibition was William Vincent "Big Bill" Dwyer. Big Bill set up his own rum running business with the help of his boyhood friends from the Hudson Dusters and the Gophers. He established the biggest rum running syndicate on the east coast and within two years the former longshoreman was a multi-millionaire. He forged alliances with other ethnics like Frank Costello, Arnold Rothstein and Meyer Lansky. Dwyer introduced Costello and Lucky Luciano to Jimmy Hines, who provided Big Bill with political protection. His distribution boss was Vannie Higgins, a flashy loud-mouthed gangster who worked closely with Frank Costello, though Costello preferred the limelight. On December 3 1925 Dwyer, Costello and 59 other men were arrested in what the *New York Times* described as the smashing of a $40 million international liquor ring. Dwyer and E.C. Cochran, who had bribed a coastguard, were found guilty - Frank Costello, tried separately was acquitted. Big Bill served a year in Atlanta and traded his liquor interests for racetrack interests, gaining a reputation as a millionaire sportsman. He was the original owner of the Brooklyn Dodgers football team and was responsible for bringing professional ice hockey to New York. Dwyer was convicted of income tax evasion in 1939 and died penniless in 1946.

As the demand for alcohol increased the mindless street criminal became the millionaire overnight. Gone were the corner boy thugs with the cap brim pulled down over the eyes. The new breed of hood dressed in sharp suits, fedora hat, spats and $100 shoes and rode around in the newest flashiest car. Huge organisations were required to move vast amounts of bootleg and co-operation was needed on a greater scale. Gangs co-operated like never before. In pre-Prohibition days there was no need for gangs from one city to co-operate with gangs in another city. Now there was. The likes of Al Capone in Chicago was dependent on alcohol supplies from Canada coming through Detroit, where the Purple Gang held sway. Capone had to come to some arrangement with the Purples and the same form of co-operation was reached in other areas involving other gangs.

While the great Irish gangs of the 19th century had faded away, Prohibition brought the Irish gangster back into the public eye. However, the majority of gangsters during the Prohibition era were Jewish and Italian, the main occupiers of the big city ghettos. No census exists but judging by the cities involved it is possible to put together a picture of the ethnic balance. As an example, Chicago's composition can be judged by the Chicago Crime Commission's first list of "Public Enemies": 1. Al Capone. 2. Tony "Mops" Volpe. 3. Ralph Capone. 4. Frank Rio. 5. Jack "Machine-Gun" McGurn. 6. James Balcastro. 7. Rocco Fanelli. 8. Lawrence Mangano. 9. Jack Zuta. 10. Jake Guzik. 11. Frank Diamond. 12. George "Bugs" Moran. 13. Joe Aiello. 14. Edward "Spike" O'Donnell. 15. "Polock" Joe Saltis. 16. Frank McErlane. 17. Vince McErlane. 18. William Neimoth. 19. Danny Stanton. 20. Myles O'Donnell. 21. Frank Lake. 22. Terry Druggan. 23. William "Klondike" O'Donnell. 24. George "Red" Barker. 25. William "Three-Fingered Jack" White. 26. Joseph "Peppy" Genaro. 27. Lee Mongoven. 28. James "Fur" Sammons.

The Cleveland police force kept a "black-list" of "criminals of a dangerous character" and broke it down by ethnic groups. Of seventy-four native whites of foreign parentage (this in 1930) twenty-seven were Jewish, fifteen were Germans, while thirteen were Italian and nine Irish.

New York was dominated by Jews and Italians in that order with the Irish clinging on to the West Side and parts of Brooklyn. In Boston both the Irish and Italians were evenly divided with the Jews in the minority. Philadelphia was mainly Jewish as was

Detroit. Cleveland was divided between Irish mobs led by Mickey McBride and Tom McGinty - and Jewish and Italian factions. In St. Louis five major gangs were dominant; Egan's Rats; the Pat Hogan Gang; the Syrian Cuckoo Gang and two Mafia gangs.

Just as Prohibition revived the Irish gangster, Repeal signalled their downfall. In Chicago those Irish hoods who did not conform to the Syndicate rules were wiped out. It was the same in every other major city. In New Orleans William Bailey, arch rival of the Mafia forces, was shot dead as he walked along a street by a shotgun-wielding Sam Carolla, who stepped from his limousine and blasted Bailey with both barrels. Carolla emerged as king of the rackets after murdering all his rivals. While in Toledo, Ohio beer baron Jackie Kennedy came under pressure from the Detroit Licavoli Family. The Mafia forces wiped out Kennedy's mob eventually catching Jackie Kennedy on a dark suburban street with his mistress, Miss Tiger Woman. The Mafia hitman walked up to Kennedy, who never had a chance to reach for his gun and shot him dead at close range. Dapper Danny Hogan, St. Paul bootlegger and political fixer was killed in a car bomb attack in 1928. In St. Louis and Baltimore where Irish hoods had been dominant since the 19th century the Mafia emerged as the victors in the bootleg battles.

In New York Irish mobsters fought a losing battle with the Jews and Italians for control of the city's lucrative bootlegging rackets. The bootlegging business in New York was half Jewish, a quarter Italian an eighth Irish and an eighth Polish. The West Side of Manhattan spawned many of Prohibition's Irish gangsters. One of the most notorious was Owen Vincent Madden. Born in 1892 in Liverpool, England - his parents were from County Tyrone - Owney Madden arrived in New York in 1903 after his father's death to live with an aunt in the notorious Hell's Kitchen on Manhattan's West Side. He began hanging around with the

Gophers, one of the main Irish gangs on the West Side. By the time he was seventeen Madden had progressed to one of the main leaders of the gang. He was an expert street fighter and was credited with devising the trick of sewing a razor blade in the peak of his cap and slashing an opponents face by merely bobbing his head. To celebrate his leadership position Madden beat an Italian man to death.

In 1911 Madden, always the ladies man, shot dead a clerk named William Henshaw who had tried to chat up one of his girls. The killing was committed in front of dozens of witnesses aboard a tram car at 9th Avenue and West 16th Street. Henshaw stayed alive long enough to name Madden as his killer. Two weeks later, after a dramatic rooftop chase across Hell's Kitchen, Madden was arrested. He was released when no witnesses came forward.

On November 6 1912 in a dance hall quarrel the small and slender Madden took on eleven hoods from the rival Hudson Dusters and ended up in hospital perforated by five bullets. Asked by police to name his assailants, he said, "It's nobody's business but mine." By the time he was released from hospital, the Gophers had evened the score a bit; six of his attackers were dead. However, Madden had a new problem. Little Patsy Doyle had passed word around that Madden was crippled for life and he was assuming leadership of the Gophers. Madden was not impressed. He was less impressed when Little Patsy started talking to the police. Madden lured Doyle to a saloon at 8th Avenue and 41st Street and put three bullets into him. Convicted for manslaughter - he pleaded self-defence - Madden served 8 years of a 10 year sentence.

When Madden was released in 1923 the "little banty rooster from Hell" had changed into a sleek, dapper, sophisticated criminal. Staked by Larry Fay, a former member of the Gophers, Madden went into bootlegging, laundry and coal delivery rackets. He formed a partnership with George Jean "Big Frenchy" DeMange, a bootlegger and speakeasy owner and former leader of the Hudson Dusters. Together they opened the Cotton Club in Harlem, the most famous jazz club in its time, where the wealthy rubbed elbows with gangsters like Lucky Luciano and Dutch Schultz. Madden became friendly with Jimmy Hines and forged alliances with the new Syndicate leaders like Luciano, Meyer Lansky, Frank Costello and Lepke Buchalter.

In 1931 Vincent "Mad Dog" Coll, a reckless Irish gangster, kidnapped Big Frenchy and acquired a $35,000 dollar ransom from Madden for his partner's release. Madden then told his men to team up with Dutch Schultz in his war against Coll. A few months later Coll was on the phone threatening Madden with death if he did not fork out again. Madden kept him on the phone long enough until two gunmen showed up to end the Mad Dog's bloody reign.

In the 1930s Madden moved into the boxing rackets and joined Broadway Bill Duffy in piloting a hapless Primo Carnera into the heavyweight championship title. Carnera never made a dollar from the deal but Madden and Duffy made a fortune. The two gangsters rigged Carnera's title fights to keep him reigning champion until it was too obvious. By 1934 Carnera had fulfilled his usefulness. One June night in Long Island Max Baer beat the hulking Carnera to a pulp. Madden also controlled the interests of five world champions, including Baer and Rocky Marciano.

In 1932 Madden was sent back to jail for a parole violation, and when he was released he was subjected to intensive heat from Tom Dewey's racket-busting campaign. He decided to retire from the rackets and open a health spa in Hot Springs, Arkansas. It was a nice quite existence, no bullets to dodge and the local politicians and police were only too willing to do his bidding. Occasionally, some old friends would drop by when they were on the run or recuperating from wounds. Lucky Luciano hid out in Hot Springs until Tom Dewey applied massive pressure and there was a national outcry. Still, Madden kept Luciano under his protection for several months, until finally twenty armed Arkansas Rangers were sent to arrest Luciano and take him to Little Rock, the state capital, from where he was extradited to New York. Lepke Buchalter also hid out in Hot Springs until he went back to New York to face the music and the electric chair. Bugsy Siegel hid there too until his murder charge was dropped. Meyer Lansky visited a lot and he and Madden opened several casinos locally.

When Luciano was freed in 1946 Madden was one of the delegates at the going-away party on board the *S.S. Laura Keene* - which brought Luciano to exile in Italy. Madden ran the local casinos with quiet expertise, and when Lansky bought the Tropical Park racetrack near Miami, he used relatives of Madden's to front him. Madden achieved a considerable measure of respectability in Hot Springs, marrying the postmaster's daughter and in 1943 becoming an American citizen, his wife pleading his case at his naturalisation hearings. "We are fighting a World War to do away with intolerance and persecution," she said. "I believe Mr Madden is entitled to some consideration."

On April 24 1965 the *New York Times* front page reported that Owney Madden, an "ex-gangster" who had given big contributions to charity, had died of emphysema.

Bay Ridge in Brooklyn produced another flamboyant Irish gangster. Vincent "Vannie" Higgins was born in 1897 in the Bay Ridge area where he grew up learning the trade of pickpocket and petty thief. After a criminal apprenticeship in street gangs, Vannie formed his own gang, branching into bootlegging and eventually teaming up with Big Bill Dwyer. After Big

Bill's downfall in 1927 Higgins branched out into other areas of Brooklyn and Manhattan where he had working associations with Legs Diamond and Anthony Carfano.

Vannie liked to boast that "I don't let my boys take no risks I don't take," and he was only too willing to lead his men into battle. He had several gunshot and knife wounds to prove it and he was utterly fearless and reckless in action. In 1928 Higgins and several gang members were involved in a shootout with some of Sammy Orlando's mob in Brooklyn's Owl Head Cafe. The police arrived and began firing in all directions. Patrolman Daniel Maloney was shot and killed in crossfire from other policemen. Higgins was seen running away from the scene with his top enforcer Bad Bill Bailey. Two weeks later Sammy Orlando was murdered and Higgins and Bailey were arrested and charged with murder. By the time the case came up for trial, the witnesses against Higgins and Bailey had disappeared.

Higgins' Manhattan incursions eventually ended up in another gang war, this time with the Bronx Beer Baron, Dutch Schultz. Vannie allied himself with Legs Diamond and Vince Coll, who were also battling the Dutchman. Higgins obtained a shipment of stolen grenades which he used to good effect blowing up several speakeasies operated by Schultz.

Higgins was a loud, brash gangster who liked to talk to reporters and pose for photographs in his specially imported suits. He had plenty of political and police connections, once flying one of his private planes to Comstock, N.Y., to visit an old friend, Joseph H. Wilson, warden of Comstock Prison. Warden Wilson had used convict labour to clear a nearby field where Vannie could land his plane. However, despite his many friends Higgins had also made many enemies. On the night of June 18 1932 Higgins was leaving the Knights of Columbus clubhouse in Prospect Park, accompanied by his wife, mother-in-law, and daughter Jean, who had just performed an Irish dancing recital. As they stepped out into the street, machine-gun fire from a slowly passing car splattered the building and pavement. Young Jean Higgins was nicked in the ear and dived, screaming hysterically, into her father's car. Mrs Higgins and her mother ran back into the clubhouse. Vannie drew his revolver and chased after the car, his wife calling for him to come back. He chased the car on foot but a burst from a tommy-gun mortally wounded him. Higgins was rushed to the Methodist Episcopal Hospital where he died several hours later, his last words were, "The rats! They tried to wipe out my family!"

As the Roaring Twenties faded men of vision like Meyer Lansky and Lucky Luciano and even Al Capone foresaw that Prohibition would soon fade away too. They realised it would be far more profitable to organise for that eventuality and also to milk the profits that Prohibition still offered. In May 1929 thirty gang leaders from across the country gathered in Atlantic City, New Jersey for a three day conference and set the foundation for the formation of the new nation-wide Syndicate. It was an impressive gathering of America's biggest criminal talent and was held in the luxury of the President's Hotel. It was a multi-ethnic attendance of Jewish, Italian, Sicilian, Irish and Polish gangsters. Enoch J. "Knucky" Johnson was the overlord of Atlantic City crime and hosted the conference. The biggest contingent came from New York among them Meyer Lansky, Lucky Luciano, Frank Costello, Dutch Schultz, Lepke Buchalter, Frank Erickson, Albert Anastasia, Johnny Torrio - who had a tearful reunion with Al Capone - Owney Madden, Larry Fay, and Bugsy Siegel. From Chicago came Al Capone and Jake Guzik; Longy Zwillman of New Jersey; Nig Rosen and Max Hoff of Philadelphia; Joe Bemstein and Louis Fleisher of Detroit's Purple Gang; Charles "King" Solomon of Boston; Moe Dalitz and Chuck Polizzi of Cleveland; Danny Walsh of Providence, Rhode Island;

Tom Pendergast, the political boss of Kansas City was the only politician invited to attend. He found it inopportune to attend himself and sent Johnny Lazia, the city's Mafia boss, to represent him.

Almost half of the delegates were Jewish, the biggest ethnics in organised crime at this time. The conference was the creation of two of crime's most talented leaders, Meyer Lansky and Johnny Torrio. (It must be remembered that Torrio had organised Chicago's gangs as early as 1920.) For three days the gang bosses hammered out their differences. Co-operation in every sphere was preached; there would be no hijackings of bootleg liquor and no gang wars, which were bad for business and usually led to police crackdowns. Plans were laid down for activities after the inevitable repeal of Prohibition. It was agreed that the gangs would branch out into legitimate "business" and more into gambling and labour racketeering.

The new Syndicate was based on mutual co-operation. Everyone would be given a chance to join, those that scorned the new enterprise would be eliminated. The seeds of a nation-wide enforcement arm, later to be known as Murder Incorporated, were sown. There were handshakes all round when the delegates left Atlantic City to spread their new gospel. In 1931 the gangsters, most notably Meyer Lansky and Lucky Luciano, organised a national crime Syndicate on a permanent and more efficient basis.

Italian and Jewish criminals had long co-operated as a matter of convenience. Both groups arrived at the same time and felt the lash of nativist discrimination. The main occupiers of the ghettos were at the time the Irish and they also discriminated against the new immigrants. A rapport developed between the Jews and the Italians that did not develop in the main with Irish gangsters, who had long dominated American crime and now felt threatened by the expanding activities of these newcomers. As a result more Irish gangsters were wiped out in the development of organised crime than any other ethnic group. In Chicago the Italians wiped out the Irish North Siders while in New York Jewish mobsters knocked off Legs Diamond, Mad Dog Coll and Vannie Higgins. In Brooklyn the Mafia also finished off the Irish White Hand Gang. It was the same story in most other major American cities. By the end of Prohibition the Irish gangster was no longer a major force in organised crime.

Prohibition was repealed in 1933. On February 16 the Senate voted 63 to 23 to submit the Twenty-first Amendment to the State Legislatures, undoing the Eighteenth. However, the great gangs of the Prohibition era remained. Many of them stayed in business, thanks to their bootleg millions. Some though could not adapt to the changing times and returned to conventional crime. In the end Prohibition give birth to and nurtured organised crime giving it its strength and power which it still retains.

CHAPTER 6

THE CHICAGO BOOTLEG WARS

From the early 1920s to the 1930s Chicago was, in the words of Lucky Luciano, himself no stranger to violence, "a real crazy place." Over five hundred people died in the Bootleg Wars waged mainly between the forces of Al Capone and the North Side Irish mob.

THE SOUTH SIDE BEER WAR.
On January 17 1920 the National Prohibition Act came into effect, banning the manufacture and supply of alcohol. It was the culmination of a campaign that had its roots in the 1840s when nativists first tried to ban alcoholic beverages favoured by new immigrants. Chicago, like many of the big cities, had voted heavily against Prohibition. It was the triumph of town and rural district over the immigrant filled cities. Because a law had been passed and drinking alcohol was now illegal it did not stop Americans from drinking. Gangsters were ready for this golden opportunity to take over supplying the huge demand.

Johnny Torrio was a diplomat and had the foresight to see

the huge profits that Prohibition offered. He foresaw the dangers of rivalry and called a meeting of all the major gangs in the city. Chicago was carved up into sections, each to be a territory of a different gang. The gangs would have political and police protection. The small time operators were mercilessly wiped out. Bootleg beer was given a set price and no one was to undercut the price or to encroach on another's turf.

The North Side was controlled by Dion O'Bannion, a quick tempered killer with a formidable army of gunmen; on the West Side were the O'Donnells, an all Irish gang; between Little Italy and the suburb of Cicero, Frankie Lake and Terry Druggan ran another Irish mob, the Valley Gang; Little Italy on the South Side was in the hands of the Gennas, six murderous Sicilian brothers; on the far South Side was another Irish mob of O'Donnells (no relation to the West Side O'Donnells) and a Polish-Irish gang, the Saltis-McErlane mob; Johnny Torrio ran rackets on the South Side as well as running brothels in the O'Donnell area and in Cicero; Ragen's Colts also operated on the South Side around the stockyards.

It was in the summer of 1923 when the first rounds of the Chicago Bootleg Wars began. Edward "Spike" O'Donnell had been in Joliet Prison, serving time for armed robbery, when territory had been allocated and his gang were only given "crumbs" as Spike said himself. On his release he let it he known that he wanted a bigger piece of the action. Spike was known to have murdered at least six rivals in his long criminal career and was pardoned in July 1923 by Governor Len Small at the request of six state senators, five state representatives and one criminal court judge. The South Side O'Donnells, Spike, Walter Steve and Tommy, began to check incursions by the Torrio-Capone mob on their territory, known as the "Kerry Patch", after Spike's release. He hired more men and they began to hijack Torrio-Capone trucks and force the sale of their cheaper beer in Torrio-Capone and Saltis-McErlane "turf". "I got a mob of blue-eyed Irish boys who are with me to stay", Spike was quoted as saying. "No Saltis is going to run us out." However, the Saltis-McErlanes proceeded to do just that. On September 7 1924 Steve, Walter and Tommy O'Donnell together with George "Spot" Bucher, George Meeghan and Jerry O'Connor visited the speakeasy run by Jacob Geis to persuade him to buy their beer and not the stuff the Saltis-McErlanes were selling. It was the last of five calls and five beatings. The O'Donnells beat up Geis and the two bartenders. Unknown to them they were being followed by Frank McErlane and two other hoods. The O'Donnells went on to Klepka's Bar where they were joined by Spike. Here they were ambushed by McErlane and Danny McFall, a Cook County deputy sheriff. McFall came in the front door pistols drawn, "Stick up your hands or I'll blow you all to hell!" he shouted. The O'Donnells ran to the rear where McErlane was waiting. O'Connor was shot through the heart and died in the street as the rest fled. McFall was indicted for murder but he was acquitted in January 1924.

Saltis-McErlane territory was in the near South West side of the city, a lucrative area of hard-working and hard-drinking stockyard and factory workers. By 1922 the Saltis-McErlanes had become a satellite of the Torrio-Capone mob. Al Capone informed Frank McErlane that if the going got too rough he would send in his troops. There was no need for them. On September 17 Spot Bucher and George Meeghan, driving two truckloads of beer, were held up and blasted with shotguns by Frank McErlane and Danny McFall. The following December McErlane killed Morris Keane, a beer truck driver and several days later killed Peter Corrigan as his beer truck drove by. The O'Donnells imported a New Jersey hitman, Henry Hasmiller, to take out their most dangerous foe, but McErlane got wind of it and on April 17 1925 walked into an Evergreen Park roadhouse and shotgunned to death both Hasmiller and Walter O'Donnell as they sat at a table.

On September 25 McErlane, using a Thompson sub-machine gun - its first recorded use in a gangland shooting - attempted to kill Spike O'Donnell. McErlane drove past a South Side store-front in a slow moving car and sprayed it with fifty rounds in an attempt to hit Spike, who survived unharmed. The alcoholic McErlane was not exactly too bright and he found that just pointing the weapon and squeezing the trigger suited him per-fect. Until the 1920s the tommy gun, produced at the end of WW1, could be freely purchased by mail or in sporting-goods stores. The tommy guns had been bought from the North Side Irish mob, whose leader, Dion O'Bannion had brought them to Chicago from Colorado shortly before his death. The Saltis-McErlanes had quietly defected from the Torrio-Capone alliance and had joined forces with Hymie Weiss, O'Bannion's successor. McErlane was reputed to have personally killed fif-teen men, but was never arrested for any of the many shootings he was seen to commit, thanks to his police and political pro-tection. (In 1926 he was jailed for bootlegging, but was released the following year.)

On October 9 another attempt by Joe Saltis and Lefty Paddy Sullivan, a former Chicago police sergeant, left Spike in no doubt that he was on the losing side. Spike narrowly escaped with his life and in returning his would-be assassin's fire, he wounded a policeman by mistake. A week later McErlane riddled Spike's car, wounding his brother Tommy. Spike on the defensive from attacks on two fronts - he had lost seven men compared to two Saltis-McErlane hoods - fled to New York, announcing, "I can whip this bird Capone with my bare fists anytime he wants to step out in the open and fight like a man." But the days of fisticuffs were over. It was the day of the pistol and tommy gun now.

A year or so later, after reaching an accommodation with Capone, the remaining O'Donnells resumed their bootlegging operations, though on a smaller scale and always under the thumb of Big Al. Spike outlived the bullet and died of a heart attack in 1962.

THE WEST SIDE BEER WAR.

The O'Donnell brothers, Myles, Bemard and William or Klondike, dominated the West Side of Chicago between Madison and Grand Avenue. Their influence expanded into the suburb of Cicero where Johnny Torrio and Al Capone were beginning to exert their muscle. The O'Donnells gang was fairly small and they knew a fight with the Torrio-Capones was suicidal, so they entered an alliance with them. The Cicero speakeasies were divided between both groups, though in the Italians favour. The Torrio-Capones also ran brothels in the O'Donnells areas. Like the North Side O'Bannions, the O'Donnells would have no dealings with prostitution. The O'Donnells even provided the muscle for the Torrio-Capones against smaller independents who refused to toe the line. One saloon keeper, Eddie Tancl, a former prize-fighter and a potent vote broker, refused to buy the Italian mob's beer, so Myles O'Donnell and James J. Doherty made a visit to Tancl's saloon in Cicero.

Myles was the youngest of the O'Donnells. Slim, fair haired and sickly, he lacked the toughness to take over when Klondike went to jail. Klondike was the natural leader of the gang. Of big build, he had a red face and black hair, and like Spike O'Donnell, who was no relation, he was of the older breed of gangster. The middle brother, Bemard was of less importance than Myles. The most vibrant members of the gang were Doherty and James "Fur" Sammons, their ace enforcers. Eddie Tancl had been a power in the pre-Torrio-Capone days and made it clear that he was not going to knuckle under. Myles O'Donnell and Jim Doherty began drinking in Tancl's saloon, the Hawthorne Inn, on Saturday night November 22 1924. They returned early Sunday morning and started drinking again. Around eleven o'clock they started an argument about a $5.50 check. Myles hit waiter Martin Simet with his gun, just as Tancl walked in. Tancl pulled out his gun and Doherty did likewise. Both O'Donnell and Doherty started shooting at Tancl and bartender, Leo Klimas. Tancl was hit by four bullets but before he fell to the ground mortally wounded he managed to get off seven shots, hitting O'Donnell with three and Doherty with two.

They stumbled out into the street followed by Klimas who tackled O'Donnell on the pavement. Klimas might have finished off O'Donnell only Doherty shot him through the head, killing him instantly. Local church-goers and shoppers threw themselves into doorways and behind cars as the violence spilled out onto the streets. By the time the two gangsters came to trial the following spring, stories had been changed and witnesses had disappeared. The jury took only nine minutes to find O'Donnell and Doherty not guilty. The prosecutor in the case was William Harold McSwiggin, known as the "hangman prosecutor". He had obtained seven death penalties in eleven murder cases in eight months. Yet no one seemed to notice that McSwiggin and Doherty were boyhood pals and had kept up their friendship.

By 1926 the O'Donnells had fallen out of favour with Al Capone - Torrio by now had retired from the rackets - by siding with the North Siders in their war with the Capones. Doherty had accompanied Schemer Drucci in his murder of Samoots Amutana in a Cicero barbershop. The turmoil in Little Italy as opposing forces fought for the leadership of the *Unione Siciliana,* was viewed by the O'Donnells as weakness on Capone's part. He could not keep his own back yard quiet, let alone the South Side. The O'Donnells began to push the sale of their beer, which was better than Capone's needle beer. Harry Madigan, owner of the Pony Inn in Cicero said, "I changed and upon my recommendation so did several other Cicero saloon-keepers." Worse still, Myles O'Donnell and Fur Sammons were heard openly boasting about it. Capone had no choice but to go to war.

On April 3 1926 John "The Fox" Ryan, a gunman for Ralph Sheldon, shot dead Walter Quinlan in a saloon on South Loomis Street. Quinlan was one of Kiondike's top men. Six years before Quinlan had murdered Ryan's father, Paddy the Bear, ruler of the Valley. Ryan undoubtedly delighted in the job, but it was not a revenge killing. It was done at Capone's urging. Police learned that both Myles O'Donnell and Jim Doherty had wit-nessed the murder. They found them at Doherty's saloon on Roosevelt. They also seized bullet-proof vests, which would soon figure in a prominent killing. Surprisingly, O'Donnell and Doherty readily identified Ryan as Quinlan's killer. On April 23 1926 Capone's gunmen armed with their new tommy guns shot up a beauty parlour belonging to Fur Sammons' girlfriend, seriously wounding Sammons and narrowly missing Jim Doherty.

On April 27 Klondike and Myles O'Donnell, Doherty and Eddie Hanley spent the day as Bob Crowe officials, watching a recount of the primary ballots. The O'Donnells had helped in the recent election of Crowe's candidates, especially Joseph P. Savage, who ran for county judge, a post that controlled the election mechanism. Later on they picked up Tom "Red" Duffy and dropped Klondike home. About 7.30 the car, Doherty's green Lincoln, stopped outside Bill McSwiggin's house. Duffy went in to get McSwiggin. Like Doherty, Duffy had also been McSwiggin's boyhood friend. Duffy worked as a small-time bootlegger and gambler for the O'Donnells. The five then drove to Harry Madigan's Pony Inn in Cicero. Unknown to them they had been spotted by Capone hoods and trailed by a five car cavalcade to Cicero.

The Pony Inn on Roosevelt stood alone in an otherwise vacant lot. As McSwiggin, Doherty and Duffy stepped out of the Lincoln a Cadillac approached from the east. Al Capone leaned out, a tommy gun in his hands and sprayed the Lincoln. McSwiggin fell in a heap at the door of the tavern, while Duffy hit by five bullets staggered into the empty lot to hide behind a tree. Doherty lay sprawled on the pavement, riddled by sixteen bullets. Myles O'Donnell and Hanley hugged the floor of the Lincoln and were not hit.

Myles and Hanley loaded McSwiggin and Doherty into the car and drove to Klondike's house. They must have missed Duffy for he was found propped up against a tree by a passing motorist who drove him to hospital where he died six hours later. McSwiggin and Doherty were found to be dead on arrival and Klondike ordered them to dump the bodies. The two bullet ravaged bodies were dumped in Berwyn where they were soon discovered.

The murder of McSwiggin caused an uproar. McSwiggin's father named Al Capone, Frankie Rio, Frank Diamond and Bob McCullough as the killers. Capone denied having any part in the killings hinting that the popular young assistant state's attorney was on the take. Interviewed by a journalist Capone said, "Of course I didn't kill him. I liked the kid. Only the day before he was up to my place and I gave him a bottle of Scotch for his old man. I paid McSwiggin. I paid him plenty and I got what I was paying for."

That the popular McSwiggin had been killed in the company of gangsters shocked Chicago citizens who were not easily shocked but that a state attorney had been gunned down like any common criminal had them clamouring for action. It was seen as a direct attack on the State. The truth was that McSwiggin was in the wrong place at the wrong time. Capone had wanted to teach the O'Donnells a lesson. He was too shrewd to murder someone like McSwiggin, which was bound to bring down the kind of heat he wanted to avoid.

The police announced that McSwiggin had been "following up a case" and arrested Al and Ralph Capone, Charlie Fischetti, Pete Payette, Harry Madigan and the three O'Donnells and charged them with conspiracy to violate the Volstead Act. The police announced that McSwiggin had been following up a lead on a missing bullet proof vest, one of five seized at Doherty's saloon. The O'Donnells even embraced this story. After three grand juries all the charges were dropped for lack of evidence and all defendants were released. The McSwiggin case was never resolved. The murders had their desired effect. Within a few months the West Side O'Donnells had drifted into obscurity with their territory being swallowed by the Capone mob. Myles O'Donnell died young, in 1932, of illness, while Klondike later flourished as part of the Outfit.

THE NORTH SIDE WAR:
THE BOOTLEG BATTLE OF THE MARNE.

Late in 1923 the Sicilian Genna brothers began to invade other areas from their base in Little Italy and undersell other bootleg gangs with their cheaply manufactured bathtub booze - the main source of income for many of the poor Italian and Sicilian families that produced it for them. Johnny Torrio, ever the diplomat, tried to keep the peace, saying there was enough money to go around for everyone. But Dion O'Bannion, the leader of the North Side mob was also getting restless. He couldn't resist hijacking Torrio's booze trucks. For O'Bannion old habits died hard.

Born in Maroa, Illinois, in 1892, Charles Dean (often spelled Dion) O'Bannion grew up in the Little Hell district on Chicago's

North Side. Little Hell was close to the Sicilian quarter and Death Corner and was formerly an Irish shantytown called Kilgubbin. Barely a half-mile square it was a maze of narrow streets. The flames from a local gasworks chimney reddened the sky at night and gave the area its nickname - Little Hell. As a young tearaway O'Bannion ran with the juvenile branch of the Market Street Gang, the Little Hellions. As a boy he had sung in the choir at Holy Name Cathedral. At night Deanie, as he was known to his friends, sang in the tough dives on Clark and Erie, bringing tears to the customer's eyes with sentimental Irish ballads. Later on he would roll the same drunks as they staggered home. O'Bannion injured his leg in a fall, while escaping from a policeman, when he was a teenager. The growth was stunted and Deanie was left with one leg an inch shorter than the other, giving him a slight limp, which he exaggerated when wishing to intimidate rivals in later life. Because of this he was known as "Gimpy" , but never to his face.

From mugging O'Bannion graduated, along with such notables as Joe Saltis, Tommy Malloy and Frank and Vince McErlane, to slugging for Maxie Annenberg, who was in charge of promoting sales of the *Chicago Tribune.* The "circulation wars" gave many of the Prohibition-era gangsters their big start. In these newspaper circulation wars rival vans were overturned and their contents destroyed, while street corner vendors were beaten up and robbed. When the opposition offered Deanie more money he transferred his loyalties to the newer Randolph Hearst *Herald-Examiner.* He would later do the same in politics.

In 1911 O'Bannion received three months for carrying a concealed weapon. It was the last time he would go to prison. He quickly learned that Chicago was the city of the fix. As a result of his work for Hearst he got to know many politicians and reporters. The likeable O'Bannion was looked upon as a colourful character and enjoyed good press from his many friends in

Chicago's newspapers. For years he brought in the vote for his hand-picked political candidates. At each election and old refrain was asked by the press and politicians: "Who'll carry the Forty-Second and Forty-Third wards?" The answer was always the same. "O'Bannion will in his pistol pockets." O'Bannion always delivered landslide returns for his candidates who, once in office, turned a blind eye to his many criminal activities. He ran these activities from Schofield's flower shop, in which he owned a half-share, at 738 North State Street, directly opposite the cathedral he sang in as a boy. It provided him as a front, but also satisfied his love for flowers. O'Bannion did a great trade, providing flowers for gangsters funerals. On many occasions he also provided the corpses - he was reputed to have murdered at least 25 people and was dubbed by the Chief of Police as "Chicago's arch criminal."

By the advent of Prohibition O'Bannion was the leader of a mighty gang on the North Side, which controlled the wealthy "Gold Coast" and the northern lakefront neighbourhoods. He formed an alliance with many Jewish gangsters of the old 20th Ward, especially those working with Samuel "Nails" Morton, and the gangs eventually merged. The O'Bannion mob was a formidable foe and comprised some of the toughest and most ruthless hoods in the city.

Among the senior members were Hymie Weiss, George "Bugs" Moran, Vincent "The Schemer" Drucci, the only Sicilian O'Bannion would ever trust, Louis "Two-Gun" Alterie, Daniel "Dapper Dan" McCarthy and the Gusenberg brothers, Frank and Pete. The North Side mob was also the most zaniest gang of the period. Deanie himself was a charming psychopath. He would do anything for a laugh.

Once he filled both barrels of a shotgun with hard clay and bet an acquaintance that he could not hit the side of a barn thirty feet away. When the shotgun exploded in his 'friend's' face O'Bannion though it hilarious. Obviously, his badly injured "friend" did not.

O'Bannion was a doting husband. He always remained loyal to his wife, always returning home for dinner - if he was not out on a robbery or murder. She told reporters that: "Dion loved his home and spent most of his evenings in it. He loved to sit in his slippers, fooling with the radio, singing a song, listening to the piano player. He never drank. He was not a man to run around nights with other women. I was his only sweetheart." O'Bannion was also deeply religious - he always carried a rosary in one pocket, a carnation in his lapel and three guns hidden on his person. (His suits were specially made concealing three extra pockets for weapons - one under the left armpit of the coat-jacket, another on the outside left and a third on the centre front of the trousers. He could shoot accurately with either hand, having been taught how by fellow Irishman, Gene Geary, another psychopath whose eyes filled with tears when Deanie sang his sentimental ballads.) Deanie would not allow his men to involve themselves in prostitution, saying it was a lowly act only fit for Italians and Sicilians. He boasted that not one brothel operated on the North Side. After all such activities were "against the Holy Mother, the Church."

O'Bannion shared his fortune with the less well off people of his wards. At Thanksgiving and Christmas, trucks loaded with turkeys and other foodstuffs were donated to the poor. His gang - unlike any other modern gang this century - was held together by deep affection, loyalty and genuine respect. When Nails Morton heard that the Gennas had hired an out of town killer, named Frank Constanza, to kill O'Bannion, he and Two-Gun Alterie were waiting for the hitman when he arrived by train. Morton shot Constanza dead and with Alterie's help threw the body into an east-bound boxcar saying, "Now the bum is heading back to New York where he belongs."

Nails Morton was a WW1 veteran, a winner of the Croix de Guerre in France. He was believed to have killed eight men, including two policemen, and was one of the most visible gangsters during the early Prohibition period. He lived the high life, dressing in expensive suits, sporting a diamond stick-pin in silk ties and carrying an ivory-handled walking stick, which contained a small, razor-sharp sword. He also developed an interest in horse riding, having been introduced to it on Two-Gun Alterie's Colorado ranch. Nails even introduced Deanie in the sport and on May 13 1923 he had an appointment to meet O'Bannion to go riding in Lincoln Park. The horse Morton had hired was a spirited mount and threw Nails, then kicked him in the head, killing him.

Morton's funeral was a massive affair, with floral tributes by the truckload. O'Bannion, Hymie Weiss, Two-Gun Alterie, Bugs Moran, Schemer Drucci and Frank Gusenberg carried the coffin of their dear friend. Even Johnny Torrio and Al Capone attended. Twenty-five thousand people lined the streets of the old Maxwell Street area. To these people Nails Morton was a war hero and a local hero, a defender of the rights of the Jewish people. That he had been a gangster and a murderer did not matter. He was one of them and a success.

To his North Side friends his "murder" was unforgivable. It was an eye for an eye. Alterie rented out the offending animal and with Weiss, Moran and Drucci, he brought the horse to the spot where nails had died. Alterie was so upset over his friends death he punched the horse in the snout. Then each of the madcap gangsters pulled their pistols and each one shot the hapless horse in the head. Alterie later called the owner and shouted over the phone: "We taught that damned horse of yours a lesson! If you want the saddle, go and get it!" When O'Bannion heard the news he bemoaned the fact that he had not been around when vengeance was exacted.

In early 1924, despite O'Bannion's criminal background, including several shootings in public view, a banquet was held in his honour by the Chicago Democratic party for "services rendered". It was dubbed the "Balshazzar Feast" by the press and clergy. O'Bannion sat beaming at the head of the great table with Moran, Weiss, Alterie, Frank Gusenberg, Con Shea, a notorious labour racketeer and killer, Maxie Eisen, another labour racketeer responsible for bringing several labour unions under O'Bannions control and Loop gambler Jerry O'Connor. Facing them were Michael Hughes, Chief of Detectives, Police Lieutenant Charles Evans, William Scott Stewart, a former assistant state's attorney, County Clerk Robert M. Sweitzer and Colonel Albert A. Sprague, Democratic nominee for United States Senator and dozens of office holders and Democratic and Republican politicians. The main reason for the banquet was a rumour that O'Bannion was switching his allegiance from the Democrats to the Republicans. The Democrats had returned William E. Dever as mayor of Chicago in the recent election. Dever was a reformer and insisted that the laws against many of O'Bannion's activities be enforced. O'Bannion let it be known that he was not impressed. At the banquet Democratic politicians made speeches in his honour and even presented him with a $2,000 platinum watch, all to no avail. Deanie and the votes of the 42nd and 43rd Wards went to the Republicans.

Among the many Chicago gang leaders there was none more resentful of O'Bannion's success and power as Johnny Torrio and Al Capone. Torrio had turned his cheek many times from O'Bannion's insults. They watched as O'Bannion rolled in the profits of his lucrative North Side rackets, and offered to include him in their share of the Stickney brothel profits for a share in his Cicero booze concession - given by Torrio as a diplomatic gesture and for the loan of O'Bannion gunmen in the

April election. O'Bannion's answer to this was a raucous laugh and another insult. O'Bannion took pride in the fact that he provided all the saloons and speakeasies in his area with good whiskey and real beer. After all he owned several distilleries and breweries and laughed at Torrio-Capone and the Gennas rotgut and home-made alky peddled on the South Side. He was forever insulting his Italian and Sicilian rivals with racist remarks calling them "dago pimps, wop wallopers, guinea goons and spaghetti benders." He had entered an alliance with the Torrio-Capone combine, but he was not happy in it. He did not like sharing his profits with the Italians, nor did he trust his partners. Among O'Bannion's most lucrative ventures with Torrio and Capone was a huge gambling casino called The Ship. When Angelo Genna left I.O.U.s totalling $30,000 - losses were usually split among the three partners - O'Bannion rang him up and snarled, "You got one week to pay up, spaghetti bender!" Bloody Angelo, as he was known due to his many murders, felt this a personal insult and informed Johnny Torrio that he was going to kill O'Bannion. Torrio ordered Angelo to pay his debt and forget the insult. Angelo paid, but he did not forget.

In May 1924 O'Bannion informed Torrio he was quitting the rackets and retiring out West to a ranch and offered to sell the Sieben brewery for half-a-million dollars. Torrio jumped at the chance to purchase his own brewery and to be rid of the unpredictable Irishman. While O'Bannion and Torrio were inspecting the premises the police raided it, arresting both gang leaders and several of their men. The brewery was closed down and O'Bannion was a half-a-million richer. Torrio as a second offender - he was fined a year earlier for manufacturing alcohol - would end up in jail. O'Bannion thought the whole escapade was hilarious. Not only did O'Bannion double-cross Torrio by tipping off the police but he openly bragged about it. Even when Hymie Weiss urged him to make amends with Torrio,

O'Bannion shrugged him off. "Oh, to hell with them Sicilians," he said.

All out war was inevitable, but Mike Merlo, the head of the Chicago branch of the *Unione Siciliana* - a Sicilian fraternal organisation with ties to organised crime - kept the peace. Then on November 8 1924 Merlo died of cancer. Wreaths and floral tributes were ordered by the dozen from O'Bannion's flower shop. On the morning of November 10 three men arrived to pick up a pre-ordered wreath. The porter, William Crutchfield, witnessed the three swarthy strangers talking and shaking hands with O'Bannion.

"Hello, boys," O'Bannion greeted them. "You want Merlo's flowers?"

"Yes ... for Merlo's flowers," one man said offering his hand. Deanie took the outstretched hand. As the man held O'Bannion's hand in a firm grip his two accomplices pulled out guns and pumped bullets into O'Bannion. He died instantly with four bullets in the head and two in his chest. The gunmen had held the guns so close there were powder burns on the corpse.

The killers were believed to be Mike Genna, the man in the middle who had held O'Bannion's hand, and Albert Anselmi and John Scalise, the Gennas top killers, known as the "Homicide Squad." O'Bannion rarely shook hands with anyone and usually stood feet apart, his hands ready to go for any of his three guns. He obviously was not expecting trouble and felt safe enough to offer his hand in friendship to Mike Genna.

O'Bannion received one of the biggest funerals ever seen in Chicago. As one newspaper commented, "Presidents are buried with less to-do." The bronze and silver casket cost $10,000 and was brought in specially from Philadelphia. The funeral procession was a mile long with twenty-six cars and trucks laden with flowers. Before the funeral forty-thousand people passed through the undertakers to view the body, while ten-thousand followed the hearse to be met by thousands more at the Mount Carmel cemetery, where Deanie was laid to rest as his friends and enemies, including Torrio and Capone, stood solemn faced.

Many Chicago dignitaries were present at the funeral, leading reform judge, John H. Lyle, to say, "It was one of the most nauseating sights I have ever seen in Chicago." The Cardinal Archbishop banned O'Bannion from being buried in consecrated ground or to have the last rites administered, despite pleas from his wife and many church figures. Father Malloy, an elderly priest, who remembered Deanie as an innocent altar-boy in Holy Name Cathedral, knelt and said three Hail Mary's and the Our Father - against his superior's orders - as the casket was lowered into the earth. Mrs. Viola O'Bannion thanked him and the old priest replied: "It was the least I could do. No matter what he became he was one of ours at the beginning."

Hymie Weiss wept openly, and honestly, at O'Bannion's funeral. The two gangsters had been the best of pals. When Torrio and Capone showed up at the cemetery with six bodyguards, Hymie kept the O'Bannion boys in check, having promised Deanie's widow there would be no violence until O'Bannion was laid to rest. Asked by a reporter if he held Al Capone responsible, Weiss threw up his hands in mock horror. "Blame Capone. Why Al's a real pal. He was Dion's best friend, too." But inside he was seething. He plotted revenge on Torrio, Capone and the Gennas. Weiss even banished Two-Gun Alterie because he kept publicly stating that the gang was going to get Torrio and Capone.

Leland Verain, a.k.a. Louis "Two-Gun" Alterie, was born in Denver, Colorado, in 1886 and was first arrested in Chicago in 1922 with Terry Druggan of the Valley Gang, after robbing $50,000 in jewellery from two local citizens. The witnesses contacted "Chicago amnesia" - a phrase coined by Dion

O'Bannion - and the case was dropped. Alterie later joined up with Nails Morton, who introduced him to O'Bannion who used him to organise (i.e. beat) several unions to elect him and other North Siders as lifetime presidents. As the O'Bannions fought the Gennas, the Valleys, West Side O'Donnells and Capone Alterie became one of their top gunmen, credited with killing at least twenty rivals. Alterie invented the machine gun ambush, wherein he would rent an apartment, usually on the second floor directly across from the home or working place of an intended victim. With his racket riches Alterie bought a ranch in Colorado where he, O'Bannion, Morton, Weiss and Moran used to drive around in ten-gallon hats shooting deer and other animals.

At O'Bannion's funeral, tears streaming down his cheeks, Alterie told reporters, "I have no idea who killed Deanie, but I would die smiling if only I had the chance to meet the guys who did, any time and place they mention and I would get at least two or three of them before they got me. If I knew who got Deanie, I'd shoot it out with the gang of killers before the sun rose in the morning, and some of us, maybe all of us, would be lying on slabs in the undertaker's place."

When these remarks were printed in the next day's paper, Mayor Dever asked in shock, "Are we still living in the Dark Ages?" He promptly launched a major crackdown on the North Side mob, which led Hymie Weiss to banish Alterie to Colorado. Alterie returned periodically to Chicago, still retaining control of his unions, until he was murdered in 1935, ironically, in a machine gun ambush.

On January 12 1925 the North Siders struck at Capone. As Big Al entered a restaurant, leaving his chauffeur and two bodyguards in his car, another car, containing Weiss, Schemer Drucci and Bugs Moran, drew alongside it raking it with gunfire, severely wounding the chauffeur. The attack prompted Capone to order a custom built, armour-plated car with bullet proof windows. Days after the Capone attack Johnny Torrio was ambushed as he drove his limousine. The chauffeur and Torrio's dog were killed, but Torrio was unhurt. Then, on January 24, Torrio was ambushed again, outside his apartment as he returned from a shopping trip with his wife. This time he was not so lucky. As Torrio walked towards his front door with an armload of packages, Hymie Weiss and Bugs Moran jumped out of a passing car. "This is for O'Bannion, you dago son of a bitch!" Weiss roared, blowing Torrio off his feet with a double blast from a sawn-off shotgun. Moran pumped two slugs from a .45 into Torrio and as he attempted to apply the *coup de grace* - a bullet to the head - his gun jammed. As Moran fumbled with the automatic Schemer Drucci honked the horn, in a prearranged signal and the two gangsters hopped into the car and fled. Moran was later identified by a witness as one of the assailants, but although arrested and released he was never brought to trial nor even indicted.

Torrio hovered near death for weeks, but survived. When he was discharged from hospital he left Chicago handing over the whole operation to Al Capone. (It is quite possible that Capone had tipped off the North Siders in the hope that they would get rid of Torrio for him.)"The Bootleg Battle of the Marne" now began in earnest. It was the bloodiest gang war in American criminal history. The gangs began to take sides: the West Side O'Donnells and later the Saltis-McErlanes went over to the O'Bannions, while the Gennas, the Druggan-Lake Gang and the Sheldon mob aligned themselves with Capone. The Gennas proved to be the first losers.

On May 26 newly wed Bloody Angelo Genna was driving to view a newly acquired house when he was overtaken by a car driven by Frank Gusenberg, with Weiss, Moran and Drucci on board. In a desperate effort to escape Genna accelerated, mounted the sidewalk and hit a lamp post. Pinned behind the wheel all he could do was watch helplessly as Schemer Drucci stepped out of the pursuing car and blasted him with both barrels of a sawn-off shotgun.

The O'Bannions then approached Samuzzo "Samoots" Amatuna of the Gennas and asked him to set up John Scalise and Albert Anselmi, the killers of their boss. Amatuna agreed but double-crossed them. At the appointed time, on June 13, Moran and Drucci were waiting in their car when another car pulled up. In it were Anselmi, Scalise and Mike "The Devil" Genna. They opened fire wounding both Drucci and Moran. They were spotted by a cruising police car and the cops gave chase. In the ensuing gunbattle two police officers were killed and one wounded. Anselmi and Scalise fled, leaving a severely wounded Mike Genna to be captured. He died two hours later of his wounds.

A month later Tony "The Gentleman" Genna was set up and killed by a disgruntled member of his own gang. The surviving brothers were demoralised and fled Chicago. Eventually, they abandoned the rackets and went into the olive oil import business. Samoots Amatuna became the new president of the *Unione Siciliana* but did not last long. On November 13 he was sitting in a barber shop in Cicero when Schemer Drucci and Jim Doherty, of the West Side O'Donnells, walked in and shot him dead.

Al Capone, still striving to maintain his mentors policy of pacification, tried a little diplomacy with Hymie Weiss, contacting him and promising him that the old Madison Street dividing line would be respected. Weiss said he would make peace only if Anselmi and Scalise (they had joined Capone's outfit after the disintegration of the Gennas) were turned over to him. "I wouldn't do that to a yellow dog," Capone said. Earl "Hymie" Weiss was a clever adversary. Born in Chicago, in 1898, to Polish Catholic parents, he was a regular church-goer. As a young criminal he teamed up with Dion O'Bannion and Bugs Moran. They were all great pals. Weiss was credited with inventing the "one-way ride". When Steve Wisniewski hi-jacked an O'Bannion beer truck Weiss exacted revenge. Wisniewski was brought for a drive along Lake Michigan and was never seen alive again. "We took Stevie for a ride, a one way ride," Weiss later told O'Bannion.

Under Weiss' leadership the North Siders took over the Gennas territory and moved southwest into Capone's territory. They expanded into the South West Side, forging an alliance with Joe Saltis and Frank McErlane, who invaded the Sheldon's turf. On August 6 1926 Saltis and Lefty Koncil shot dead John "Mitters" Foley, Ralph Sheldon's top enforcer. Two days later, Al Capone narrowly survived an attack by the O'Bannions. Capone's car had been tailed by the North Siders and when he stepped out of his car at the Four Deuces, the mob's head-quarters, they opened fire with revolvers and a shotgun. Capone literally dived through the door of the saloon. His driver, Tony Ross, was not so lucky. He was killed instantly. The Capones retaliated within days with two unsuccessful attempts on Weiss and Drucci outside the Standard Oil Building.

On September 20 Weiss made his most daring assault on Capone territory. Al Capone and his most trusted bodyguard, Frank Rio, were dining in the Hawthorne Inn in Cicero, when the ever alert Rio heard the distant sound of a tommy gun. The restaurant crowd fell silent as a car drove by, a man hanging from the window firing a machine gun. When the firing stopped, all the patrons, including Capone and Rio, ran to the windows to see what was happening. There were no bullet holes. The machine gunner had been firing blanks. Rio understood instantly. It was a ruse to draw out Capone and his men. Rio knocked Capone to the floor, falling on top of him, just as the first of ten cars, filled with a least fifty North Side hoods, armed with machine guns, shotguns, rifles and revolvers drove slowly by in single file. As each car reached the Hawthorne Inn its occupants let loose a fusillade of fire. The gunners raked the Hawthorne, left to right, then right to left, then up and down to cover the two floors of the building. All the windows in the Hawthorne were blown in and thirty-five cars parked nearby were riddled with bullet holes. As the last car in the cavalcade arrived Pete Gusenberg casually got out carrying a tommy gun. He knelt before the entranceway and fired a full drum of 100 .45 bullets into the shattered lobby. When the drum was empty he strolled to the car and got in. A horn sounded a signal to leave and the cavalcade drove down 22nd Street towards Chicago.

Thousands of bullets had been fired into the building but miraculously no one had been killed. Louis Barko, a Capone gunman, had been hit in the shoulder and a woman sitting in a nearby car with her infant son in her lap was struck by a bullet that creased her forehead and injured her eyes. Capone paid for all her medical bills and doctors saved her eyesight. Surveying the damage to the Hawthorne Inn a shaken Al Capone knew that Weiss was capable of making good his threat that he would kill Capone and anyone that stood in his way. Capone conferred with his best hitmen in an effort to rid himself of his chief antagonist.

On October 11 1926 Hymie Weiss attended the trial of Joe Saltis and Lefty Koncil, who had been charged with the murder of Mitters Foley. As allies of the North Siders it was in his best interests to see that the two killers were acquitted, which despite the testimony of five eye-witnesses, they were. Weiss left the courthouse with Sam Pellar, his chauffeur, Paddy Murray, his bodyguard and beer salesman, Benny Jacobs, a private legal investigator and a politician of the Bloody Twentieth Ward and Saltis' defence attorney, William W. O'Brien, a celebrated mob lawyer, who had been shot in a Chicago saloon and then upheld the code of the underworld by refusing to name his assailant. The five men drove up State Street and parked their Cadillac outside Holy Name Cathedral.

As the five men crossed the road towards O'Bannion's old flower shop, now Weiss' headquarters, they were caught in a withering crossfire from two machine gun nests placed strategically on both sides of the street in second-storey windows. The crossfire was devastating. Weiss and Murray were killed instantly; Weiss was riddled with twelve bullets, while Murray was hit by fifteen. The other three were all seriously wounded but later recovered. O'Brien was hit by four bullets and crawled across the road to a doctor's surgery. All three were interviewed in their hospital beds but could not understand why anyone would want to shoot them

At his funeral Weiss' widow was upset that there were only eighteen car loads of flowers while O'Bannion had twenty-six. Bugs Moran explained that since O'Bannion's demise some thirty members of the gang had joined him leaving the amount of donors considerably less. (While not all were members of the North Side mob the Chicago Crime Commission gives a total of approximately 97 Irish hoods who were killed 'gangland style' during Chicago's bootleg wars. The Chicago Crime Commission body count began in 1919 and was one of the most remarkable of its organised crime projects.)

A few days after Weiss' funeral, at the instigation of Joe Saltis, a peace conference was called. All the rival gangs met in the Hotel Sherman and the territories were reapportioned. Present were Capone and Jake Guzik, his financial advisor and his South Side ally, Ralph Sheldon. From the North Side came Schemer Drucci and Bugs Moran and their allies, Ed Vogel, Potatoes Kaufman, Frank Citro, Billy Skidmore, Barney Bertsche and Jack Zuta. Labour racketeer Maxie Eisen was representing

Joe Saltis and Frank McErlane, who were residing in jail. Also present were Klondike and Myles O'Donnell whose ambitions had been quietened by the McSwiggin killing and Antonio Lombardo who was the chief mediator. The North Siders kept their old territory, the 42nd and 43rd Wards, but had to give back all the territory seized by Weiss and O'Bannion. The South Side was divided between Sheldon and the Saltis-McErlanes while the operations of the O'Donnells, Billy Skidmore, Barney Bertsche and Jack Zuta came under Capone's control. Capone was now at the pinnacle of his power, or as one newspaper called him "The Mayor of Crook County."

For a time it looked like the cease-fire might last. With Weiss gone the O'Bannions were keeping a low profile. Like Capone they were only bidding their time. However, on December 30, seventy days into the truce, Hilary Clements, from the Sheldon mob, was caught selling beer in Saltis-McErlane territory and was killed by Lefty Koncil and Charlie Hubacek. Both Joe Saltis and Frank McErlane were in prison and instead of referring the affair to arbitration, in the manner that had been decided at the Hotel Sherman conference, Saltis ordered Clements killed. Capone had been using Sheldon to gain a foothold in the South West Side and Sheldon protested to Capone about the killing. Koncil and Hubacek were lured into a trap and shot dead. Saltis decided it was time to make his peace with Capone.

However, the O'Bannions were not content with keeping the peace either. They were now lead by Schemer Drucci, who it was rumoured was becoming more and more unstable. Vincent Drucci was born in Chicago in 1895. As a youth he teamed up with Dion O'Bannion, Hymie Weiss and Bugs Moran's safecracking gang. Though a Sicilian himself Drucci was more at home with the predominantly Irish North Siders. He had a special hatred for Sicilian gangsters, particularly those working with the Gennas. He was nicknamed "The Schemer" because of his wild plots and hare-brained ideas about killing his rivals. Al Capone thought of him as his deadliest rival. Drucci made several attempts to kill Capone, once tracking him to Arkansas. Legend has it that the Schemer nearly got him once. He cornered Capone alone in a Turkish bath and almost strangled him before his bodyguards turned up. Drucci ran away - stark naked - jumped in his car and escaped. Frustrated that all his efforts had so far failed Drucci and his henchmen kidnapped Theodore "The Greek" Anton, an old and trusted friend of Capone's. Immediately, Capone realised the inevitable consequences. He remained in a booth in the Greek's restaurant, crying inconsolably, waiting for news of his friend. Anton's tortured and bullet riddled body was later found in Cicero. Capone swore vengeance on Drucci but the honour went to Chicago's finest.

With election day looming all the Chicago gangs were backing Big Bill Thompson, under whose corrupt reign the gangs had prospered. On April 4 1927 Drucci led a raid on the offices of a William E. Dever stalwart, wrecked the place and beat up a secretary. The unarmed Drucci was arrested by police and put in a squad car along with his two henchmen, Albert Single and Henry Finkelstein. Detective Dan Healy, sitting in the front seat, questioned the three thugs. "I don't know nothin', coppers!" Drucci snarled.

Dan Healy was an utterly fearless and incorruptible policeman, one of Chicago's finest and toughest detectives. He hated all the Chicago gangsters and went out of his way to provoke them. Once he bumped into Joe Saltis, who was a towering giant of a man. Saltis tried to push Healy out of his way and ended up getting beaten senseless by the young detective. On the way to the Criminal Courts Building, Drucci told Healy he would not serve an hour in jail, that his lawyer would have him out in no time. The North Siders lawyer, Morris Green, was actually waiting at the courthouse to bail Drucci out. Healy told Drucci to shut up and sit back. Drucci became agitated, threatening Healy, who pulled out his revolver and held it on Drucci. After more threats Drucci punched Healy, who promptly fired four bullets into the gangster. By the time the police car pulled up outside the Criminal Courts Building Drucci was dead. On seeing his client's dead body Green stormed into the offices of William Schoemaker, Chief of Detectives, demanding that Healy be arrested for murder. "I don't know anything about anyone being murdered," Schoemaker replied. "I know that Drucci was killed while trying to disarm an officer. We're having a medal made for Healy."

Drucci's slaying put George "Bugs" Moran in control of the O'Bannion mob. Moran, born of Irish and Polish parents, in Minnesota, in 1893, grew up in the predominantly Irish North Side of Chicago. He served his time with street gangs and had been jailed three times before he was twenty-one. He joined up with O'Bannion in 1914. Deanie loved him like a brother and they became a natural team, both of them possessing the same streak of homicidal "wit". Moran was nicknamed "Bugs" because he was thought to be as "mad as a bed-bug". Moran's sense of humour made him popular with the press. He lost no opportunity to openly insult Al Capone to reporters, referring to him as "The Beast", "The Behemoth", or "The Pimp." Like his mentor, O'Bannion, he was a regular church-goer and refused to allow brothels to operate on the North Side. It was Moran who is credited with devising the motorcade system of murder. A convoy of cars, filled with hoods, usually armed with tommy guns, swept past the target's home, business or hang-out. As each car slowly drove past, dozens of bullets were fired in the general direction of the target. It was usually effective, but sometimes an innocent bystander might get caught up in the attack, which did not bother gangsters at all. Dozens of citizens were killed or injured in the Chicago bootleg wars.

For two years there was relative peace between Moran and Capone as both respected the truce. (Though there were still plenty of gangland killings among the rest of the Chicago gangs.) Capone had pledged not to send his men north of the Madison Street dividing line and Moran had agreed that his men would not go south of the line. Capone had been busy strengthening his mob and in early 1929 began encroaching on Moran's territory. Moran found an ally in Joe Aiello and his West Side gang of Sicilians, who had been battling Capone for the last year. With the disgruntled Billy Skidmore, Barney Bertsche and Jack Zuta also backing them, the Moran-Aiello alliance felt strong enough to finish what they had started.

On January 8 1929 Joe Aiello and the Gusenberg brothers, Frank and Pete, called on Pasqualino Lolorado, the new president of the *Unione Siciliana* - a position Aiello coveted. Lolorado thought Aiello a friend and invited the three hoods into his North Side home where the four sat down to share a bottle of whiskey. An hour, or so later, Mrs. Lolorado heard the honk of a car horn outside. This was followed by the sound of several gunshots from the parlour. The three killers ran outside to their getaway car. Mrs. Lolorado found her husband lying dead on the floor, his face shot away.

As Capone's power grew Moran kept up his attacks, hijacking Capone's liquor trucks, bombing saloons that sold Capone bootleg and killing his best strong-arm men and seriously wounding his top gunman, Machine-Gun Jack McGurn. Moran tried to have Capone knocked off on many occasions, by having prussic acid dropped in his soup, by ambushing his chauffeur driven car and by bribing his bodyguards to kill their boss. He also put a $50,000 contract on Capone. Nervous and under strain, Capone moved to his Palm Island estate in Florida, to direct his $50 million a year operations and plan a bold stroke to wipe out once and for all "those Irish bastards."

The morning of February 14 1929, St. Valentine's Day, was freezing cold in Chicago with a flurry of light snow falling. In a warehouse at 2122 North Clark Street seven men were waiting for Bugs Moran and a delivery of hijacked whiskey which had been offered by phone the night before. In the dingy warehouse, known as the S.M.C. Cartage Co., there were four trucks, one of which had been jacked up. A mechanic, also a safecracker and thief, Johnny May, was working under the truck, while his dog, and the gangs mascot, Highball, was tied to an axle. Six more men were sitting or standing around talking, laughing and drinking coffee. They were Frank and Pete Gusenberg, Moran's top gunners; James Clark, real name Kashellek, a German born immigrant, a thief and gunman; Adam Heyer, an accountant and Moran's business manager, who also owned the garage; Al Weinshank, Moran's associate in the dyeing and cleaning business and Reinhard H. Schwimmer, an optometrist, who was not a hood but a "hanger-on", a man who liked to be seen with gangsters.

As Moran and his two bodyguards, Teddy Newberry and Willie Marks, approached the warehouse they saw a black Packard touring car pull up and four men, two in police uniform and two in plainclothes, enter the building. Thinking it a routine raid the three sidled into a doorway, watched for a moment, then beat a hasty retreat to a nearby coffee shop. Already in the garage was Al Weinshank, a man of heavy build and similar height to Moran, and who was wearing a brown hat and coat closely resembling Moran's. It seems probable that the spotters seeing who they believed to be Moran going into the warehouse and contacted the hit team, who were waiting in the Circus Cafe, on North Avenue, for the phone call that sent them to 1222 North Clark Street.

Inside the garage the men thought it was a raid, too, offering no resistance when they were told to line up against the wall, their hands held high above their heads. The two plainclothes cops produced tommy guns from under their coats and opened up with a deadly fusillade, spraying hundreds of bullets at head, waist and knee height. At that range some of the bullets went through the men and hit the wall. The seven men fell away from the wall riddled with bullets. The two uniformed men then produced sawn-off shotguns and blasted any of the victims showing signs of life. With that the four killers left, the two uniformed men marching the two plainclothes men out as if they were under arrest. They climbed into the touring car and went southward on Clark Street.

The noise of the tommy guns had been heard by neighbours, who thought it was pneumatic drills at use in the garage. (The noise of the shotguns was thought to be cars or trucks backfiring.) It was only when Highball, the German Shepherd, began to howl and would not stop, that a neighbour investigated. The police were called and shrank back in horror. The seven men were lying in pools of blood. Clark and May had been shot at close range and their heads were blown apart, their brains spilling out on the ground. Startled detectives found that one of the men, Frank Gusenberg, was still alive. He was rushed to Alexian Brothers Hospital.

With a dozen bullets in him Frank Gusenberg knew he was dying. He was questioned by Detective Frank Sweeney, a boyhood friend. Gusenberg had started as a hi-jacker for Dion O'Bannion and became a gunman for Hymie Weiss and Bugs Moran, killing an estimated twenty men. Now even on his deathbed he would not reveal who shot him. He died several hours later, without breaking the code of the underworld. his death brought the toll to seven, the worst gangland killing in American criminal history. The city of Chicago, which was used to shootings, bombings and daily murders was shaken at its roots. Al Capone thought it would solve all his problems. Instead the St. Valentine's Day Massacre would prove to be his undoing.

Capone, of course, had the perfect alibi - he was at the offices of the Dade County solicitor in Miami to answer questions about his income. Moran was certain who was responsible. "Only Capone kills like that," he declared to reporters and checked himself into hospital, where he thought he would be safe. While there were many suspects for the massacre, only one was known for certain to have taken part. Fred "Killer" Burke was a killer for hire who worked for the St. Louis gang, Egan's Rats. He was arrested in Green City, Missouri, in 1931 and sentenced to life for the 1929 murder of a police officer in Michigan. A tommy gun and bullets, identical to the ones extracted from the massacre victims, were found in his home near St. Joseph, Michigan, when it was raided in 1929. Burke, a suspect in twenty murders, (one of the tommy gun's found had also been used in the 1928 murder of Capone enemy Frankie Yale in New York) was never formally charged with the killings, opting to be extradited to Michigan for the patrolman's murder. He died in prison in 1940.

Public outcry was so intense against Capone, he thought it convenient to take refuge in jail until the heat was off. Coupled with the fact that Teddy Newberry and Willie Marks were constantly shadowing him - even following him to the Atlantic City conference - Capone arranged to have himself arrested. As Capone and his ever present bodyguard, Frankie Rio, left a movie theatre in Philadelphia they were arrested and charged with carrying concealed weapons. Both gangsters pleaded guilty. With a $50,000 reward on his head Capone felt he would be safer behind bars. The two were given the maximum sentence, one year. It was the beginning of Capone's downfall. His political and police contacts began to avoid him. His close associate, Jake Lingle, street reporter for the *Chicago Tribune,* whose connections with Police Chief William Russell gave him inside information that Capone badly needed, deserted him for the Moran gang. Capone had Lingle murdered on June 30 1930 instigating another scandal of murder and corruption. Then one of Capone's most trusted business associates, Edward J. O'Hare, secretly defected, providing IRS investigators with vital information needed in preparing a major case against the gang boss.

On October 23 1930 Joe Aiello, Moran's Sicilian ally was machine gunned to death by Capone mobsters. It was another blow for Moran. Two months before his new business manager, Jack Zuta, was gunned down by Danny Stanton. The North Siders despised Jack Zuta for his cowardice and his prostitution rackets, yet tolerated him because, next to Jake Guzik, he probably had the best business brains in the underworld. He was a meticulous accountant and among his papers police found a complex record of the takings of the Moran gang, prompting tax officials to begin investigations. More damaging were papers detailing a payoff schedule to several politicians and law enforcement officials, including Police Chief William O. Freeman, police sergeant Martin C. Mulvihill. Judge Joseph W. Schulman, State senator Harry W. Starr and alderman Dorsey Crowe.

In 1931 Al Capone was sentenced to eleven years in jail for income tax evasion. (In that same year the Chicago Crime Commission issued its second roster of 28 Public Enemies naming Joe Fusco as No.1 and Ted Newberry as No.2. Capone was not even mentioned.) He was replaced by several men from the Outfit's 'board of directors', among them Frank Nitti. Along with Machine-Gun Jack McGurn, real name James DeMora, Nitti was one of the chief planners of the St. Valentine's Day Massacre and was high on the North Siders death list. In 1932 two police officers invaded Nitti's headquarters and after handcuffing the unarmed gangster shot him three times in the back and neck. Nitti lingered near death but miraculously survived. Later, under testimony the policemen said they were acting under orders from the new Chicago mayor, Anton Cermak. Elected as a reformer Cermak was anything but. He waged war on the Capone mob not to clean up the city but to replace them with his own favourites. Allegations were made that Cermak and Teddy Newberry plotted to kill Nitti and that Newberry had offered $15,000 for the elimination of Nitti. Cermak also urged Roger Touhy to make war on the Capone mob with the assistance of the police department.

On January 7 1933 Ted Newberry's body was found in a ditch near Bailey Town, Indiana. A little over a month later, on February 15, Mayor Cermak was shot and seriously wounded while riding in the same car as Franklin D. Roosevelt, who was not hit, in an attempted assassination in Florida. Cermak lingered for three weeks on his deathbed maintaining he was the real target, not Roosevelt as the whole country thought. The assassin, Joseph Zangara, was captured at the spot and later executed in the electric chair. Zangara, it turned out, was an ex-Italian army man who had several awards for pistol-shooting. There were a lot of unanswered questions and shades of the Kennedy assassination case. Maybe Zangara did get the right target after all.

Despite Capone's jailing Bugs Moran's power declined and with the repeal of Prohibition his power began to fade. Unable to adjust to the post-Prohibition world, his gambling operations were swallowed up by the Outfit and Moran had to resort to conventional crime to support himself. By 1940 Moran was no longer a criminal force. All his friends were gone, even his wife had left him. He was reduced to committing burglaries to survive. After WW2 he moved to Ohio, where in 1946 he received ten years for robbing a mere $10,000 - a sum he would have carried around in his pockets in Prohibition days. He was released and went straight back to prison for another bank job, this time on a federal rap. He died, aged 65, of lung cancer in relative obscurity in Leavenworth prison on February 25 1957 receiving a paupers funeral in a potters field outside the prison walls.

Al Capone was released from Alcatraz prison in 1943 with advanced syphilis. He retired from the rackets, living a reclusive life in Florida. He died in 1947. The Syndicate Capone and Johnny Torrio created went from strength to strength, becoming one of the most powerful mobs in the country.

George "Bugs" Moran, centre, talking to his defence attorney in court where he faced forgery and counterfeit charges 1939.

Photo: Corbis-Bettmann/UPI

Tammany Hall 1937. New York Democratic Party Headquarters.

Photo: Corbis-Bettmann/UPI

Roger "The Terrible" Touhy, second left, leaving Marshall's Office 11/8/1954 en route to County Jail, Chicago.

Five Points, New York 1840s.

Owney Madden at the time of his arrest and removal to the Tombs Prison, New York 1932.

Charles F. Murphy stands in front of Tammany Hall, New York 1914.

Vincent Coll, centre, thanks his lawyers Raymond J. Reilly, left, and Samuel Leibowitz after his acquittal on child murder charge 1931.

Dion O'Bannion, leader of the Chicago North Side Mob.

Jack "Legs" Diamond, centre, and his attorneys leaving federal court after being convicted of owning an unlicensed still 1931.

Photo: Corbis-Bettmann/UPI

Joseph John "Mad Dog" Sullivan is escorted from the Federal Building in Rochester, New York after his arraignment on robbery charges 1982.

Photo: Associated Press

Tammany boss and former Whyos leader, "Big Tim" Sullivan greets Marion Armstrong by a sign that reads "Vaudeville Comedy Club", New York.

(L to R) Johnny Dunn, Daniel Gentile and Andrew "Squint" Sheridan as they left Criminal Courts building in a car headed for Sing Sing after being convicted of murder 19/1/1948.

Frank McErlane, Chicago mobster labelled "the most brutal gunman to pull a trigger".

Photo: William Helmer Collection.

"The Gun That Made the Twenties Roar"

The Thompson sub-machine gun. First used by Frank McErlane in 1925 and later adopted by most organised crime gangs by the end of the decade.

Photo: Authors Collection.

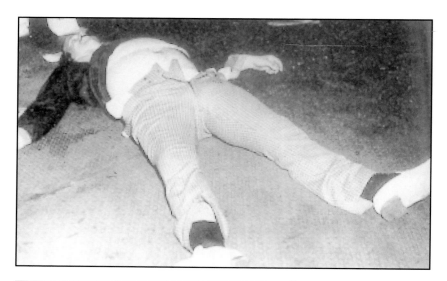

The body of James McBratney lies sprawled on the floor of a Staten Island tavern after he was murdered by John Gotti and two accomplices 22/5/1973.

Photo: U.S. Justice Department

Freelance killer Elmer Burke, leaves a cell in Boston Police Station 16, on 18/6/1954 in the company of Officer Francis Crawford who arrested him as a "suspicious person".

Photo: Associated Press

John "Cockeye" Dunn, labour racketeer and murderer. Photo: Corbis-Bettmann/UPI

WHITE HAND GANG LEADERS.
Right: William "Wild Bill" Lovett and above right: Richard "Pegleg" Lonergan.
Photo: Authors Collection.

The SS Normandie burns at her West Side Manhattan berth 2/9/1942.
Photo: Corbis-Bettmann/UPI

ST. VALENTINE'S DAY MASSACRE 1929.

Six of the seven victims: (from top) Pete Gusenberg, Albert Weinshank, Adam Heyer, John May, Reinhardt Schwimmer and James Clark (against wall). Frank Gusenberg was still alive when police arrived and died several hours later in hospital.

James J. "Whitey" Bulger. Boston mobster and FBI informer still on FBI Ten Most Wanted List.　　Photo: FBI

Original Caption: "Mr. Croker's Idea of Expansion". Political Illustration of overweight Richard Croker, Boss of Tammany Hall, mounted on a donkey while he pulls two bulldogs on leashes.
Photo: Bettman/CORBIS

New York Draft Riots 1863. Mob looting houses on Lexington Avenue at the height of the Draft Riots.

Jimmy "The Gent" Burke being led handcuffed from a law enforcement vehicle in New York, after being arrested as a parole violator 12/4/1979.

CHAPTER 7

MAD DOGS & IRISHMEN

As the new breed of gangsters syndicated themselves in the late 1920s and early 1930s those that opposed these moves had to be eliminated. Two of those were the Irish gangsters Legs Diamond and Mad Dog Coll. They sneered at the new Syndicate declaring they could do what they liked. But progress would not be halted and the two lone wolves would pay the ultimate price. In Chicago Frank McErlane, "the most brutal gunman to pull a trigger", bucked the system, but could not be tamed. These three Irishmen cut a bloody swathe through the underworld and died within months of each other; Diamond and Coll by the bullet, while ironically, the fierce McErlane died, not by the gun, but of pneumonia.

The Clay Pigeon of the Underworld: Legs Diamond.

Jack "Legs" Diamond was often known as "the clay pigeon of the underworld" such were the many times he survived murder attempts. In his long criminal career Legs Diamond made few friends and many enemies. He was born John T. Nolan, in 1896, in Kensington, a slum area of Philadelphia, the first son of John and Sarah Nolan, poor immigrants from County Cavan.

Sarah Nolan died young in 1913 and the family moved to New York. Here Jack and his younger brother, Eddie, fell in with the Hudson Dusters. Jack Diamond got his nickname as a young thief, because of his ability to outrun his pursuers. He did not always get away and served several short stints in the reformatory for burglary and assault. On his release he was approached by Dick Butler, whose mob were the terrors of West 30th Street, and together he and Eddie joined up hi-jacking along the Hudson River waterfront. The pickings were rich for America was working overtime sending goods to the Allies. In 1918 Legs was asked to do a little more for the war effort - he was drafted. Legs could not adapt to army life and deserted. When he was caught he was given a five-year sentence in Leavenworth. He served a year and a day and was released in 1920 returning to New York, where he began muscling in on many of the petty criminals that swarmed the Lower East Side.

In 1922 the Diamonds ended up labour slugging in the city's garment district wars. They teamed up with Jacob "Little Augie" Orgen in his war with Nathan "Kid Dropper" Kaplan for control of the garment district labour rackets. The Little Augies were a mixed crew of Jews, Irishers and Italians and had such bloodthirsty stalwarts as Lepke Buchalter and Gurrah Shapiro - later heads of Murder Inc., - in their employ. In 1922 and 1923 twenty-three people were killed in the Orgen-Kaplan gang war. Victory came to the Little Augies when Legs Diamond masterminded the murder of the feared Kid Dropper in August 1923.

Diamond persuaded Orgen to file an assault complaint against Kaplan. While Kaplan was being led out of Essex Market Court, on the Lower East Side, a young hood, named Louis Kushner, shot him dead in front of police, reporters and onlookers. Legs had promised the impressionable Kushner a top position with the Little Augies. Instead Kushner received a twenty-year term for manslaughter. Diamond, along with Lepke

Buchalter and Gurrah Shapiro, had escorted Kushner to the courthouse and stood looking on as he shot Kaplan. For his reward in setting up Kid Dropper Legs Diamond gained his bootleg and narcotics rackets, while Augie took over Kaplan's labour rackets, becoming the city's top labour racketeer, working for employers or unions, or whoever paid the highest.

Legs consolidated his rackets and also muscled in on some small time hoods, who retaliated in October 1924. While walking along 110th Street, in Upper Manhattan, Diamond was ambushed by two gunmen. His head was peppered by buckshot and he took a bullet in his heel. When he recovered Legs continued working for Little Augie, mostly as a bodyguard. In 1926 Arnold Rothstein, the big time gambler and fixer of the 1919 World Series, was called in to end the garment districts longest strike. For six months 50,000 workers had withdrawn their labour, paralysing the city's biggest industry. Rothstein persuaded the gangs, hired by both sides, to leave the streets and hammered out a deal between the unions and employers. For Little Augie it was his death knell. Lepke Buchalter saw that Augie was only scratching the surface and realised that there were huge fortunes to be made if they had control of the unions. Lepke approached Legs to help him, but Diamond would not commit himself.

On October 15 1927 Little Augie and Legs Diamond were on the corner of Norfolk and Delancey Street, on the Lower East Side, when a black touring car pulled up. A fusillade of shots felled the two gangsters. Augie was killed and Diamond severely wounded. Hit in the arm and leg, Diamond crawled into a nearby doorway, where ambulancemen found him. Doctors said he lost so much blood he would not live. He did and sent a message to Lepke that the garment district was all his. Legs was happy enough to inherit Augie's bootlegging and narcotics rackets.

With his new found riches Diamond began living the high life, buying large touring cars and living in expensive apartments, surrounding himself with loyal gangsters and gorgeous show-girls. He was constantly seen on Broadway with a different girl on his arm. He dined in the best restaurants and tipped lavishly, bragging about his conquests and his own underworld impor-tance. His wife, Alice Schiffer, to whom he married in 1920, stayed loyally at home, living a lonely and semi-secluded life in Brooklyn, while Legs lived it up. Once when reporters asked her about Legs' mistress, Marion "Kiki" Roberts, she pointed to her wedding ring and said, "She may have some of my husband's attentions, but I have the man." Kiki Roberts was a voluptuous, stunning red-head, a Ziegfeld Folly at seventeen.

Legs became a high-priced bodyguard for the underworld's Mr. Big - Arnold Rothstein - who paid him $1,000 a week to pro-tect him from sore losers, to escort heavy winners home and to persuade debtors to pay up. Meanwhile, Rothstein helped Legs to expand his bootlegging and narcotics rackets. Rothstein sup-plied funds for Diamond to buy trucks, warehouses and political and police protection. On November 4 1928 Rothstein was fatally wounded in Manhattan's Park Central Hotel. Gambler George "Hump" McManus was indicted for the murder but was later acquitted. The slaying was then attributed to Legs Diamond. Legs was believed to have double-crossed Rothstein on a narcotics deal. Rothstein blamed Eddie Diamond and sent a hit-squad to Denver, Colorado, to kill him. (By the time the hit squad arrived in Denver Rothstein was already dead.) Eddie Diamond was battling tuberculosis and Legs sent him out West to the warmer climate. On November 6 Eddie's car was riddled by machine gun fire. He escaped injury and returned to New York. Denver police arrested Eugene "Handsome" Moran and James Piteo, former bodyguards of Rothstein, and charged them with assault. They were released on bond and promptly skipped town, along with Frank "Blubber" Devlin, who was also wanted.

Back in New York Rothstein's empire was quickly swallowed up. Harry Vesey, a Queens beer runner formerly associated with Rothstein was murdered near the Hoboken waterfront by the Diamond mob while the five men involved in the Denver shooting joined the list of former Rothstein associates who were rubbed out. The first to die was Gene Moran. His body was found in his burnt out car in Newark, New Jersey. Blubber Devlin, James Pieto, Fatty Walsh and Moe Schubert were killed one after the other, most of them by the Diamond's ace hitman, Joe McDonald.

Due to his connections with Rothstein, Legs had become something of a Broadway sport, even opening his own place, the Hotsy-Totsy Club on Broadway between 54th and 55th Streets. The Hotsy-Totsy Club was so notorious Lucky Luciano ordered his men not to drink there, as he could not guarantee that they would not come out feet first. Legs often invited gang rivals to peace meetings there. Many of them ended up murdered in the back room and were escorted out as "drunks", their bodies dumped in alleyways. Legs could be seen most nights in the club, drinking and chatting up the girls. He was an elegant dresser, sometimes wearing a silk hat, a cloak, white tie and tails, a white carnation and a cane. Diamond always positioned himself at a table so he could be facing the door and study who came in.

On the night of June 13 1929 Legs was in his usual spot, drinking with his chief enforcer, Charlie Entratta a.k.a. Charlie Green. Diamond was in a foul mood. Several waterfront toughs, led by William "Red" Cassidy, entered the club and propped themselves at the bar. The group loudly demanded service and insulted several customers, including Simon Walker, an ex-boxer recently paroled from Sing Sing. A fight broke out between

Walker and Red Cassidy and his brother, Peter. Diamond and Entratta stepped up to the group and told them to behave politely. Red Cassidy insulted Legs and swung a punch. Seeing that the argument was getting very loud the manager, Hymie Cohen, ordered the band to play louder. The band struck up a deafening rendition of *Alexander's Ragtime Band.* By now Legs had pulled a .45 and shot Cassidy in the groin. As he fell to the floor Legs put two more in Cassidy's head for good measure. Entratta joined in shooting Simon Walker. Cassidy, mortally wounded, was carried downstairs by his friends and put into an ambulance. He died before reaching hospital. When the police arrived they found the place a shambles. The only customer left was Simon Walker. His head was resting on the bar and two loaded .38 revolvers were stuck in his waistband. He was also dying.

Diamond and Entratta went into hiding and directed a purge against the witnesses to the killings. The three main witnesses disappeared, one was found shot dead in New Jersey. It was enough for the others to change their stories. Entratta was arrested by police in Chicago and brought back to New York for trial. But of the forty men and women in the club that night no one could remember who had done the shooting. In fact no one had even seen a gun. Entratta was acquitted for lack of evidence. Then, and only then, did Diamond reappear. He walked into police headquarters to surrender, saying he was out of town and he had just heard he was wanted in connection with some shooting. Despite its failure in convicting Entratta the state went ahead with prosecuting Diamond. With no evidence the case collapsed and Diamond yet again went free.

But there had been complications while Legs was in hiding. Eddie Diamond had finally lost his battle with tuberculosis. Legs went to the funeral disguised as a priest. The police waited for Legs to appear, even putting a man undercover in the upstate sanatorium. Eddie was buried from a house on West 93rd Street in Manhattan and it was here it was thought Legs appeared disguised as a priest. There were other problems: the Hotsy-Totsy Club was closed down and Dutch Schultz had moved in on Diamond's midtown bootlegging rackets. Legs had a loyal following of ruthless gunmen led by Charlie Entratta; Jimmy Hart, Tony Fusco, Jimmy Dalton, John Herring, James Hines and John Scaccio. The war between Diamond and Schultz waged for more than two years, with Schultz getting the worst of it. Diamond controlled all the major highways in upstate New York along which bootlegged bonded whiskey was transported from Canada. Legs entered an alliance with other Irish gangsters, like Mad Dog Coll and Vannie Higgins, who were also battling the Dutchman. Legs got a shipment of grenades from Higgins, which he used to good effect on the Dutchman's speakeasies and breweries. When Schultz was lured to a peace meeting it turned out to be an ambush and one of his top aides, Joe Noe, was killed.

Schultz was a top member of the newly formed Syndicate and they backed him, supplying him with any information they had on Diamond. The Syndicate had been formed in 1929 by top mobsters like Meyer Lansky, Lucky Luciano and Frank Costello. They were men of vision. They proposed to run organised crime like any big corporate firm. Legs Diamond had no such foresight. All he wanted to do was take what he could and to hell with everyone else. Legs' antics might be good press for him but it was bad for organised crime. It brought too much heat from the cops and crusading politicians. If Schultz came out the winner in the war for midtown Manhattan it would suit the Syndicate's plans.

By 1930 Diamond was at his peak. He had become a powerful and greatly feared mobster. He decided to expand his rackets beyond New York City to Green County, in the heart of the Catskill resort country, sixty miles north of Manhattan. Legs thought it would be easy to take over the bootlegging operations in the area. He assumed the local bootleggers would not have the muscle the city mobs had. The Diamond mob set up headquarters in Acra. Legs bought a huge mansion and in advance of his arrival his men put up such a show of armed strength the place became known as "Fort Edward". The house was set back seventy-five feet from the road. It had two towers and on top was a revolving spotlight, which at the sound of approaching traffic at night was immediately switched on, bathing the area in a brilliant light.

It did not take the Diamond mob long before they had the local bootleggers on the run. Legs tried to camouflage his campaign of violence behind a front of goodwill. He paid for the funeral of a local child whose parents did not have the money to pay for it; he sent his chauffeur-driven limousine to bring a poor farmer to visit his seriously ill daughter in an Albany hospital; he personally brought sweets to sick children and tipped lavishly wherever he went. Simultaneously he was conducting a violent campaign against the local moonshiners and cider makers. On August 22 Harry Western, a hotelier in Saugerties, disappeared after meeting Legs Diamond. A Diamond gang member, Harry Klein, was arrested driving Western's bloodstained car. He was sent for trial on a car theft charge - the only thing police could pin on him.

Legs decided to take a holiday to avoid the heat the Klein trial was causing. He also needed a rest, for he had contacted pleurisy from the wounds he received in the Little Augie shooting. Legs announced he was going to Europe for a well earned break. Police believed he was setting up a drugs route from Europe. On August 30 Ireland, the country of Diamond's parents, announced that it would refuse landing permission to Legs Diamond and four friends alleged to be with him - Charlie

Entratta, Charlie Luciano, Salvatore Arcidicio and Al Treager. The alien branch of the Irish government said that when the White Star liner *Baltic* docked that evening, permission to enter the country would be refused to the notorious group.

Scotland Yard, who had notified the Irish Minister of Justice that Diamond was on board the *Baltic*, said that if Ireland would not let him land he would have to come on to Britain, where he was wanted for questioning in connection with a stock swindle. However, Legs was not on board the *Baltic*. Instead he had booked passage on the liner *Bergenland*. When the ship docked in Plymouth Legs and his entourage were politely told they were not wanted. Legs sailed on to Antwerp, where the Belgian authorities detained him for twenty-four hours before allowing him to travel on to Germany. There he was refused a visa and deported back to America. Arriving in Philadelphia from Hamburg Legs was arrested by local police as a "suspicious" character.

In October in a third known murder attempt Legs was shot and seriously wounded at the Hotel Monticello on West 65th Street. Legs had arrived in New York from the Catskills to meet his showgirl mistress Kiki Roberts. For three days the lovers remained in secrecy until the morning of October 12 when a knock came to the door. Legs opened it, as if he was expecting someone, and spoke to two men for several minutes. Kiki Roberts was in an adjoining room when she heard several gunshots. She rushed in to find Legs lying in a pool of blood. She phoned for an ambulance and Legs was rushed to hospital where the doctors said he had no chance. But Diamond confounded the odds and lived again. Chief suspect in the murder attempt was former Diamond ally, Vannie Higgins.

It was not long before Diamond was back in business. He expanded his campaign against the Catskill cider distributors and their suppliers. The cries from the outraged public were heard in the state capital and Governor Franklin D. Roosevelt ordered Attorney-General John Bennett to head up an investigation. But the underworld got to Diamond first. On the night of April 26 1931 as Legs left the Aratoga Inn, near Cairo, he was hit by several shotgun blasts. The proprietor of the roadside inn, James Wynne and Diamond's bodyguard, John Scaccio, raced outside guns drawn. But all they saw was the fading lights of a car roaring away. The seriously injured Diamond was rushed to Albany hospital where for days he lingered at death's door. Miraculously, he again recovered.

When Dutch Schultz heard the news that Legs was back on the mend he reportedly said, "Can't anybody shoot that guy so he won't bounce back up." When he did recover Legs moved about with reckless abandon. By now he believed no one could kill him. "There hasn't been a bullet made that can kill me," he boasted. Once when told two killers working for Owney Madden were searching the Broadway bars for him, he stood his ground and said, "What the hell do I care." He was named the "Clay Pigeon of the Underworld," by one witty reporter, while the *New York American* called him "The Most Picturesque Racketeer in the Underworld." *The Post* said he was "The Most Publicised of Public Enemies" and the *Daily Mirror* named him "The Most Shot at Man in America." Racket-buster Tom Dewey named him his Public Enemy and gained a conviction in August against Legs for operating an illegal still. He was sentenced to four years and fined $10,000 but freed on bail, while he appealed the conviction.

But Diamond had made one too many enemies. Strapped for cash for his numerous court cases - his safe deposit box had been seized by investigators in a Cairo bank - he began muscling in on Larry Fay's Manhattan night-clubs. Lucky Luciano and the board of the Syndicate agreed that Legs would always want more. He was bad for business, was too greedy and created too much heat. He would have to be stopped once and for all. Orders went out for Diamond to be shot on sight. His chief lieutenant, Charlie Entratta, was first to go. Three gunmen walked into his bottling plant in Brooklyn and shot him dead.

In December 1931 Legs was again in court, this time on a kidnapping charge. Two local bootleggers, Grover Parks and James Duncan, were kidnapped by the Diamond mob in the village of Catskill. They were tortured by John Scaccio and several others, who burned them with cigarettes and red hot pokers. Both men were released after agreeing to work for Diamond. The two immediately went to the police and told their horrific tale. Diamond and Scaccio were arrested and went on trial in Troy, N.Y. When it was obvious Scaccio was going down, Diamond withdrew his defence attorneys and let his henchman face the music alone. No point wasting money on a lost cause, he reasoned. Scaccio was convicted and received ten years.

Diamond was acquitted for lack of evidence. To celebrate his release on December 16 Legs, his wife, Alice, and several friends and relations went to an Albany speakeasy where after several hours drinking, Diamond excused himself, saying he would be back in half an hour after he met some "newspaper pals." He got a cab to see Kiki Roberts, who he had put up in a nearby apartment. He stayed with her for three hours, leaving at 4.30 a.m. taking the same cab back to his nearby boarding house on Dove Street. His wife was staying at another address. This was usual procedure for Diamond. He always rented several single rooms in the city so no one could find him too easily. Legs staggered into his room and collapsed drunk on the bed and fell into a deep sleep. Minutes later, two men appeared in the room and switched on a flashlight. One gunman held the unconscious Diamond by the ears, while the other shot him three times in the head. This time there was no mistake. Legs Diamond was definitely dead.

Despite all the money Legs had made over the years Alice Diamond was left penniless. Legs had spent the last of it on legal fees for his defence. His widow had to borrow money for the funeral - allegedly from Owney Madden - and for the eight-foot cross of pink and white chrysanthemums that was her tribute. His mistress, Kiki Roberts, tried without success, to arrange for Legs to be buried in a Catholic cemetery. On July 1 1932 Alice Schiffer Diamond was found dead in her Brooklyn home with gunshot wounds to the head. She had reportedly been claiming that she knew her husband's killers and also had been target shooting in her yard with a pistol. Like her husband's murder the killing remains unsolved.

The Mad Mick: Vincent Coll.

Vincent Coll was born on July 20 1908, the youngest of five children, in a little stone cottage near Bunbeg in Co. Donegal. His father and mother had returned to Ireland after meeting and marrying in New York. Donegal was one of the most impoverished counties in Ireland and the people of the area depended on money sent home from families abroad. The Colls, like their neighbours, lived on shellfish, fish and potatoes. Two of their children died of hardship there and the family decided to return to America in 1909. They settled in a Bronx slum. A few years later Vince's father left home never to return. When Vincent was seven his mother died of pneumonia. Vince and his older brother Peter were entrusted to the care of the Mission Of The Immaculate Virgin on Staten Island. The Mission was renowned for its brutality and the young brothers had to look out for each other. Vince was "unruly" and did not conform to authority and ran away several times. He probably had a psychopathic personality and when he was released, at sixteen, he was already a fierce young tough, brutalised by years of "care and reform". He went to live with his older sister, Florence, in a tenement on 11th Avenue, in Hell's Kitchen on Manhattan's West Side. With his brother, Peter, Vince roamed the streets from an early age stealing from pushcarts and stores. Even as a youngster Vince exhibited a violent and vicious nature. As a teenager he was tall and rangy, appearing to be much older than he was. At seventeen Vince was sent to the state reformatory at Elmira, N.Y., for robbery. By then he had already been involved in a number of street gang deaths. On release, aged 19, he went to work for the Bronx Beer Baron, Arthur Flegenheimer, or as he preferred to be known - because it made him sound tougher - Dutch Schultz.

Schultz depended on brute force to survive in the tough world of bootlegging and Vincent Coll supplied that brutality. He had no compunction in using violence. The ambitious Schultz and his gang of young toughs began to expand into the territory of rival bootleg gangs. The Schultz mob had several confrontations with a Bronx Irish gang, led by brothers John and Joseph Rock, and several of the Dutchman's beer truck drivers were attacked. Schultz went straight to the source. Joe Rock was kidnapped by the Colls and the Weinberg brothers, Bo and George, and brought to a garage. He was strung up by his thumbs and beaten severely. The thugs then smeared pus in his eyes and taped them over. Eventually Joe Rock went blind in one eye. When he was released his brother got the message; he retired from the rackets.

Despite Schultz making a huge fortune he was notoriously mean. The Colls, as trusted gunmen, were only getting a mere $150 a week - a pittance to what Schultz was making. But the Colls were ambitious and Vince believed he had leadership qualities and began planning to start his own mob. Vince robbed the Sheffield Farms dairy in the Bronx and when he was upbraided by Schultz he asked him for a bigger slice of the action. But the Dutchman shared his profits with no one. So while still working for Schultz they started convincing some of his men that they would be better off working for them. Vince and Pete enlisted Arthur Palumbo, Frank Giordano, Edward Popke, a.k.a. Fats McCarthy and several other young guns, most of them of Italian extraction. One that resisted Vince's offer was Vincent Barelli, a top Schultz lieutenant, with rum-running connections in Canada. The Colls went to school with a girl named Carmine Smith, whose sister Mary was Barelli's girlfriend. Because of this Mary Smith brought Barelli to a meeting with the Colls, where Vince promptly put three slugs in Barelli. Since Mary Smith was now a witness he also shot her dead.

As a suspect in the killings Vince Coll was arrested for a violation of the Sullivan law - carrying a concealed firearm - and promptly jumped bail after Schultz put up the $10,000 bond. Schultz was furious and planned to teach the Colls a lesson. The Colls began hijacking the Dutchman's beer trucks and selling them off to the many small-time operators in the city. A full scale war broke out when Schultz hoods shot up a Coll speakeasy killing one man while the Colls retaliated by machine-gunning to death two Schultz beer salesmen on East 116th Street in Harlem. On May 30 1931 twenty-four year old Pete Coll was shot dead as he left his girlfriend's apartment in Harlem. As he drove down St. Nicholas Street, near 111th Street, another car, containing four men, drew alongside and fired several shots through the windshield. Pete was hit four times in the chest and back and died instantly, his car crashing into a wall. Vince was overwhelmed with grief and in retaliation personally killed five of Schultz' men, the first within hours of Peter's death. The loss of his brother affected Vince deeply. It was probably the only key relationship he had. The brothers had survived all the reform schools together and had started out their criminal careers side by side. Peter, though older than Vincent, had lived in his shadow. He was reserved and introverted and had a stabilising influence on his hell-bent brother. Now, with the only stabilising person in his life gone Vince Coll went completely off the rails.

Coll had less manpower than Schultz and had to make up for it by paying top rates for hoods to join him. To finance his war he kidnapped Big Frenchy DeMange, partner of Owney Madden, outside DeMange's Club Argonaut, at West 50th Street and 7th Avenue, on June 15 and collected a $35,000 ransom for his release. Owney Madden promptly placed a $50,000 bounty on Coll's head. (Dutch Schultz had also put a $50,000 contract on Coll.) Coll joined forces with Legs Diamond, who was also warring with Schultz and on July 16 state troopers and New York City police arrested eight men and six women, alleged members of the Coll gang, on a farm in Coxsackie, near the Acra estate of Legs Diamond. They also found an arsenal of weapons and a blood stained car. Coll became such a thorn in the side of Schultz that he walked into the Morrisiana Precinct Station in the Bronx and offered the detectives there a house in Winchester to anyone who would kill "The Mick", as Coll was then known. The offer, tempting as it was, was naturally refused and Schultz went away cursing, insisting that he paid enough graft to the precinct that the cops should willingly do his bidding.

In the underworld Coll was known as "The Mad Mick" and in the press as "Mad Dog" after the attempted killing of Joey Rao, one of Schultz' top men. On July 28 a car driven by Frank Giordano, and containing Vince Coll and several others, tried to kill Rao and other Schultz men in Spanish Harlem. They blazed away with a tommy gun and automatics but hit none of them. Unfortunately, five children playing in the street were hit and one, five year old Michael Vengalli, his stomach shot away, died. Vince Coll was identified and public revulsion demanded that he be caught and punished. Coll went on the run, hiding out in the Adirondacks and New York. He dyed his auburn hair and grew a mustache. His men were arrested one by one and one of them, believed to be Mike Basile, told the cops where Vince was. Twenty policemen surrounded the Cornish Arms Hotel in Manhattan and arrested Coll. He hired Samuel Leibowitz, the top criminal lawyer of the day to defend him. On October 5 1931 Vince Coll and Frank Giordano were indicted for the murder of little Michael Vengalli.

A month before his capture Coll had taken on a mind-boggling contract to kill Lucky Luciano, Vito Genovese and several other top Mafiosi. It was proof, if proof was needed, that Coll was not playing with the full deck. To think that he could kill Luciano and Genovese and not incur the full wrath of their mobs was madness. The contract was a direct result of Salvatore Maranzano's bid to dominate the American Mafia. After Maranzano had emerged victorious from his mob war with Joe "The Boss" Masseria he had tried to take over all the New York Mafia mobs and declare himself "boss of bosses." This did not fit into the plans of Lucky Luciano, Vito Genovese and Frank Costello. Without the help of these "young Turks" Maranzano would not have succeeded in killing Masseria. But his reward to them was to kill off any opposition. He hired Vince Coll to bump off Luciano, Genovese, Costello and several others, including Dutch Schultz, whose rackets he offered to Coll on completion of his contract. Maranzano decided to have a non-Italian do the hits for him so he could then pose innocent. He gave Coll $25,000 as a down payment and promised him another $25,000 on the elimination of his first two victims.

On September 10 1931 Luciano and Genovese had an appointment to see Maranzano at his office in the Grand Central building on Park Avenue. Vince Coll also had an appointment. He was to arrive at the same time to kill Luciano and Genovese. Shortly before the appointed time four men walked in, flashed badges and announced they had questions to ask Mr. Maranzano. The "police officers" were really Jewish gunmen on loan from Meyer Lansky. They lined Maranzano's bodyguards up against the wall and disarmed them. Then two of them, Samuel "Red" Levine and Benjamin "Bugsy" Siegel, went into Maranzano's office and stabbed and shot him to death. The hit team charged out and raced downstairs. On the way down the emergency stairs Red Levine met Vince Coll coming to perform his own killing. As a fellow professional Levine said, "Beat it, Vince. The cops are on their way." Coll did not mind. He had been paid in advance. Coll turned and left, $25,000 the richer.

Coll and Giordano's trial for the Harlem "Baby Massacre" began on December 16 and lasted until the 28th. The case against them looked airtight until Samuel Leibowitz worked his courtroom magic. Leibowitz made it look like the eyewitnesses rather than the defendants were on trial. He disclosed that the state's star witness, George Brecht, was an underworld informer, had a criminal record and a history of providing false testimony. Brecht's testimony that he had seen Vince Coll firing the tommy gun was demolished by Leibowitz. The case collapsed and Coll and Giordano were acquitted for lack of evidence. (Giordano had been convicted of the murder of Joe Mullins a month earlier so the verdict meant nothing to him. He was returned to the death house.) Coll was not freed until a few days later after a writ of *habeas corpus* freed him on the Sheffield Farm robbery and Sullivan Act charges. Outside the courthouse Coll hugged his girlfriend, twenty-three year old Lottie Kreisberger, then turned to waiting reporters and said, grinning, "I have been charged with all kinds of crimes but babykilling was the limit. I'd like nothing better than to lay my hands on the man who did this. I'd tear his throat out. There is nothing more despicable than a man who would harm an innocent child." The reporters and onlookers said nothing. They knew what everyone else knew, that the Mad Dog had indeed killed an innocent child. The public were outraged and the police continued to harass Coll, arresting him and his men at every opportunity, releasing and then re-arresting them.

Now the Syndicate decided it was time for Coll to go. He was too dangerous and creating too much heat and bad press. Dutch Schultz and Owney Madden wanted him dead. And Luciano and Lansky agreed. A $50,000 contract was put on his head, along with the bounties already offered by Schultz and Madden. On February 1 1932 four gunmen entered a house in the North Bronx where they believed Coll would be. He was not there but some of his gang were, playing cards. Two of them, Fiore Basile and Patsy del Greco, were shot to death, along with Mrs. Emilie Torrizello. Another woman and Basilie's brother, Louis, were seriously wounded. Coll turned up thirty minutes later, but left the scene when he saw the ambulances and police cars.

By this time Vince Coll was a wealthy man, raking in thousands of dollars from his bootleg empire and his hijackings of booze trucks. He had married his girlfriend, Lottie Kriesberger, on January 4, and they lived in an enormous apartment at the upmarket Cornish Arms Hotel, on the north side of West 23rd Street between 8th and 9th Avenues.

Across the hall from Vince's apartment lived two of his best bodyguards, while more bodyguards occupied apartments on floors below. In the end one of these men fingered him. On February 9 1932 Coll left his apartment building, a trusted bodyguard, beside him. They walked a few doors down on the south side of West 23rd Street to the London Chemist's Shop, a drugstore where Coll invariably made his business calls, as he believed his own phone was tapped. (He was right.) He was also being tailed by two detectives in an unmarked car but he had given them the slip.

Coll went into the phone booth while his bodyguard sat at the soda fountain. While Coll was engrossed in his telephone conversation threatening Owney Madden that he would kill him if he did not give him money, a black limousine pulled up outside. Coll's bodyguard, thought to be Mike Basile, slipped off his stool and walked quietly outside. Two men, Leonard Scarnici and Anthony Fabrizzo, got out of the limousine nodded to the bodyguard and walked outside. Fabrizzo ordered the customers to remain calm, while Sarnici strode toward the telephone booth. Coll's eyes bulged as he saw Scarnici remove a tommy gun from under his coat. In his cramped position he could not react in time. Scarnici raked the booth from top to bottom, then zigzagged his fire back and forth. Coll died instantly, his body riddled with bullets - fifteen in all - his right arm practically severed. The two gunmen calmly left the scene, hopped into the limousine and sped away. The detectives parked in their car a block away gave chase but lost the car when it turned on to 8th Avenue and sped away at 70 m.p.h. Lottie Coll arrived on the scene soon after, wearing the same dress she had wore on her wedding day. Now she was widowed for the third time.

The huge crowds and costly funerals enjoyed by many prominent gangsters were denied Vince Coll, who since the Harlem "Baby Massacre" had become "The most hated killer since John Wilkes Booth." He was denied a Catholic funeral and was buried beside his brother Peter in St. Raymond's Cemetery in the Bronx. Only a handful turned up at his burial, and only two wreaths were laid on his grave - one from his sister and another that proclaimed "From the boys". However, even after his death Vince Coll still grabbed the headlines. On June 30 1932 Frank Giordano and Dominic "Toughy" Ordierno were executed in

Sing Sing for the 1931 murder of Joey Mullins, a minor hood who worked for Dutch Schultz. The day before the scheduled execution Giordano made a desperate move to save his life. He asked to speak to the warden and revealed that he had been the driver of the car the day young Michael Vengalli was killed. Vince Coll, Giordano claimed had indeed fired the fatal bullet. This information was passed on to Governor Franklin D. Roosevelt, who asked the warden to hold off the execution for twenty-four hours. Roosevelt reviewed the case and Giordano's "evidence" the next day but decided that the information was quite useless as Vince Coll was already dead. He decided that the two killers should meet their fate in the electric chair and they were both executed.

On November 20 1932 Tony Fabrizzo, one of the freelance hitmen attracted by the large bounties placed on Vince Coll, was shot dead at his home in Southwest Brooklyn. He was allegedly murdered by Murder Inc. hitmen in retribution for the bombing attempt on Bugsy Siegel, but according to police Fabrizzo was about to reveal the workings of a "professional gun troop hiring out to the underworld chiefs". Fabrizzo said his last assignment was as "an assistant" on the Vince Coll killing. Fabrizzo's partner, Leonard Scarnici, was later arrested for the murder of a policeman in Rensselaer, N.Y. Scarnici confessed to this murder and 13 others, including that of Coll and of leading the attack on Coll's lair in the North Bronx. He was executed in Sing Sing in 1935.

On June 23 1933 Lottie Kreisberger Coll, Joseph Ventre and Alfred Guarino were arrested and indicted for robbery and murder. The authorities believed that Lottie had been trying to raise funds and recruit a gang to avenge the killing of her husband, Vince. In an attempted hold-up of a Bronx loanshark on June 21 a young woman was fatally wounded by a stray bullet. Guarino was later sentenced to 20 years to life in Sing Sing for second-degree murder, while Lottie Coll received six to twelve years in Bedford Reformatory and Ventre seven to fifteen years in Sing Sing for manslaughter. When she was released Lottie Coll disappeared without trace. So ended the Mad Dog Coll saga which had begun a little less than a year ago.

The most vicious killer of his time: Frank McErlane.

Frank McErlane was born in Chicago in 1894, the son of Peter McErlane, who had left the South Derry village of Bellaghy in the 1880s to earn his fortune in America. Frank grew up in the near South West Side of Chicago, an area of hard-working heavy-drinking stock yards and factory workers. As a young hoodlum he got his start with Moses Annenberg in Chicago's newspaper circulation wars. One journalist described the Annenberg-McErlane relationship: "McErlane went on to become the most vicious killer of his time. Moe Annenberg went on to become the father of the ambassador to the Court of St. James." According to another reporter Frank looked like a salesman - "a butter and egg man." He was a portly five foot eight and 190 pounds, with blue eyes, a rosary ever-present in his pocket. But his face had a habitual glower and when he was drunk, which was often, his eyes would glaze over, at which sign it was wise to depart his company. Chicago police believed he was responsible for fifteen murders. The Illinois Crime Survey tagged him "the most brutal gunman who ever pulled a trigger in Chicago." Chief of Detectives William O'Connor ordered that "known criminals" be tested for insanity. Frank McErlane and his brother, Vince, wriggled out of the psychiatrists' grip on *habeas corpus* writs.

In 1923 Spike O'Donnell began muscling in on the Saltis-McErlane turf (with the arrival of Prohibition the McErlanes had entered a partnership with Polack Joe Saltis) and neighbouring territory belonging to the Sheldon mob. Both gangs became allies to repel the invasion. On September 7 1923 Frank McErlane, Ralph Sheldon, Danny McFall and another unidentified gunman ambushed the O'Donnells at Joseph Klepka's saloon. Jerry O'Connor was shot dead by McErlane and the O'Donnells fled. Ten days later Frank McErlane and Danny McFall ambushed Spike's top enforcers, George Meeghan and Spot Bucher, as they drove a beer truck, and shot them dead. On December 1 McErlane and William Channell hijacked two O'Donnell beer trucks, kidnapping the drivers, Morris Keane and William Egan, who they put in the back of their sedan.

"Where are you gonna get rid of these guys?" Channell asked.

"I'll take care of that in a minute," McErlane said and laughed sadistically. He turned and shot Keane twice with a sawn-off shotgun. Then he calmly reloaded and fired two more rounds into Keane. He reloaded again and said to Egan, "I guess you might as well get yours, too." He shot Egan in the face and leg, reloaded, then shot him in both sides. Then the fat, but agile, killer, climbed over the front seat into the back, opened the door and kicked out Keane's body. He dragged over Egan and shoved him out as the car travelled at 50 m.p.h. Amazingly, Egan survived -though half his face was blown off - and lived to tell the tale. Later, he withdrew his evidence and McErlane walked free.

The O'Donnells imported a New Jersey hitman, Henry Hasmiller, to do away with McErlane, but Frank got word of it and walked into a roadhouse and shot-gunned to death Walter O'Donnell and Hasmiller as they sat at a table. By this time the Sheldon and Saltis-McErlane alliance had fallen apart and now they were gunning for each other. Undeterred by his failure to kill Spike O'Donnell with his new weapon, the tommy gun, McErlane riddled the Ragen's Colts clubhouse on October 5 1925 and killed a Sheldon hood, Charles Kelly, making him the first victim of the gangsters new weapon of terror. Three days before Christmas, Sheldon associates Dynamite Joe Brooks and Eddie Harmening, an ex-county policeman, were waylaid as they left a bar, forced into Harmening's car and brought to Marquette Park in the far South West. Frank McErlane, sitting in the passenger seat, shot them dead, in retaliation for a gun attack on McKeone's saloon in which two Saltis-McErlane hoods had died.

On April 22 1926 McErlane was arrested and held for extradition on a murder charge to Indiana. The charge arose out of an incident on May 24 1924 when McErlane and two friends, John O'Reilly and Alex McCabe, were drinking in a Crown Point saloon. McErlane was drunk and his two friends ragged him to show his marksmanship. McErlane picked a random target at the far end of the bar, lawyer Thaddeus S. Fancher, and killed him with a head shot. The three fled but O'Reilly and McCabe were caught. McErlane escaped back to Chicago. O'Reilly was given a life sentence, while McCabe was convicted and appealed. Thanks to Governor Len Small, Frank was not even arrested until two years after the murder, while the chief witness against him was bludgeoned to death with a hammer. McErlane stayed in an Illinois jail until August, when he was extradited. He showed up for one court appearance drunk, his warder equally intoxicated. A year later, and with much changed testimony, he was acquitted.

While McErlane was in prison the Chicago bootleg wars had continued and after Hymie Weiss was killed a peace conference had taken place at the Hotel Sherman. Labour racketeer Maxie Eisen had represented McErlane and Joe Saltis, who was also in jail. The South Side was divided between Saltis-McErlane and Ralph Sheldon. In 1929 a disgruntled McErlane left his partnership with Joe Saltis, after been denied a bigger cut of the bootleg profits. He once distinguished himself by being held on five simultaneous charges; drunk and disorderly, carrying a concealed weapon, firing a shotgun indiscriminately (at imaginary enemies) around the neighbourhood, driving with forged licence plates and biting his sister on the cheek. His domestic life was no better. On January 28 1930 McErlane was rushed to hospital, his leg shattered by a bullet from an automatic that medics found lying on the floor. He said it was an accident, but it was believed his mistress/wife, Elfrieda Rigus, who preferred to be known as Marion Miller, shot him during one of their rows.

A month later while Frank lay in his bed in the German Deaconess Hospital, his leg still in traction, two uninvited visitors burst into his room guns blazing. McErlane snatched a .38 from under his pillow (police thought about a concealed weapon charge) and fired back, five of his shots shattering the door jamb and frightening his would-be killers, who fled. One even dropped his .45 automatic. McErlane was hit three times, though none of the wounds were serious. Asked by police who shot him, McErlane replied, "I'll take care of this matter myself." The .45 was traced to Sam Malaga, bodyguard of John O'Berta, a rival of McErlane. John "Dingbat" Oberta was an Italian, who spelt his name O'Berta when it suited him to sound Irish. He had replaced McErlane as Saltis' main partner, though he had been part of the Saltis-McErlane combine from the early days. He had married the widow of labour racketeer, Big Tim Murphy, who was murdered in 1928. They had met at the funeral. O'Berta had been Republican committee man for the Thirteenth Ward and had also run as an alderman and state senator. McErlane blamed him for the murder attempt and on March 5 O'Berta and Sam Malaga were found shot dead in the Dingbat's Lincoln. O'Berta had fired three shots from his sawn-off revolver before dropping from a hail of dum-dum bullets and shotgun pellets.

Next Frank "took care" of his girlfriend, Elfreida Rigus. On October 7 1931 he shot her four times, leaving her in the back seat of her car next to her German shepherd and fox terrier, which he also killed. Chicagoans, used to murders, were more upset by the killings of the dogs than that of Elfreida. The case was dismissed for lack of evidence. No death would have been too bad for the savage McErlane but he died, on October 8 1932, not by the bullet, but in a state of pneumonia-induced delirium, held down by four attendants as he ranted and raved.

CHAPTER 8

THE MACHINE
ORGANISED CRIME AND POLITICS

I rish Catholic attachment to the Democratic Party was based partly on opposition to the strong evangelical Protestant and anti-Catholic strains which ran through the Whigs, Know-Nothings and Republican parties and partly on acute consideration. The Democrats, especially on municipal levels, offered jobs, charity, protection against discriminatory legislation and law enforcement in return for loyalty at the polling booth. The Irish political personality had been shaped by centuries of confrontation with British imperialism and the Irish immigrant in America was highly politicised and a natural for the rough-and-tough politics of the mid-nineteenth century. A powerful new entity known as "the machine" emerged in American politics in the mid-1800s. City government was fragmented, and power scattered and haphazard. Each city was divided into wards or districts and then further divided into precincts. New York's Tammany Hall and similar political machines had a strict hierarchical structure. Every city block had one or more active political workers, known as "wardheelers", who kept in touch with local sentiment; the labourer looking for a job; the family facing eviction; the son in trouble with the law; the illiterate trying to write a letter; all were in need of help and the wardheeler was there for that purpose. The machine operated through its ward-heeler in every block. Above him was the precinct captain and above him was the district leader. The district leaders elected an executive committee whose chairman was the party leader, or "boss". The machine formed, in effect, a shadow government paralleling the legal, official government. At the time the government had no social service agencies or financial aid to allocate to the unemployed or poor. The machine provided these facilities instead. It was a system devised by the Irish immigrant and it worked.

The machine derived its strength on its ability to provide jobs on public works and on private companies depending on government grants and on its control of the predominately Irish police force, and thereby its ability to influence the enforcement of laws against gambling and prostitution. The machine collected its "taxes" through bribes paid in exchange for franchise and "kickbacks" on construction contracts. Political insiders knew where public improvements were to be made and profited by buying the land in advance. They also owned or had interests in the sand and gravel companies that provided the building materials.

The saloon, as an important aspect of social life, played a major part in machine politics. The church and the saloon were important factors in Irish social life. The saloon was a centre of neighbourhood activity and an important social base for political activity. The saloon-keeper and the politician were often the same person. A saloon keeper was in a good position to influence his customers and the way they voted. The machine politician was usually a popular figure. He was well known in his ward and made it his business to know everyone, regardless of nationality or creed. He could fit in anywhere; with the labourer, the street thug or the widow. He was a fish among fishes. In the days before social welfare he provided important services to his constituents - jobs, food, charity and assistance with the law and public agencies - that otherwise would not be available. There was, of course, a small price to pay for such assistance - a vote for the machine. And vote the ghetto dweller and immigrant did. Many saloon-keepers, landlords and gambling house owners became political powers in many cities. They also became very rich.

Yet the years from 1845 to 1870 were hard ones for the Irish Democrat. The party still generally excluded Irishmen from elective offices and when they were nominated for minor posts, Protestant Democrats often "scratched" them from their ballots. The few Irishmen who did attain political power during this period, like Richard Connolly and Peter Sweeney, were second generation Irish-American with atypical education. The great mass of Irish Democrats had to be content with municipal jobs and an occasional foot on the lower rungs of the civil service ladder. Irish participation as "repeater" voters or as "sluggers" bullying native voters away from polling places, did nothing to dispel the Irishman's reputation for untrustworthiness and violence. In 1870 the New Jersey legislature abolished elective government in Jersey City after Irish Catholics were elected to municipal office. In 1885 the Massachusetts legislature stripped Boston's police force from city control when Hugh O'Brien became the city's first Irish Catholic mayor. Irish America's growing political influence was first reflected by the succession of "Honest John" Kelly to the leadership of New York's Democratic party, a success repeated in most eastern American cities by 1890.

Once in power the machine made alliances with legitimate and illegitimate businesses. Organised crime services to the machine were as significant as legitimate business contributions. In Kansas City, mobster John Lazia was an important aspect of the Pendergast machine. James Pendergast began his political career as a saloon keeper. He became a dominant force in the First Ward, and his ability to deliver the vote enabled him to provide police protection for organised gambling.

The police, acting on his behalf, forced independent operators into the gambling syndicate or out of business. The Pendergast machine flourished under Tom Pendergast, brother of James, who forged an alliance with John Lazia's North Side Italian mob. The machine provided police protection for the mob's activities and was rewarded on election day when hired thugs picked up prostitutes, thieves, deadbeats and floaters and brought them to the polling booths to vote for Pendergast. In the 1934 election four people were killed and dozens beaten up as thugs ran riot. When John Lazia ran into trouble with the tax authorities and rumour had it that he was going to inform on the machine for a lenient sentence he was murdered, probably on the orders of Tom Pendergast. Lazia's murder proved Pendergast's undoing for his political and criminal successor, Charlie Binaggio, also ousted the Pendergast machine.

In Chicago in 1873 saloon keepers, gamblers and brothel owners helped Mike McDonald put gambler Harvey D. Colvin in as mayor, ushering in a corrupt regime that lasted until the 1890s. When King Mike died in 1907 his political mantle was taken by the "Lords of the Levee" John Coughlin and Michael Kenna. John Coughlin was born in 1860, to Irish immigrant parents in Chicago's First Ward. He began his political career as a rubber in the exclusive Palmer Baths, where he made friends with powerful businessmen and politicians.

He opened a string of bathhouses with his connections and in 1892 he was elected alderman for the First Ward. "The Bath" Coughlin was a powerfully built six-footer while his partner, Kenna, was a little over five foot and of small stature. Born in the

First Ward in 1858 he opened a saloon and became a precinct captain. He was the brains behind Coughlin. During the severe winter of 1893 Kenna provided care for thousands of homeless and destitute. They were registered in the First Ward and brought back for each election. This majority gave Coughlin and Kenna the ability to deliver the ward and the First Ward majority was so overwhelming that it could effect city, county and even state elections.

With the help of the police and the notorious Quincey Street Boys, Coughlin and Kenna ran the First Ward as their own private fiefdom. Under pressure from the Republicans, who had gained a majority on the council, the Lords of the Levee organised the Annual First Ward Democratic Ball - which netted them $25,000 in ticket sales. The ball was an outrageous affair; gangsters and prostitutes mingled with politicians and policemen. Each year the balls grew bawdier until finally, in 1910, the mayor banned it, when the Catholic archbishop threatened to denounce the ball from the pulpit.

In 1915 Big Bill Thompson was elected mayor of Chicago. He promised the reformers strict enforcement of the gambling laws and he promised the gamblers an open town. Big Bill found it was more profitable to do the latter. Under Thompson, Chicago was to know an era of corruption like never before. Thompson was a friend of the gangster, the gambler and the bootlegger. He was Al Capone and Dion O'Bannion's choice for mayor even though the two were mortal enemies. In 1931 Thompson was defeated by Anton J. Cermak, the founder of the Chicago machine. Cermak concluded that the Irish domination of the Cook County Democratic party did not make numerical sense. He organised an ethnically balanced machine that became the most powerful in Chicago's history. Cermak ran on a reform ticket and vowed to rid Chicago of Al Capone, but he was no better than his predecessor. He made alliances with Bugs

Moran and Roger Touhy, and other bootleggers, corrupt policemen and politicians. Two of his policemen even tried to rub out Frank Nitti, Capone's successor. At their trial they revealed they were acting on orders from Cermak.

Cermak was a protege of George E. Brennan, Democratic party boss in Illinois and a State Representative. He modelled his organisation on the Tammany Hall machine. Early on in his political career Cermak had learned the power and political influence that gambling provided for organised crime. Once in power Cermak decided to control organised gambling himself and briefed his new Police Commissioner that all policy on gambling would come directly from the mayor's office. He selected Big Bill Johnson to manage the West Side gambling concessions and ex-Moran gangster, Ted Newberry, for the North Side. He planned to replace Marty Guilfoyle, on the North West Side, because he derived his concession from the Republicans. In 1933 Cermak was mortally wounded, while sitting beside President-elect Franklin D. Roosevelt. Many believe Cermak was the real target and not Roosevelt.

Cermak's successors were Edward J. Kelly and Patrick Nash. After capturing the mayoral election Kelly and Nash created Chicago's first truly functional political machine that would survive until recent times. The Kelly-Nash machine modelled itself on Tammany Hall and more discreetly learned how to make Chicago "the city that worked". Fronted by Kelly as mayor for fourteen years the machine was more ruthless and more efficient than any of its predecessors.

While gang murders decreased to an acceptable level corruption increased: 7,500 gambling establishments operated openly and the thousands of speakeasies continued after repeal as legitimate saloons although openly flouting the licensing laws; labour racketeering increased and the Capone mob became one of the most powerful in the country. Chicago under the Kelly-Nash machine was to know a more corrupt alliance between the underworld and the government.

Tammany Hall.

Tammany Hall began its long career in 1789 as a fraternal society. Named after a legendary Indian chief, the society became a full fledged political organisation in New York linking itself to the Democratic party. With the arrival of thousands of Irish immigrants, in the 1840s, Tammany Hall was quick to see their value as new votes. Despite nativist and anti-Catholic sentiment in Tammany Hall the Irish soon rose to leadership positions and would dominate "The Hall" for the next ninety years. One of the first Irish Tammany "greats" was Boss Tweed. William Marcy Tweed was born in New York in 1823. He worked his way from nowhere to become chairman of the Democratic Central Committee at Tammany Hall in 1856, and by a series of clever and illegal moves manipulated the city's revenues through his own and his supporters pockets. He consolidated his position by registering thousands of immigrants as Democrats in return for a low-level welfare system and by handouts and payoffs to the queues of critics waiting to be bought. However, one could not be bought. The political cartoonist and editor of the *New York Times* refused half-a-million dollars to keep quiet. His revelations turned public opinion against Boss Tweed and led to his downfall.

Tammany made natural alliances with the street gangs of New York. They were used as repeaters and sluggers on election day. To keep gang members in funds between elections the political bosses found them employment in saloons, gambling houses and brothels under their patronage. By the end of the 1850s Tammany controlled the vote in the slums of the so called "Whiskey Wards" - the Fourth and Sixth Wards. The first man to organise the slums into a voting bloc was the gambler and knife-fighter, Isaiah Rynders. He owned six groggeries in New York where he had a loyal following of thugs and cut-throats. His primary function was to meet newly arrived immigrants and provide them with jobs and lodgings in return for their votes. Rynders was a friend of Tammany and the Irish but his first allegiance had been to the Nativists. His chief rival was the boxer and gambler, John Morrissey, who worked for Tammany boss, John A. Kennedy. Morrissey's initial task was to surround the polls with Dead Rabbits, at a dollar a head, to prevent the Bowery Boys from creating havoc, thus sowing the seeds of a feud that would last for decades.

After the downfall of Boss Tweed the Tammany crown passed to Honest John Kelly. Under Kelly's reign graft was handled more discreetly. When Honest John passed away in 1886 a more boisterous leader emerged in the form of Richard "Boss" Croker. Born in Ireland in 1843 Croker emigrated with his family three years later and wound up in a shantytown in what is now Central Park. He became a leader of the Fourth Avenue Tunnel Gang, who lived in niches in the train tunnels leading out of Grand Central. He was elected alderman in the 1860s and went on to become Superintendent of Market Fees and Rents. Croker more than anyone was the model of the rough and tumble Irish political boss. He made his reputation as a slugger and on one occasion he led several hundred local toughs to commandeer the Philadelphia elections of 1868. In 1874 he was involved in a political row on a street corner in the Gas House District in which he pulled a gun and shot dead an innocent bystander in crossfire. He was indicted for murder but with the Tammany connection, and a little luck, his case resulted in a hung jury.

Under Croker's leadership Tammany became the Democratic party in New York. (The Irish also dominated the New York police force, which was in effect an arm of Tammany

Hall. Corruption in the police force was high and prior to WW1 a fee of $250 to Tammany was required to secure a job as a policeman.) Gambling and house prostitution was under the protection of Tammany state senator, Big Tim Sullivan and Police Chief William Devery. Along with Frank Farrell, Devery and Sullivan headed up a syndicate that handled protection for gambling establishments. Frank Farrell was a gambler and owner of several gambling houses while Big Bill Devery, despite being Police Chief, was known as "the meanest gambler in New York." Sullivan was author of a state law (the Sullivan Act) pro-hibiting the carrying of concealed firearms without a permit. This law was enacted to enable Tammany to better control the behaviour of the street gangs.

After several scandals Tammany lost the 1894 election, but, after the reform impulse ran its course, Boss Croker's machine was back, seeming as invincible as ever. Tammany's loss of the election - and its regain - could be blamed on the change in the city's racial balance. By 1900 the Jewish population of the Lower East Side had doubled to over half-a-million. It was no accident that Tammany's headquarters, known as the "Wigwam", now stood on 14th Street, facing the northern extremity of the Jewish district. Timothy "Big Tim" Sullivan had now become Tammany's main chieftain, surpassing even the great Boss Croker, who was devoting his energies to his race horses and would retire the following year to a huge estate in the English countryside. He spent his last days in Ireland and England raising bulldogs and racing horses. In 1910 Croker's Orby became the first Irish-trained horse to win the Epsom Derby.

Big Tim Sullivan was a gifted street brawler and organiser. He became a saloon-keeper in his teens and host to the Whyos, pursuing a lucrative sideline as a repeat voter and controller of the Whyos votes. He soon had four saloons, one of them across the street from the Tombs Police Court and another on Chrystie

Street, which became headquarters for the Whyos. With his feet in both camps Sullivan entered politics. Elected to the legislature while still in his twenties Croker promoted him to head of the Third Assembly District in 1892. From his saloon, the Occidental, on Broome Street, Sullivan held court handing out food and clothing to the poor, settling disputes and doling out favours and jobs, receiving in turn the votes of the masses. The population of Sullivan's district was changing rapidly as Eastern European Jews and Southern Italians replaced the Irish and Germans on whose electoral support Tammany had always depended. It became Sullivan's job to convert his new constituents to Tammany's way of thinking. He often went out among them attending weddings, bar mitzvahs and funerals, honouring their holidays - or creating them, as he did for his Italian constituents, Columbus Day.

Sullivan knew his constituency for he was a child of it. "I was born in poverty," he would say to his critics, "one of six children, four boys and two girls. The boys used to sleep on a three-quarters bed, not big enough for two, and the girls on a shakedown on the floor. Some nights there was enough to eat and some nights there wasn't. And our old mother used to sing to us at night and maybe it would be the next day before we would think she had been singing but that she had gone to bed without anything to eat. That's the kind of people we come from and that's the kind of mother that bore us down here. If we can help some boy or some father to another chance, we're going to give it to them. The thieves we have done here ain't thieves from choice, they are thieves from necessity and necessity don't know any law."

What votes Sullivan couldn't pick up on his electioneering strategy, his gangster pals furnished through repeating and more forceful methods. The use of the street gangs was nothing new to Tammany, but now the ethnic makeup of them had changed and the Democratic party needed them now more than ever. The Whyos had evolved into the Five Points Gang, led by an Italian, Paolo Vaccarelli, who called himself Paul Kelly. The Five Pointers now did Sullivan's dirty work. In the 1901 campaign for the Second Assembly District Paul Kelly approached Sullivan and offered his services. The hotly contested election was between an old-time alderman, Paddy Divver, and Sullivan's candidate, Tom Foley. Sullivan gave Kelly the go-ahead and scores of Five Pointers descended on the district battering Divver supporters with blackjacks and clubs, making it the most violent primary in the city's history. The police stood idly by as Kelly's thugs cast their votes. One hood boasted that he had voted 53 times. The election was won by a three-to-one majority for Foley.

Big Tim Sullivan ended his days in a New York asylum while the Tammany mantle went to Charles F. Murphy, a former saloon-keeper. Under Murphy's reign Tammany advanced further winning election after election in Manhattan and the boroughs and eventually taking over the state government as well. He also changed the machine's operations; open gambling and prostitution were ended; immunity for gangsters was withdrawn and the power of the police was curtailed. The use of the police as graft collectors was abolished and replaced by a representative of the gamblers, Arnold Rothstein.

Arnold "The Brain" Rothstein was one of the first Jews to become involved with the Tammany machine. As a teenager he worked for Tim Sullivan as a bagman. Later Rothstein began running dice games and became a bookmaker and the owner of a gambling house, retaining his association with Sullivan, which brought him political and police protection. Rothstein became a big-time gambler, handling "lay-off" bets from other bookies. He was the brains of fledgling organised crime in New York around Prohibition and served as the inspiration for Meyer

Wolfsheim in F. Scott Fitzgerald's *The Great Gatsby*. Throughout Prohibition, until his murder in 1928, Rothstein continued to play the role of broker, not only between Tammany and the gamblers, but also between two of New York's political-criminal factions. One faction was headed by James J. Hines, with ties to Dutch Schultz, Owney Madden, Bill Dwyer, Vannie Higgins and Larry Fay. The other faction was headed by Albert C. Marinelli with ties to mainly Italian gangsters like Lucky Luciano, Frank Costello and Albert Anastasia.

Charlie Murphy was the last truly great of Tammany and when he died a battle began in the inner council of the Hall between Jimmy Hines, who considered himself heir apparent to Murphy, and Al Marinelli, who was representing the growing Italian interests in the city. Traditionally, the Irish had ruled and governed New York since the 1870s, but by 1920 the Italians outnumbered the Irish two-to-one and the balance of voting power was shifting. Charlie Murphy had managed to balance the two racial groups, but with his death Tammany was to become a battleground between the opposing factions.

Jimmy Hines, born in 1877, was a third generation politician, following in the footsteps of his grandfather, who served under Boss Tweed and his father, who worked for Richard Croker. In 1907 he was alderman for the Eleventh Assembly District and six years later chief clerk of the board of aldermen. It was all uphill after that. Before Prohibition the Tammany ward boss protected the gangsters from law enforcement. The ward boss was at the top of an unofficial structure with the gangsters at the bottom. Prohibition changed all this, making millionaires of former street thugs, who could now buy politicians by the bunch. Hines, a man of foresight, changed with the system. He was the connection between Tammany and the Syndicate.

Most mob payoffs to Jimmy Hines were funnelled through Dutch Schultz and Frank Costello. When Hines attended the

1932 Democratic convention in Chicago, Costello shared a suite with him. His payroll from organised crime was estimated to be around $5,000 a week. One of his principal jobs was protecting the numbers racket for Dutch Schultz and after the Dutchman's murder in 1935, he performed the same duties for the Luciano-Costello combine when they swallowed up Schultz' rackets. This arraignment continued until racket-buster Tom Dewey launched an all-out war on New York's top mobsters. On May 25 1938 Hines was charged with being a "co-conspirator and part of the Dutch Schultz mob". Dewey alleged that Hines was the bagman for the mob and paid off police, judges and even the district attorney, William C. Dodge. Hines first prosecution ended in a mistrial when the leading witness, George Weinberg, committed suicide. He was convicted in a second trial in February 1939. After a year of appeals Hines was sent to Sing Sing. He was one of the most powerful politicians ever to be imprisoned. He was paroled after four years on condition that he refrain from entering politics. Jimmy Hines died in 1957 at the age of eighty, the last Irish great of Tammany Hall.

Another Tammany star was New York mayor, James "Dandy Jim" Walker. When Louis Kushner shot dead the notorious Kid Dropper in front of dozens of police, reporters and onlookers his defence lawyer was Jimmy Walker. The district attorney, another Tammany man, agreed with Walker that it was manslaughter not murder and Kushner received a 20 year term - though he only served 10 years - rather than the electric chair. When Walker became mayor he ushered in an organised reign of corruption. He named Grover Whelan as police commissioner, who in his first six hours in office, abolished the police confidential squad charged with unearthing police and political corruption. Walker was a hard-drinking playboy and delighted in being seen in New York's fashionable spots. Due to serious charges of corruption Walker resigned and John P. O'Brien was chosen to serve out Walker's remaining year in office.

O'Brien, another Tammany man, was under the thumb of Jimmy Hines and Al Marinelli. When he was asked by reporters if the mayor was going to name a new police commissioner, he said: "I haven't had any word on that yet." In 1933 O'Brien was succeeded by Fiorello La Guardia and payoffs to the police commissioner's office, reportedly $20,000 a week, ceased. Under John J. Ryan, and then Lewis J. Valentine, the New York police department would be virtually corruption free for the next eleven years. Despite the reform Tammany remained untouched. The Hall still selected the municipal judges and county district attorneys and police hierarchies - except the police commissioner - and other lesser officials responsible for enforcing the law.

When La Guardia declined to run for mayor again in 1945, William O'Dwyer, on the strength of his tough anti-crime repu- tation, won the election. O'Dwyer had represented Tammany's best hope of a comeback after years of scandal and disgrace. He was born in Ireland, had been a policeman, a lawyer and a judge before being elected district attorney in Brooklyn in 1939. He was a charming Irishman with the "gift of the gab" and a demonstrated vote-getter. In 1940 his office announced that they had cleared up fifty-six unsolved gangland murders dating back several years. O'Dwyer revealed for the first time the exis- tence of a Syndicate enforcement arm known as "Murder Incorporated". With Abe "Kid Twist" Reles as the star witness, O'Dwyer smashed Murder Inc., sending its leader, Lepke Buchalter, and several others to the electric chair. While under police guard in Coney Island's Half Moon Hotel Reles "fell" to his death from a sixth floor window. Lucky Luciano later claimed that Frank Costello paid $50,000 to law enforcement officials to throw the former hitman out the window. Far from being the scourge of organised crime, O'Dwyer was a tool of Tammany

Hall and had ties to Syndicate leaders, including Frank Costello. In March 1951 he appeared before Senator Estes Kefauver's Senate Rackets Committee. Though no charges were ever filed the Kefauver hearings ruined O'Dwyer's political career. He resigned as ambassador to Mexico, a post he taken up in 1950.

By the 1940s and 1950s the Washington administration had started a welfare system that brought street politics away from the masses and Tammany Hall and its counterparts in every other city withered and died. The Irish ward boss faded into history and except for pockets in working class districts Irish domination of politics faded, too.

CHAPTER 9

ON THE WATERFRONT

For recently arrived emigrants the New York waterfront pro-vided attractive employment and as a bustling port there was no shortage of work. The loading and unloading of ships was hard work and in those early days, hazardous work. Many Irish emigrants straight off the boat sought employment on New York's busy waterfront. They worked ten or twelve hours a day to unload and then load a ship for perhaps fifty cents an hour. Employment was usually found through a hiring boss, who had control of a pier. The hiring boss usually gained control of his pier through bloodshed.

There was constant warfare for control of the waterfront. To control the docks meant control of the rackets there; gambling, loansharking, pilfering, kickbacks and the loading racket - which involved a flat rate levied against the importers and another charge levied against the hauliers for every crate they loaded. With lead pipes and brass knuckles the gangs fought each other for the right to plunder the docks. On Manhattan's piers gangs like the Whyos, Gophers and Hudson Dusters mur-dered their rivals by the dozen for a piece of the action. Across the river in Irishtown - an area wedged in between the East

River on the north, the Navy Yard on the east and the Washington Street entrance approach to the Brooklyn Bridge off to the west - Irish gangs battled each other and newer gangs of Italians for control of the docklands.

'Runners' were to be found in every port of entry in America but it was in New York that their inequities were at their worst. On arrival the emigrant was accosted by a runner and unless he was met by relatives he was frightened and confused. The runner's first move was to recommend the comfort and economy of a boarding house managed by one of his friends; sixpence for a meal, the same for a bed and luggage was stored free. Only too often the emigrant allowed himself and his luggage to be led away. At the boarding house everything was charged at an exorbitant price and the unfortunate emigrants were virtually kept prisoner until all their money was gone. Runners supplied victims at so much a head to boarding-houses of ill repute. They worked in gangs and bloody fights were waged for the possession of the terrified emigrants, the strongest party carrying off the prey. Corruption on New York's waterfront was powerful, involving corrupt officials, runners, saloon keepers, gang lords, passage brokers and forwarding agents and was not checked until 1855 when all emigrants were landed at Castle Garden pier, under the eye of armed police, instead of being landed at different quays.

The Longshoreman's United Benevolent Society, formed in 1852, was exclusively Irish. During the strikes of 1852, 1855, 1862 and 1863 blacks were brought in to take the place of striking Irishmen. These waterfront labour wars led directly to the 1863 Draft Riots.

Black workers had traditionally been an important part of the workforce on the docks of New York, Boston, Philadelphia, Baltimore, Charlestown and New Orleans. By the 1850s the New York waterfront had become an Irish preserve. Blacks could only find work during strikes and under police protection – even Germans were unwelcome.

Until 1900 about ninety-five per cent of the longshoremen on the New York waterfront were Irish. By 1912 Italians comprised about thirty-five per cent and by the end of the decade that had risen to seventy-five per cent. The Irish retained the docks on Manhattan's West Side, while the Italians dominated the East Side, most of Brooklyn and the New Jersey waterfront. The International Longshoreman's Association was formed in the 1890s with the aid of labour racketeer Paolo Vaccarelli, better known as Paul Kelly, leader of the Five Points Gang. In the pre-WW1 era of union organising and union busting Kelly leased out his army of thugs to businessmen as strike-breakers and to other mobs as sluggers and enforcers. By 1914 the ILA had complete control of the New York waterfront.

The docks provided racketeers with golden opportunities to make a fortune. Smuggling, loansharking, gambling, large-scale pilfering and deals with employers eager to keep costs down enriched the gangsters plaguing the waterfront. One of the principle incentives for organised crime to infiltrate the ILA was the "loading" racket. Due to lack of rail connections to harbour piers, cargo had to be moved from the pier floor to waiting trucks. Since demand for cargo loading was dependent upon immediate need when ships arrived, loading guaranteed extra-ordinary profits and was a lucrative racket. Through control of the loading racket the mob extorted millions from trucking companies.

Control of the waterfront labour force meant control of the waterfront. Once in control of the labour force, through control of the union, everything else followed. When a ship docks it must be emptied quickly. Apart from the cargo including perishable goods, ships "turnaround" time is crucial to profitability. To unload quickly meant having an oversupply of labour. The "kick-back" racket arose from the surplus of men at the daily "shape-up". The longshoremen usually gathered around the hiring boss, who was usually a mob hood and union official. He selected the necessary number of men required. The "kick-back" was the part of the day's wages paid to the hiring boss for the "privilege" of working. There were other money makers for the mob on the waterfront. There was large-scale thieving and smuggling, especially of narcotics, and gambling and loansharking, which bled the poorly paid longshoreman dry. Steamship and stevedoring companies also had to bribe the ILA and gang bosses for labour peace, just to stay in business.

The mobsters and union bosses made a fortune while the longshoremen barely scratched an existence. New York dockers earned far less than those in San Francisco, who belonged to another union. The ILA paid no strike pay, no sickness or death benefit. In the 1940s the ILA president, Joe Ryan, was paying himself $25,000 a year while rank and file members barely earned $2,000 a year. Every politician in New York knew the ILA was riddled with corruption, but none would raise their voice because Ryan and his cohorts could make or break politicians with their campaign funds, donations and their control of block votes.

While Paul Kelly led the gangster dominated ILA into the waterfront it was under Joe Ryan that organised crime control of the docks became complete. Ryan was a fierce anti-Communist and became the ILA president in 1927, a post he retained until 1953. As a result on the West Coast, Australian born Harry Bridges, a merchant seaman with leftist views, withdrew from the ILA and formed his own union. Bridges arrived in San Francisco in 1920 and seeing the poor working conditions on the docks stayed to improve them. He led the largest strike action in American history in May 1930. When strike-breakers tried to force the lines, two people were killed and dozens injured in the ensuing riots. The union fought back with a call for a general strike, which closed the city down for four days, inspiring solidarity in other Bay area communities. The strike ended with the longshoremen winning their demands. Joe Ryan refused to back another strike in 1934 and Bridges withdrew from the ILA and formed his own union, the International Longshoreman's and Warehouseman's Union, which was then, and still is today, entirely free from mob influence.

The mob kept control over the ILA by using violence. One of Joe Ryan's most brutal allies was Johnny "Cockeye" Dunn, who ruled sixty of Manhattan's downtown piers for ten years by murdering more than thirty people. Dunn was to go swaggering and unrepentant to the electric chair in Sing Sing in 1949 for killing a disobedient hiring boss. Through violence and intimidation the mob ruled the biggest port in the world. From the 1930s to the 1950s a succession of Irish gangsters ran the West Side piers while the Brooklyn docks were controlled by Albert Anastasia and his brother, Tough Tony, who was also president of Local 1814, the biggest ILA branch in Brooklyn. The New Jersey waterfront around Hoboken and Newark was dominated by the Genovese crime family.

In 1952 a series of articles written in the *New York Sun* by Malcolm Johnson caused a public outrage. Organised crime had been levying the equivalent of a five per cent tax on all cargo annually moved through the port. The cities of New York and New Jersey, who owned most of the large piers, began a campaign to clean up the waterfront and set up a Waterfront Commission to fight mob influence and control of the port.

The commission was empowered to license stevedoring concerns and regulate waterfront employees. Those with serious criminal records were banned from the docks. The commission was given subpoena power and investigate authority in New York and New Jersey and was aided by federal investigations into the ILA.

The West Side docks at this time were controlled by thugs like Eddie McGrath, John O'Hara, Hughie Mulligan, Apples Applegate, Mickey Bowers and his Pistol Local 824, snake-eyed John Keefe and Sudden Death Ward. They held the waterfront in a grip of fear, for to defy the mob meant certain death. Leading the campaign for reform was "The Waterfront Priest" Father John Corridan, a tough, fast-talking, revolutionary Kerryman. As the influence of the Corridan group spread through the waterfront it was met by violence. There were shooting attacks, beatings and intimidation. Christy Doran, a hiring boss on Pier 42 and a member of the reform campaign, "fell" to his death from a cliff at a church picnic. On notorious Pier 32, Michael Brogan, an assistant hiring boss, disappeared shortly after his local, 895, voted five to one to quit the ILA. Three weeks later his body was found in the Hudson River. Brogan's death was blamed on Eddie McGrath, an ILA organiser for fifteen years and a mob leader with a record of twelve arrests for crimes ranging from petty larceny to murder. McGrath had fled to Florida after his brother-in-law and gang-partner, Cockeye Dunn was executed. From Miami he was running the rackets on the Lower West Side piers, including Pier 32.

On September 23 1953 the ILA was expelled from the American Federation of Labour because of corruption. In November its president, Joe Ryan, resigned while under investigation for misappropriating union funds. However, as a token of gratitude for his years of service, Ryan was awarded a yearly pension of $10,000. Reformer William V. Bradley was elected president in his place. Both the AFL and the West Coast based ILWU unsuccessfully attempted to wrest control of the 40,000 longshoremen from the ILA. In May 1954 elections were held to decide whether the longshoremen would remain in the ILA. On the morning of May 27 the returns were in. The ILA had polled 9,110 votes to 8,791 for the reform movement. In Jersey City buses scheduled to carry anti-ILA dockers to the polling stations failed to show up due to threats made against the drivers and owners of the buses. Along with murder and intimidation this had added to the reform movement's defeat. The ILA remained in power.

The real losers were the 8,791 longshoremen who had gambled their livelihood - and some their lives. Scores left the docks to escape the vengeance of the mob; they shipped out as seamen or sought employment elsewhere. But some stayed to carry on the fight and lived to see the end of the shape-up and a more reform-minded leadership under William Bradley. The Waterfront Commission abolished the shape-up and the hiring boss - the biggest causes of gang rule on the docks. Workers were hired not by the employer but by the union which nominated the hiring boss. Each hiring boss ruled his own pier. He decided who worked and who did not.

The commission barred men with serious criminal records from holding union office. It also tried to reduce the number of surplus longshoremen looking for non-existent work. The ILA had never tried to reduce union membership. They kept the books open and union dues kept coming in. This suited the employers as with so many men fighting for so little work, wages could be kept at a minimum. Now with the reduction of surplus longshoremen wages rose.

For a time it looked like the waterfront was finally free of mob domination. However, barred mobsters soon found their way around the rules by giving themselves highly paid "no-show" jobs for which no license was needed. The mob remained though more subtle and more sophisticated. The ILA shifted from exploiting its members to carving up the cargo traffic among the stevedoring companies and taxing them on their shares. Corruption between businessmen and ILA officials was rife. It was all business so there was no longer any need for extortion or violence. The ILAs new president, William Bradley, failed to co-operate with the waterfront racketeers and after being issued with death threats declined to run for re-election.

On July 17 1963 Thomas W. "Teddy" Gleason was unanimously elected president. While being questioned by a grand jury about corruption in the ILA he took the Fifth Amendment. Earlier in his career Gleason and Connie Noonan, boss of a waterfront numbers racket, had allegedly engaged in a number of business deals, including selling armed planes to the Dominican Republic. (Cornelius "Connie" Noonan was president of ILA Local 1730. In 1959 he was indicted on charges of corruption.) Gleason also opposed an administrative bill to force convicted criminals out of union leadership positions. When Ronald Reagan addressed the ILA - Reagan was the first U.S. President to address the ILAs national convention - on July 18 1983 he had great praise for Teddy, who he said "sticks by his friends and he sticks by his country, the kind of integrity and loyalty that is hard to come by today." When Gleason retired in 1987, at the grand old age of 87, the presidency went to his associate and ILA executive vice-president John Bowers.

Today Manhattan's West Side piers are almost dead. The old piers where longshoremen fought and died for the right to work are quiet now. The bars where union bosses and mobsters ran their rackets are home to New York's gay population.

The Mob Joins The War Effort.

On December 9, two days after the Japanese attacked Pearl Harbour, Germany and Italy declared war on the United States. Within two months seventy-one American merchant ships were sunk by German submarines. U.S. Navy Intelligence suspected that the U-boats were being refuelled and resupplied off the U.S. coast by German and Italian sympathisers, who were also providing information on Allied shipping movements in and out of eastern ports.

On February 9 the *S.S. Normandie,* a former French liner being converted to a troopship, was burnt out at her Manhattan berth. Sabotage was suspected. One Intelligence officer, Lieutenant Commander Charles Haffenden, suggested that the Navy contact the men that ran the waterfront - the mobsters.

The first man to be contacted was Joe "Socks" Lanza, known as the "King of the Fulton Fish Market". He was facing trial for extortion and enthusiastically agreed to help. He would provide navy agents with union cards so they could work undercover and his men would watch out for any suspicious activity among the fishing fleets. Navy intelligence was delighted and wanted to extend the arrangement to the West Side docks, the Brooklyn piers and the New Jersey waterfront. Lanza told them all he could only deliver the small downtown fishing piers. If they wanted co-operation on all of the New York waterfront there was only one man who could do it; Lucky Luciano. The once "King of the Underworld" was in Dannemora prison serving a 35 year term for organised prostitution. On advice from the Navy he was visited by his lawyer, Moses Polakoff, and gang partner, Meyer Lansky, his associate for over twenty years. For his co-operation Luciano wanted one thing - his freedom. He gave instructions for his name to be used in approaching the Irish and Italian ILA bosses, including Cockeye Dunn on the West Side and Albert Anastasia on the Brooklyn docks.

When Dunn's name was put forward he was in jail facing an extortion charge. The Navy got him released on bail. He was business agent of Local 21510 AFL, Motor and Bus Terminal Checkers, Platform and Office Workers Union, but he was also a power on the West Side waterfront ruling no less than sixty piers. Dunn had a lot of influence and was a genuine terror - he was reputed to have murdered over thirty people. He threw himself wholeheartedly into the war effort. The Navy gave the mob the

go-ahead to "take care of business" on the waterfront. Two suspects staying at a West Side hotel were extremely interested in
what off-duty sailors were talking about. Their names were
given to Dunn to check out. Shortly after they disappeared.
Questioned about them Dunn said, "They'll never bother us
again." The Navy boys didn't press him for details but asked him
to consult them before acting on his own initiative.

Dunn and an associate, Jeremiah Sullivan, had murdered
the two potential spies, a service they were more than eager to
provide. The war years were the best years for Dunn, murder
and violence for a good cause. His friend and associate,
Jeremiah Sullivan, was only too willing to help, too. Sullivan,
a.k.a. John McCue, was the right-hand man of Joe Ryan, the
ILA president. Sullivan had served a ten year term in Sing Sing for
second degree murder. Like Dunn, he was delighted to mingle
with respectable people like Commander Haffenden. He could
not help them enough. If the Navy reported difficulties with shipping delays Sullivan paid a visit and busted arms, legs and
heads to get things moving. Dunn and Sullivan's strong-arm tactics worked. For the rest of the war there was no sabotage,
union disputes or shipping delays.

The arrangement with the Navy extended as far as Harlem,
where Tough Willie McCabe, who was running the numbers
racket for Lucky Luciano, helped out keeping an eye on Axis
sympathisers and spies who hung out in restaurants, clubs, bars
and brothels with mob connections. McCabe reportedly said,
"I'm doing this for the Boss". Obviously, he meant Luciano.

Naval Intelligence attempted to play down the co-operation between them and the mob, but without men like Dunn
and Sullivan they would have never got the co-operation they
needed. There were genuine spies and troublemakers on the
docks and all of them were dealt with harshly and effectively. It
may have been illegal and certainly it was immoral to have

murderers and criminals working for the government, but in the end it saved countless lives. The Navy was not proud of the affair and most of the records were destroyed and much of the details lost.

When the Allies laid plans to invade the island of Sicily, Lucky Luciano was again approached. He enlisted the Sicilian Mafia to help the Allies when they landed. For his part in helping the war effort Luciano was given a pardon in 1946 but was not allowed to spend his freedom in America. Instead he was deported to Italy, where he died in 1962. The early release of Luciano and Tom Dewey's role in it, was the subject of much controversy. In the 1950s the affair was examined by a senate investigating committee which cleared Dewey of any blame in Luciano's release. Nevertheless, the report was hushed up by Naval Intelligence.

CHAPTER 10

MOB WARS

Manhattan Melodrama.

Paul Kelly became the first modern-day organised crime boss, taking over the Five Points area and neighbouring districts. Paolo Antonio Vaccarelli became a bantamweight prize-fighter in the 1890s, adopting an Irish name for the ring at the time when the sport was dominated by the Irish. With Big Tim Sullivan as his political benefactor Kelly became a rising underworld power with 1,500 thugs at his and Tammany Hall's disposal. Kelly was no ordinary street thug. He spoke Italian, French and Spanish fluently. He dressed well, usually tie and tuxedo, and was well groomed and well mannered. Many of his top men had been recruited from other Five Points gangs. His chief lieutenants were Kid Twist Zwerbach, Johnny Spanish, Richie Fitzpatrick, Razor Riley and Biff Ellison.

Kelly's main rival was Edward "Monk" Eastman, a brutal, unrefined thug, who with Tammany's influence dominated the Lower East Side. Now, like Five Points, it was no longer an Irish slum, but a melting pot of Jews, Italians and other European immigrants. Five-foot-five inches the cretinous Eastman always wore a small hat on his bullet shaped head and a tight-fitting suit to accent his powerful body. By the turn of the century Eastman's army of 2,000, mainly Jewish thugs, faced Kelly's forces across the Bowery. Tammany Hall played a double hand by encouraging the much more refined Kelly to edge into Eastman's territory. Moreover, Tammany began to support Kelly further by giving his rackets political protection and encouraged the police to put pressure on Eastman.

In early 1901 a confident Paul Kelly ordered Eastman to be shot on sight. Gun battles and gang fights became a regular occurrence. In July 1903 Eastman and several henchmen were arrested while beating up a coachman. Newspaper reporters miraculously appeared on the scene and while Eastman was being led away in handcuffs he shouted so all could hear, "You're arrestin' me, huh? Say, you want to look where you're goin'! I cut some ice in this town! I made half the big politicians of New York!"

When he was quoted in the next days papers Tammany Hall realised the dangerous potential of supporting a thug like Eastman. Though Eastman was defended and cleared of assault by Thomas Grady, a Tammany state senator, the bosses gave Kelly the go-ahead to eliminate him. After a pitched gun battle involving about one-hundred hoods, which left three dead and nine wounded, Big Tim Sullivan ordered Manhattan sheriff, Tom Foley, to arrange a truce between the two mobs. Foley met with the two gang leaders and told them that unless a truce was agreed Tammany could not guarantee their political protection. The two gangsters agreed to settle their differences with a boxing match. They met and fought for two hours with the marathon fight ending in a draw. It solved nothing. Within weeks the mobs were back at each others throats.

Kelly's problems with Eastman were conveniently settled the following year by Eastman himself. On February 2 1904 he mugged a wealthy young man and was apprehended. Despite being very wealthy, Eastman always liked to join his men in penny-ante capers. Boasting that he would be out in hours Eastman was surprised when he found his political protection was gone. His appeals to Sullivan and Foley fell on deaf ears. He was tried and convicted and given a ten-year sentence in Sing Sing.

With the jailing of its leader the Eastman gang began to split in violent in-fighting. Richie Fitzpatrick and Kid Twist Zwerbach had defected to Eastman several years before and now both of them sought to take over the mob. Both Fitzpatrick and Zwerbach were dedicated killers, but Kid Twist was more cunning and was also known as Kid Sly Fox. He offered to meet Fitzpatrick in a saloon on Christie Street and over a drink divide up Eastman's empire. Fitzpatrick, wishing to avoid unnecessary bloodshed, agreed. He arrived in the saloon at the appointed time. He saw Zwerbach sitting alone at a table and as he walked over Kid Twist raised his glass in salute. The lights suddenly went out and gunfire blazed in the darkness. When the police arrived they found the saloon empty, except for Fitzpatrick, who lay dead on the floor with his hands crossed neatly over his chest. Zwerbach was arrested, but released for lack of evidence. He took over Eastman's crumbling empire, but did not last long. He was shot dead four years later by members of the Kelly mob.

Eastman's imprisonment seemed to be the end of Paul Kelly's problems. His empire went from strength to strength. But some of his lieutenants were not happy with their subservient roles. In 1908 Biff Ellison and Razor Riley made their move to take over Kelly's throne. James T. Ellison was so formidable he could command as many as three annual balls at the Tammany Wigwam. (It was common practice for gangs to sponsor benefit dances in their own behalf to raise funds. Some gangsters like

Biff Ellison organised a benevolent association of which he was the sole member. Shopkeepers and businessmen were expected to purchase blocks of tickets - it was unhealthy not to. The James Ellison Association held an "annual" three times a year which netted its benefactor $3,000.) He was angry with Kelly for not having made him the bouncer of the New Brighton Dance Hall, on Great Jones Street, after Kelly's chief bouncer "Eat-'Em-Up" Jack McManus had been bludgeoned to death with an iron bar in a dispute at the dance hall. Razor Riley was enraged when Kelly blamed him for starting a fight and personally threw him out of the New Brighton.

On the night of November 12 Ellison and Riley walked into the New Brighton, which was Kelly's headquarters. Kelly was seated near the dance floor talking to his two bodyguards, Bill Harrington and Rough-House Hogan. Harrington saw the two draw guns and shouted, "Look out, boss!" pushing Kelly out of the line of fire. Riley started shooting, hitting Harrington in the head, killing him. Hogan returned fire and the two killers dived for cover. Kelly came up guns blazing at Ellison who returned his fire. The lights were switched off and the gunfire continued, with screaming patrons running for the exits. Police arrived and exchanged fire with Ellison and Riley, who made good their escape in the confusion. Kelly was taken to a private hospital with three bullet wounds. He later turned himself in but no charges were pressed due to his Tammany connections.

Both Ellison and Riley were slightly wounded. Riley holed up in a dank basement in Chinatown where he contacted pneumonia and died before the police could find him. Ellison eluded the police and Kelly until 1911 when he was arrested and sentenced to 8-20 years in Sing Sing for Bill Harrington's murder. He went insane in prison and was committed to an asylum where he died a few years later. The New Brighton was closed by the police and Kelly moved to Harlem, concentrating on labour racketeering. With reform in full swing and the Tammany politicians protecting themselves his empire slowly disintegrated. Kelly died in bed in 1927, no longer a power in the underworld. His old enemy. Monk Eastman, was murdered in 1920 by Jerry Bohan, a corrupt Prohibition agent.

The White Hand Gang and the Dago invasion.

From the beginning of the century to the late 1920s a grim war was waged on the Brooklyn waterfront between the Irish and Italian gangsters for control of the lucrative waterfront rackets. Around 1900 the various Irish gangs put aside their differences and combined into the White Hand Gang, so named because they were fighting the Italian Black Hand gangs. The Mafia had first surfaced in New York in the 1880s. Many of its members operated extortion rackets and were referred to as Black Hand gangs, because they initialled their threatening letters with a black hand.

Irish gangsters had long organised the Brooklyn docks terrorising the shipping companies and the longshoremen. The Brooklyn waterfront was five miles long with over sixty piers. Its lucrative rackets were coveted by the recently arrived Italian criminal gangs. Pier by pier the Italians began to unseat the Irish. Even the Irish neighbourhoods began to feel the encroachments of the new immigrants. Red Hook, a tough Irish neighbourhood, housed Brooklyn's Little Italy, while Irishtown, wedged in between the East River and the Brooklyn Navy Yard, was bordered by a growing Italian community. As the Irish vacated the most impoverished areas the Italians moved into them.

The Italian gangs, led by Al Mineo and Francesco "Frankie Yale" Uale, slowly gained the upper hand, though with a great loss of life. By the end of WW1 the White Handers, under Dennis "Dinny" Meehan, retained a firm hold on the Brooklyn Bridge-

Red Hook sections of the waterfront. Stevedoring companies, barge and warehouse owners paid out weekly protection to the White Hand to prevent the wholesale theft of cargo from warehouses, or the hijacking of goods-laden trucks and the destruction of barges and wharves. Anyone who did not pay suffered severely. All of the longshoremen had to pay the White Hand a daily commission for the right to work. The majority of the longshoremen were Irish and paid willingly seeing their salvation in the vows of the White Hand to keep the waterfront free of Italians. If the White Hand were replaced by the Mafia it was inevitable that the Irish workforce would be replaced by the Italians.

When Prohibition became law the Mafia in Brooklyn was well prepared, importing bonded whiskey from allies in Detroit and Cleveland and peddling home-brewed beer and wine to Brooklyn's many saloons and speakeasies. The Irish gangsters under Dinny Meehan had no foresight to see the riches Prohibition offered. Like many old style gang lords Dinny Meehan was unintelligent enough to grasp what the Volstead Act meant. But others did.

In the early hours of the morning of April 1 1920 two gunmen crept up to bedroom of Meehan's apartment building on Warren Street. It was a three-storey, six family, red brick apartment building in a run down neighbourhood. Meehan could easily have afforded to live in better accommodation, but like many of the home-grown gangsters, then and now, he preferred to live in his home environment. While lying in bed, Meehan was shot once in the neck. The bullet hit the collarbone and deflected upwards into his brain. His wife, Peggy, was critically wounded in the stomach. Meehan had a big send-off, with over a thousand mourners and six cars laden with flowers. The only thing was, nobody was too sure who killed him. His Mafia rivals got the blame, but some believed the killing was carried out by his own men, who were eyeing the bootleg booze rackets.

Chief contenders for the leadership position were Meehan's top lieutenants, William "Wild Bill" Lovett and Timmy Quilty. The White Handers were a democratic bunch and decided to settle the issue by a dice throw! The contest was held in a crowded Furman Street saloon. Quilty rolled first and came up with a seven. "I'm the boss!" he shouted. Lovett glared sourly, then pulled an automatic pistol and fired several bullets into Quilty. "Now, I'm the boss," he said and glared around, his automatic still smoking. No one disputed him.

Lovett was never charged in the Quilty murder nor in any other of the many killings he carried out. He was an innocent-looking killer. His slight, five-foot seven-inch, one-hundred-and-fifty pound frame belied the terror he inspired on the waterfront. He had been badly wounded serving as a machine-gunner with the 11th Infantry Division in France during the war and had been awarded the Distinguished Service Cross for bravery. Wild Bill joined the White Handers when he returned from France and soon rose to a top position. He was a dangerous man to friend and foe alike and once shot a pal for pulling a cat's tail. The day Prohibition began Lovett walked into Guerney's saloon on 4th Avenue. Demanding his usual shot of whiskey he grew incensed when the bartender told him he could no longer sell alcohol. When the barman stood his ground Lovett shot him dead in front of thirty customers. Only two made statements and neither of them ever made it to court. Lovett was not charged. In all he was arrested nineteen times for charges ranging from disorderly conduct to murder. However, he only spent a total of seven months in jail for his numerous crimes.

Under Lovett's leadership the White Hand went on the offensive extending their power to all the docks from Red Hook to Greenpoint forcibly ejecting the Italians who had gained a foothold. As a first warning Wild Bill wounded a foe. If he found the collector again on his turf he killed him. The White Handers also began hi-jacking the Italians supplies of Old Grandad whiskey imported from Detroit. The Italians were not going to take this lying down and on February 14, St. Valentine's Day, they struck back. Two gunmen walked into Sagaman's Hall in South Brooklyn and opened fire on the mainly Irish hoods cele-brating with their wives and girlfriends. Three people died and a dozen were injured; two of them, Kevin Donovan and Jimmy O'Toole, were White Hand gangsters, while the third victim was Mary Reilly, girlfriend of Pegleg Lonergan, a top White Hander. Mary Reilly had been known as "Stout-hearted Mary" because she had raised seven younger brothers and sisters after their parents had drowned in 1916 in a boating accident. The White Hand swore revenge. It was not long in coming.

Twelve days later four White Handers invaded Stauch's Dance Hall in Coney Island where dozens of Mafiosi and their wives and girlfriends were attending a Saturday night dance. The doorman was shot dead and in a fusillade of shotgun and pistol fire two men and one woman were killed, while several more revellers were wounded, none seriously. One of the gun-men, Danny Bean, was shot dead as the White Handers beat a hasty retreat. The revenge attack was masterminded by Pegleg Lonergan, whose girlfriend had died in the Sagaman's Hall attack.

Richard Lonergan, known as "Pegleg", was a zany killer who had lost his right leg below the knee in a boyhood train looting expedition. The twelve year old Lonergan was outfitted with a wooden leg which helped him to walk but inspired kids to nick-name him "Pegleg". The name stuck, though as he got older no one said it to his face. His friends called him Dick. In his late teens Lonergan fell in with the local toughs who would later form the White Hand Gang. He was a psychopathic killer, with, according to police sources, over twenty murders to his credit. His wife-beating father met his death with a baseball bat blow to his head and it was rumoured that Pegleg was batting for the home team at the time. Romance came hard for Pegleg and it was not until he met Mary Reilly that he found acceptance from the opposite sex. When the Mafia killed his soon-to-wed Lonergan was devastated. His only ambition was to avenge her and kill as many Mafiosi as he could. With the Stauch's Dance Hall massacre to his credit, Lonergan's status in the White Hand Gang rose. Soon he would be trust into the leadership position.

Wild Bill Lovett was the subject of several murder attempts by his Italian rivals, fellow Irish gangsters and thugs hired by the dock owners. He carried several bullets in his body from such attempts. He boasted that no one could kill him, not the Germans, nor the Italians, nor even his Irish rivals. On January 3 1923 he was shot through the window of a shack on Front Street. Lovett was hit in the chest, shoulder and leg. One bullet lodged above his heart. He was on the critical list for two days, then he began to make a remarkable recovery. Asked by police who shot him he said, "My enemies." Shortly after, a hood named Eddie Hughes, believed to be the gunman in the murder bid, was found shot dead.

Lovett was discharged from the hospital after two weeks and while making his recovery fell under the spell of Anna Lonergan, sister of his top lieutenant Pegleg Lonergan. Anna was a beauty and was known as "The Irish Rose of the Brooklyn Waterfront." Lovett proposed marriage to her, but she said he would have to give up the rackets as she did not want to be a young widow. Bill vowed to give up the rackets and settle down and they were married on August 17 1923, spending their honeymoon in the Catskill Mountains. Pegleg Lonergan stepped in as leader of the White Hand. Lovett and his new bride bought a bungalow in Little Ferry, New Jersey, living under the name of

Brady to mislead any enemies. Bill went to work as a welder in Jersey City shipyard, earning $250 a week. He was a good welder but his boss thought it healthier to pay him more than he was worth. Lovett kept his promise to his wife until October when there were rumours on the waterfront that he was coming back.

On October 31 1923, Halloween, Lovett came home from work and told his wife he was going into Brooklyn to see some of the boys. He wound up drinking at the Loader's Club, a speakeasy at 25 Bridge Street, frequented by White Handers. He met an old friend, a longshoreman named Joe Flynn. After they had finished off a couple of bottles of bootleg rye Flynn staggered home while Lovett fell asleep on a wooden bench, using Flynn's jacket as a pillow. After eleven the bartender, looking out on an empty bar, went home leaving the porter to lock up. The porter unable to wake Lovett left him stretched out on the bench and went home. About 1 a.m. Lovett was woken by the noise of a forced entry. Three men burst in, two of them emptied their revolvers at Lovett, only hitting him with three bullets, none of them life threatening. Lovett staggered around until Willie "Two Knives" Alterri, a top assassin for Frankie Yale, buried a cleaver in his skull, finally killing him.

The next day the newspapers reported that the cleaver killer had said, "Trick or treat, Bill", before bringing the cleaver down on his skull. Lovett's Mafia foes spread the word that Wild Bill had been killed on the orders of Pegleg Lonergan, so that he could maintain his hold on the White Hand Gang. The assassin Willie Alterri was richly pensioned off to his native Sicily for having knocked off the Brooklyn Mafia's most formidable foe. Joe Flynn was arrested because his jacket was found on the premises, but he was released without charge.

Lovett had a huge send-off. Nearly two-thousand mourners were at his burial in Cypress Hills Cemetery, where he was buried among thousands of America's war heroes, dating as far back as the Revolution. He was given full military honours as befitting a war hero and was buried with his Distinguished Service Cross draped around his neck. His wife, Anna, was inconsolable and at one stage she tried to throw herself into the grave, only to be restrained by Pegleg and other mourners.

The White Handers took swift revenge for Lovett's death, killing three of their rivals within days. The waterfront war raged on until January 1925 when Frankie Yale, sick of the slaughter, brokered a cease-fire. Yale had known Lonergan since 1915, though they had not spoken since the outbreak of the war in 1920. There was a trade-off. The Italians agreed to give up the Furman Street and Greenpoint piers, while the Irish would give up the Greendocks from 17th to 36th Street. Peace prevailed for five months until Lonergan realised that the docks he had agreed to control had far less traffic than the Italian-operated docks. When he led his men back onto the Greenpoint piers they were met by determined resistance from the Mafia. The White Handers, though fighting a losing battle, fought back furiously, narrowly missing Yale one night as he left a South Brooklyn speakeasy. Yale planned for one bold stroke to wipe out the White Hand once and for all.

It came at Christmas 1925 with inside information that the White Hand were planning a bold stroke of their own. On Christmas Day Yale annually held a stag party for his gang members and Pegleg Lonergan planed to invade the Adonis Social Club, where it was held, and knock off a few top Mafia hoods, possibly even Yale himself. The Adonis Club, overlooking Gowanus Bay on 20th Street was a meeting place for working class Italians and local Mafia hoods. It was run by Angelo "Fury" Argolia, a partner of Frankie Yale. The Adonis occupied the ground floor of a wooden frame building with an apartment comprising the top half. A long corridor opened into a bar while a door there led into a large back room used for dances, weddings and other receptions. A battered piano stood in one corner while rickety chairs and tables cluttered the rest of the room. The only seasonal decorations were a few pieces of mistletoe and a banner circling the wall with "Merry Christmas and a Happy New Year" scrawled on it.

Around 3 a.m. Pegleg Lonergan and five gang members arrived and made their way to the back of the Adonis Club. The five hoods were Aaron Harms and Cornelius "Needles" Ferry, Lonergan's top aides and James Hart, Patrick Maloney and Joseph Howard, three truck drivers pressed into service as gunmen, proof that Lonergan was hard pressed for muscle. Lonergan hoped to strike late when most of the crowd had gone home. The Italians were well prepared for them. There were few visible Mafia hoods. The usual Adonis employees were there - Sylvester Argolia, brother of Fury, the club singer, Helen Logan, the pianist George Carozza and the cigarette girl, Elvira Callaghan. At one table sat the Chicago gangster Al Capone and some of his men, among them the Homicide Squad, Albert Anselmi and John Scalise. Capone was in New York for the holidays. His son was undergoing surgery for an ear affliction at the Manhattan clinic of Dr. Lloyd on St. Nicholas Place. Capone was married to a local Irish girl, Mae Coughlin. (Irishmen married late in life, so it was not unusual to find many Irish girls with Italian partners - Johnny Torrio was also married to an Irishwoman, Ann McCarthy from Kentucky.) Lonergan knew of Al Capone and knew that he had once worked for Frankie Yale and had fled to Chicago after leaving a White Hand gangster near dead, but he would not have recognised him.

Seeing no one they could recognise Lonergan and his men lounged about drinking and making many loud and insulting remarks about "dagos", "wops", "ginzos" and "guineas". When a local Irish girl, May Wilson, whose husband was serving a term in

Elmira, walked in with John Stabile, one of Fury Argolia's partners in the Adonis, Lonergan rounded on her. He ordered her
out and "to come back with a white man". Minutes later, at a
nod from Capone, Sylvester Argolia walked up to Aaron Harms
and struck him on the head with a cleaver. At that signal Fury
Argolia hit the main light switch leaving the rest of the Irish
hoods illuminated by a small chandelier over their table. Guns
blazed in the darkness. The White Handers ran for cover, but two
did not make it. Lonergan was first to fall, hit by two bullets, one
in the back of his head. Needles Ferry fell on top of his boss,
both of them in a heap a few feet from the piano, where they
were going to take cover. Patrick Maloney and Joseph Howard
ran out the door with the panic stricken customers. Aaron
Harms also made out it to the street, but he collapsed and
died. In addition to the cleaver wound he sustained he had
also been shot several times. James Hart was luckier. He had
been grazed in the ear and one bullet buried itself in his thigh.
He too made it outside and was found by police crawling
along the street on his hands and knees.

The police also found Harms lying dead and followed his
blood trail into the Adonis. Inside the place was a shambles,
with overturned tables and chairs. Two .38s, the murder
weapons, were found in one corner. The attack had come so
unexpectedly Lonergan was found with a toothpick still in his
mouth and a loaded .38 in his shoulder holster. A .45 automatic, fully loaded, was found in Needles Ferry's back pocket.
(Ferry acquired his nickname due to his fondness for heroin.)

Ten people were arrested, among them the three surviving
White Handers and "Alphonse Capone" a "bouncer" and an
alleged Chicago gunman, according to the Brooklyn Eagle.
Frankie Yale hired Samuel Leibowitz, the great criminal lawyer
who later defended Mad Dog Coll and the Scotsburgh boys.
On his advice none of the defendants would answer questions.

James Hart claimed he had not even been in the Adonis and said he was fired on from a passing car. The people living above the Adonis had heard nothing. With no witnesses everyone arrested was let out on bail and all charges were soon dropped. Anna Lovett, Lonergan's sister and widow of Wild Bill, said, "You can bet it was no Irish American like ourselves who would stage a mean murder like this on Christmas Day." While Al Capone said, "I've never met an Irishman, I didn't like." He returned to Chicago where he continued battling the North Side Irish mob. The Brooklyn Mafia, however, were grateful to Capone for triggering the shootout. The White Hand stripped of their last important leader slowly disintegrated and within three years the Brooklyn waterfront was entirely in Mafia hands.

An affair of honour: The Boston Irish Gang War.

In 1961 a violent dispute broke out between two of Boston's most powerful Irish mobs - the McLaughlin mob who controlled Charlestown and the Navy Yard and the McLean Mob based in South Boston, or "Southie" as it is known to its predominantly Irish population. The cause was an "affair of honour" - a woman. George McLaughlin, a brother of Bernard McLaughlin, leader of the Charlestown mob, insulted a girlfriend of two young associates of James "Buddy" McLean, the Winter Hill mob leader, at a Labour Day picnic party. The two McLean men beat up the drunken George McLaughlin, leaving him half dead in an alleyway. Several days later George and another brother, Edward, a.ka. "Punchy", arrived in McLean territory looking for the two. They met Buddy McLean in a Broadway bar and informed him they were going to get revenge. McLean tried to calm the headstrong pair down, but to no avail. He then told them to leave while they still could. About two weeks later, McLean's car would not start. A mechanic found two sticks of dynamite wired to the motor.

In broad daylight on October 31 1961 Buddy McLean walked up behind Bernie McLaughlin in City Square, Charlestown and shot him in the back of the head with a .45 automatic. McLean took off to Florida to let the heat die down. An eyewitness to the killing was subsequently murdered while another changed her story after the McLeans threatened her family. Buddy McLean was arrested and released after a Grand Jury refused to indict him due to lack of witnesses.

Bernie McLaughlin's killing sparked off a long and bloody war that police estimated cost the lives of at least 48 people. Buddy McLean had a lot of friends who worked with the Mafia in Boston, or as it was referred to in criminal circles, "The Office". Among them were Steve "The Rifleman" Flemmi and his brother Vinnie "The Butcher" and Joseph "The Animal" Barboza, a ruthless hitman of Portuguese extraction, who was one of the Mafia's top enforcers. These men were semi-independents who were allies of The Office. Others teamed up with the McLaughlins like Steve and Connie Hughes, two ruthless young thugs who had dreams of running South Boston and challenging the power of The Office.

The Irish war also suited Mafia boss Raymond Patriarca, who maintained that the more the Irish knocked each other off, the more he could control Boston's rackets. Raymond Patriarca had come to power in 1954 and unlike many Mafia crime lords he was quite prepared to forge alliances with non-Italians. The New England Mafia is small but ruthless and non-Mafia allies hold "licences" to be bookies, loansharks or fences. The Mafia takes twenty-five to forty per cent of receipts. Patriarca claimed the whole of New England as his territory. He was totally ruthless. He once ordered an elderly Mafioso to murder his own son, and when the man refused had him expelled from the Family. On another occasion he was said to have put out a contract on his own brother because he did not notice an FBI bug had been installed in his office. Jailed in 1938 for five years, Patriarca was pardoned a few months later by Governor Charles F. Hurley, a move that led to Massachusetts legislative calls for an inquiry. Hurley's right hand man, Executive Councillor Daniel Coakley, was later impeached and barred from ever holding public office in the state - the first person to suffer the fate since 1821 - after the inquiry found he had presented a false petition for Patriarca's pardon and guided it past government officials. After this episode Patriarca was known as a man with the connections.

As the war escalated George McLaughlin's closest friend, Harold Hannon, was found floating in Boston harbour; he had been beaten and then strangled with piano wire. George had to go into hiding when in a drunken fit he shot a clerk between the eyes at a christening party and was put on the FBI's Most Wanted List. In November 1964 Punchy McLaughlin was ambushed and shot in Brookline and only recovered after nine hours of surgery. Punchy was a hard man. He was a power in the Longshoreman's Union and widely feared on Boston's waterfront. He had lost his left ear in a waterfront fight and in naval fashion was tattooed with an eagle across his chest, a sailboat and three birds on his arms and a woman smoking a cigarette.

The problem with gang wars is that they tend to cost money and are bad for business. The McLaughlins began to feel the pinch. They had lost more men and their rackets were drying up. In desperation they began shaking down bookies and night-clubs in South Boston under the protection of Jerry Anguilo. He complained to Raymond Patriarca, whose protection he paid big money for. Patriarca sent his underboss, Henry "The Referee" Tameleo to arrange a peace deal between the two factions. A peace meeting was arranged in January 1965 at the Ebb Tide bar, a Mafia hangout. Buddy McLean and his men came in one door and the McLaughlins, George and

Punchy, came in another door. The McLaughlins were carrying brown paper bags.

"What have you got in the bags?" a curious Tameleo asked George McLaughlin.

"We got our guns ... we're not going to come in here unarmed with them" he said, pointing to the McLeans. "We're not crazy."

Tameleo was furious. This meant that his word was not good enough. Tameleo was a respected mediator in organised crime circles. He had negotiated a settlement in the Gallo-Profaci war in New York in 1961 and this earned him his nickname.

"You bring guns to a peace meeting?" he roared. "Get out of here! All of you. Get out. Go kill each other."

Tameleo stormed out and reported back to Patriarca. He said McLean wanted a settlement but the McLaughlins were gun crazy. Patriarca had a good working relationship with McLean so he ordered his men to team up with the McLeans and wipe out the McLaughlins. George McLaughlin was quickly picked up for the murder of the clerk and in August 1965 Punchy was again shot. Again he survived, though his right hand was amputated. On October 20 Joe Barboza and Joseph "Chico" Amico caught Punchy alone in the Spring Street Metropolitan Transit Authority turn-around in West Roxbury. He was waiting for a bus to take him to court to his brother's trial. He had the customary brown paper bag in his hand which carried his gun. This time he did not survive. Joe Barboza put several bullets in his head to make sure.

On October 30 Buddy McLean, Tony D'Agostino and Americo Sacremone left Pal Joey's Lounge on Broadway, in Somerville. As they got into their car Steve Hughes stepped out of the shadows of the Capitol Theatre and fired three shots from an automatic shotgun, hitting all three. McLean died instantly. D'Agostino and Sacremone were wounded. When they recovered they were sent back to jail for violating their parole, by associating with a known felon. Steve Hughes and his brother Cornelius, or Connie, were fearless gunmen and the McLaughlins top hitmen. They were both stockily built, with brown hair and hazel eyes. The brothers were ambitious and plotted to take control of the Irish mobs and challenge the power of Patriarca. Their effectiveness as assassins had a telling effect on revenues. They had to be stopped. When Steve killed Buddy McLean it signed their death warrants. McLean was a good businessman and well liked in underworld circles. Patriarca ordered his men to finish off the war.

Connie Hughes was the first to go. On May 25 1966 as he was driving along the Northeast Expressway in Revere, a car with two men in it pulled alongside him. The Mafia hitman, in the passenger seat, fired several bullets from a high-powered rifle at Hughes. He was killed instantly. When Steve heard the news he went on a killing spree, but he was fighting a losing battle. His boss, George McLaughlin, was on Death Row in the Massachusetts state prison for murder leaving the battered gang under Hughes' control. On September 23 as Steve Hughes and Sam Lindenbaum, a gambling associate, drove along Route 114 near the Three Pines Restaurant in Middleton, Mass., a car with Joe Barboza and Chico Amico pulled alongside them. Barboza leaned out the passenger window and shot both of them dead with a high powered rifle that had armour piercing shells. With most of the main participants dead and George McLaughlin in prison peace returned to Boston.

Ragen's Colts at war.

Ragen's Colts was formed in the 1890s as a baseball team, the Morgan Athletic Club. In 1908 it was taken over by Frank and Mike Ragen and was first known as the Ragen Athletic and Benevolent Society. The baseball club became Ragen's Colts, a catchier name that soon identified the entire organisation. Their territory ran from 43rd Street to 66th Street, from Cottage Grove, east, almost by the lake to Halstead on the west. The Colts became a powerful political machine on behalf of the Democrats and were providers of muscle for local politicians. Over the years the list grew of aldermen, sheriffs, city and county office-holders that owed their election to the Colts. Frank Ragen, the club's leader, used the Colts muscle to reach the post of Cook County Commissioner. "When we dropped into a polling place", one Colt bragged, "everybody else dropped out." The membership was mainly Irish and the sons of stockyard workers. In his youth, Chicago mayor Richard J. Daley had been a Colt. The gang were active during the Chicago newspaper circulation wars and at a youth level were involved in the roughing up of rival delivery boys. The circulation wars initiated many of Chicago's top gangsters into organised crime and many of these got their start with Ragen's Colts; Hugh "Stubby" McGovern; Danny McFall, who despite two murders to his credit was named a deputy sheriff; William "Gunner" McPadden; Joseph "Dynamite" Brooks, named for his favourite method of murder; Frank "Dutch" Carpenter; Harry Madigan, owner of the Pony Inn, in Cicero; Frank and Ralph Sheldon; Walter Stevens, the "Dean of Chicago hitmen" and Danny Stanton, who would later achieve major underworld fame with the Capone mob.

Like most of the Irish, and other ethnic gangs, Ragen's Colts were fiercely racist. (They also prided themselves on their patriotism and 500 members went into the armed forces during WW1.) They planned a trip to Oklahoma to attack the Ku Klux Klan for their anti-Catholic activity and one of their more prominent members, boxing referee and hoodlum, Davy "Yiddles" Miller, denounced the Klan as "nigger lovers". The Colts ensured that no blacks crossed to their side of Wentworth Avenue, the demarcation line between black and white neighbourhoods.

(They were also active against local Polish and nativist gangs.) They played a large part in the 1919 Race Riots that nearly destroyed the city.

On Sunday afternoon, July 27, some blacks crossed the unmarked boundary of the segregated 29th Street beach (of Lake Michigan) on the South Side. They were promptly chased away by bathing Colts and a rock throwing battle began. When a home-made raft with five black youngsters floated into the white section they were quickly stoned. A seventeen year old, Eugene Williams, was hit by a rock, fell overboard and unable to swim was taunted by the crowd who watched as he drowned. A black policeman tried to arrest the alleged rock thrower, George Stauber, but was thwarted by a white police- man. Word of the police action resulted in a gathering of sev- eral hundred blacks near the beach. One black was arrested as police tried to disperse the crowd. Another black man, James Crawford, fired into a group of policemen. The police fired back killing Crawford and the riot was on.

Shortly before dark, according to subsequent testimony before a coroner's jury, a swaggering youth from Halstead Street warned a group of blacks: "Remember it's the Ragen's Colts you're dealing with. We have two-thousand men between Halstead and Cottage Grove and 43rd and 66th Streets. We intend to run this district. Look out." As night fell gangs of whites, most notably Ragen's Colts, invaded the Black Belt beating up and shooting blacks on sight, dynamiting and looting shops and homes and setting dozens of buildings on fire. Blacks came out to defend their neighbourhoods and war vet- erans used their service weapons to keep the mobs at bay. Rampaging blacks retaliated by attacking white neighbour- hoods. By the end of July 28 17 people were dead and over 200 injured. The rioting continued until August 1 before the National Guard restored order. The coroner's jury described it as "five days of terrible hate and passion let loose". Fifteen whites were killed and 178 injured. Twenty-three blacks were killed and 342 injured. Seven blacks - but no whites - were shot dead by police. Anti-black rioting spread across the country in 24 additional areas resulting in a further 76 blacks killed, mainly in lynchings. The jury recommended a ban on such clubs as Ragen's Colts. (The Clubs had come under attack in an editorial in the *Defender* on July 12. At the time there were estimated to be around 75 Irish clubs, or gangs, of which Ragen's Colts was the best known, while there were nearly 1,000 Italian gangs and 150 Polish ones.) For a time the Colts charters were revoked, but under political pressure from Frank Ragen they were reinstated.

With the coming of Prohibition the Colts shifted their attention to bootlegging. Ralph Sheldon formed a "business" branch of the Colts supplying bootleg to the South Side. (Political protection, of course, came from Frank Ragen.) Sheldon, born in 1902, was a slight consumptive youth, only eighteen when Prohibition arrived but already a veteran malefactor. He first appeared in court at sixteen for highway robbery, a charge he beat, although his two companions were not so lucky. This impelled the judge to rebuke the jury for a "miscarriage of justice." The most prominent member after Sheldon was Danny Stanton, at twenty-four, the oldest of the new group. The hulking Stanton had been a stockyards hand, driver and muscle for labour racketeers, slugger for the Checker Cab company and a war veteran, cited for valour in France with the Illinois 131st Infantry.

With a membership of 2,000 (their motto: "Hit me and you hit two-thousand", was only a slight exaggeration) the Colts supplied most of the troops for the Sheldon mob and also provided a fine pool of fierce talent for other Prohibition-era gangs, including the Capone mob. In the 1924 Cicero election Al Capone borrowed 200 enforcers from his allies, including a contingent of Ragen's Colts. The Colts kidnapped an election clerk, Joseph Price, beat him up and kept him gagged and bound at Harry Madigan's Pony Inn, the scene of many a kidnapping. (Madigan accumulated eight charges of kidnapping during elections.)

Sheldon, Stanton and the rest had a reflexive aversion to Italians, but on the other hand they had no ready source of bootleg and they recognised the profits possible at Johnny Torrio's wholesale supply price of $35 a barrel, which included political protection. After a period of hijacking which could not supply the demand Sheldon joined the Torrio combine. The gang clashed with their nearest neighbours, the South Side O'Donnells and the Saltis-McErlanes. The O'Donnells, Spike, Steve, Walter and Tommy ran the Kerry Patch on the South West Side while Polack Joe Saltis (the boys knew him from the time he was a neighbourhood bar-tender and the butt of their jokes and horseplay) and the psychopath Frank McErlane were west of Sheldon in the Back of the Yards district.

On September 7 1924 Ralph Sheldon, Danny McFall and Frank McErlane shot up the O'Donnells at Klepka's Bar killing Jerry O'Connor. Ten days later McFall and McErlane blasted the O'Donnells top enforcers, Spot Bucher and George Meeghan. Despite working together in routing the O'Donnells the Sheldon-Saltis alliance was very shaky. On October 4 1925 Frank McErlane, using a tommy gun, shot up the Ragen's Colts club-house killing Charles Kelly. On November 15 Joe Saltis was shot and wounded and ten days later Sheldon's men attacked McKeone's saloon, a Saltis-McErlane hangout. Three men died in the ensuing shootout. On December 2 fourteen machine gun bullets riddled Sheldon's car and two days later Danny Stanton was hit by two bullets, though he was not badly hurt. Three days before Christmas, two Colts, Dynamite Joe Brooks and Eddie Harmening, a county policeman, left a saloon together. They were surrounded by several men, among them Frank McErlane. The two were forced at gunpoint into their car and driven to Marquette Park in the city's far South West Side, where McErlane sitting in the passenger seat fired six bullets into Brooks and two into Harmening.

On February 2 1926 a dynamite bomb exploded prematurely destroying Ralph Sheldon's empty Cadillac. Seven days later, Frank McErlane machine-gunned Buff Costello's bar, a Sheldon hangout, wounding top Sheldon lieutenant John "Mitters" Foley and another hood, Bill Wilson. On April 26 the bodies of Frank DeLaurentis and John Tuccello, two minor Capone operatives, who were peddling bootleg in Saltis-McErlane turf for Sheldon, were dumped outside Sheldon's house in their own car with their brains blown out. McErlane was in jail, arranged for murder, leaving Joe Saltis to organise the killing. In July Saltis brought Jules Portuguese, a Sheldon hanger on, whose car had been used in the Dion O'Bannion murder, for a one way ride.

On August 6 he lured Mitters Foley from his home with a bogus phone call and forced his car to the curb. Foley jumped out, tried to make a run for it but tripped. Saltis stood over him and blasted him in the chest with both barrels of a shotgun. Foley had been selling bootleg in Saltis territory. Saltis, Lefty Koncil, John Oberta and Eddie Herbert were identified by eyewitnesses and indicted for murder. Saltis asked North Side boss Hymie Weiss for help and Weiss spent $100,000 to get him off, also running two eyewitnesses out of town. With Weiss' death in October a peace conference was called in the Hotel Sherman. Al Capone, Tony Lombardo and Jake Guzik and their allies, among them Ralph Sheldon, met the North Side leaders Vincent Drucci and Bugs Moran. The 1923 dividing lines would stay and the gangs would stay out of each others territories. Sheldon would stay north and east of the stockyards while Saltis kept his Back of the Yards. Capone kept his territory and the North Siders theirs while lesser gangs carved up the rest.

For a time it looked like the cease-fire might last. However, Hilary Clements, from the Sheldon mob, was caught selling beer in the Back of the Yards and taken for a one way ride. His brother appealed for his body to be returned for Christmas, but it was not discovered until December 30, fourteen days after he was kidnapped. Sheldon appealed to Capone. Instead of referring the affair to arbitration in the manner which had been decided at the Hotel Sherman conference, Saltis had jumped the gun and ordered the slaying of Clements. While Saltis hid out - he had secretly sided with the North Siders in their war with Capone - at his summer resort and estate in northern Wisconsin, Sheldon bumped off Lefty Koncil and Charles Hubacek, in retaliation for Clements.

Saltis made his peace with Capone and Sheldon and peace returned to the South Side. On August 4 1927 the twelve remaining members of Ragen's Colts met at their clubhouse and voted to disband the club. Some of these men went on to found the Chicago Maroons football club, who later became the Chicago Cardinals. Soon after Ralph Sheldon, suffering from tuberculosis, retired from the rackets leaving his mob under the leadership of Danny Stanton.

On December 31 1928 Stanton lost two of his top men, former Ragen's Colts shoulder hitters, Stubby McGovern and Gunner McPadden, who were shot dead by George Maloney, of the Bubs Quinlan mob. The Stantons operated as a satellite of the Capone mob, eventually being absorbed by the Outfit. Stanton became a power in the Outfit, though he never lost the knack for murder. On August 1 1930 he trailed North Side mobster Jack Zuta to a hotel in Delafield, Wisconsin, on the orders of Al Capone. While Zuta stood facing the nickelodeon in the hotel's dance hall five men walked in. Two covered the exits, one the bar staff, another the dancing couples while the last, Stanton, approached Zuta.

As the nickelodeon played *'Good for you, bad for me'* Stanton ordered Zuta to "Turn around." As he did Stanton fired several bullets into him, the first ripping into Zuta's open mouth. The other two gunmen stepped over to the fallen body and pumped another sixteen bullets into him.

On June 24 1943 Danny Stanton was shot dead in a Chicago bar, victim of a dispute within the Outfit. John Moore, a.k.a. Claude Maddox, was questioned about the killing but was never charged.

The Greene Wars.

Organised crime in Cleveland, Ohio, had always been ethnically mixed with a strong representation of Italian, Irish, Jewish and black gangs drawn from a big working class population. Cleveland got its first taste of organised crime in the early 1900s when rival newspapers hired street thugs to knock each other out of business. Arthur "Mickey" McBride and Tommy McGinty, the circulation managers of the *News* and the *Plain Dealer*, used hoodlums to hijack trucks and to fight street battles to force the sale of their papers. McBride recruited the Mayfield Road Mob - out of which grew the Cleveland Mafia - to do his enforcing. He went on to monopolise Cleveland's taxis, own its football team, and in league with the Mafia, control the continental racewire service, which by both legitimate and illegal means obtained information from race tracks on racing results and transmitted them to bookies across the country for a fee. McGinty, an ex-prize fighter, used his connections with Moe Dalitz, to rise to nation-wide notoriety in the casino gambling rackets.

When Prohibition came Cleveland situated on the shores of Lake Erie, straddling the Canadian border, became one of the main centres for smuggling alcohol into the country. By 1924 Tommy McGinty was King of the Bootleggers and continued as such until the end of Prohibition. With Moe Dalitz and the Lonardo Family in full swing Cleveland in the Roaring Twenties was as dangerous a place as Chicago. By the late 1970s Moe Dalitz and the rest of the Jewish elements had long since departed to Bugsy Siegel's desert paradise of Las Vegas, leaving the Italians, under various leaders and finally John Scalish, as the dominant force.

In 1976 John Scalish died of natural causes and James T. "Blackie" Licavoli succeeded him. However, John Nardi, a capo for many years and a power in the Teamsters union, believed the leadership position was his by seniority. He plotted to take the mantle from Licavoli and enlisted the aid of Danny Green and his West Side Irish mob. Together they moved to take over the Cleveland rackets.

Daniel John Patrick Greene was born in 1930 in Texas and placed in a Catholic orphanage as an infant. When he was eighteen he joined the US Marines, learning to box and becoming an expert marksman - skills he would later utilise in his long criminal career. After he left the service he ended up working on the docks in Cleveland. In the early 1960s he took over the local branch of the ILA, using his position to shake down stevedore companies. Despite his criminal activities and the looting of the unions fighting fund, Green was admired by the longshoremen. He was a charismatic leader and a good speaker at union meetings. Good looking and well-built Greene jogged regularly, did weightlifting and maintained a good diet. Later he quit smoking and drinking to keep in shape. When his red curls began to recede, the ever vain gangster endured painful hair transplants.

Greene lost his union position in 1968 when a newspaper exposed his waterfront rackets and he was charged with embezzlement. He pleaded guilty to the lesser crime of falsifying union accounts and was given a suspended sentence. It was around this time that Greene began secretly working for the FBI. He dropped out of sight for awhile and then came back on the scene forming his own company, Emerald Industrial Relations, and began shaking down construction companies by offering to end labour disputes that his own men had caused. Many employers paid up to avoid costly strikes. Union official and convicted cop killer, Tony Liberatore, befriended him and made him a business partner in organising rubbish hauliers to form the Cleveland Solid Waste Trade Guild. Uncooperative hauliers were forced to join the guild by intimidation and violence. One independent, Michael Frato, a one time close friend of Greene's, refused to join the guild. In 1971 Arthur Snepenger, believed to be working for Greene, was blown up when a bomb he was planting on Frato's car exploded prematurely. One morning a, few weeks later, Frato ambushed Greene. Frato pulled up in his car and fired a shot from a carbine at Greene, who was jogging near his apartment. Greene, an expert marksman, pulled out a .38 and shot Frato in the right temple. Charged with manslaughter, Greene pleaded self defence and was acquitted.

Greene was also friendly with an old Mayfield Road mobster, Alex "Shondor" Birns, an ageing Jewish gangster and Mafia ally. When Birns went to jail his mistress took over control of his numbers rackets while Greene became his enforcer. His job was to ensure peace among the black numbers players. While enforcing Birns' will Greene ignited a stick of dynamite and threw it at a rivals car. The dynamite bounced off the car and exploded wrecking Greene's car and bursting his eardrum. Greene and Birns bought a bar and night-club in a black neighbourhood with $75,000 borrowed from a New York family. They needed someone to run the place and quarrelled over their choice.

Birns forced his choice through. The club was raided and Birns' man was caught disposing cocaine down the toilet. The club was closed and Greene refused to pay back the loan saying it was for services rendered when Birns was in jail. In retaliation Birns put out a contract on Greene.

In the first attack the gunman missed while a bomb planted on the axle of Greene's car rolled off and failed to explode. Shortly afterwards, on Good Friday 1975, Birns was blown to pieces when he got into his Lincoln and turned on the ignition. Pieces rained down on members of the local church congregation as they left their service. Birns Mafia allies retaliated on May 12 by throwing a bomb in a shop under Greene's second floor apartment. The bomb demolished the shop. Greene fell from the second floor to the basement, landed on the refrigerator and walked away with hardly a scratch on him. His girlfriend was blown out of the bed but was relatively unscathed, too.

It was now that John Nardi approached him and told him that they had the same enemy and that they should combine forces. As the war between the Mafia and Greene escalated he declared the Irish to be superior to the Italians. He began wearing green clothes, drove a green Lincoln, wrote in green ink and flew an Irish flag outside his new house. He began lecturing his gang on Irish history. Greene was a handsome "Irish type", though it is a subject of controversy whether he had any Irish blood. Always willing to talk to the media, he refused to speak about his background. It was rumoured he was part Scotch, part Jewish, but no part Irish. However, with several young relatives and some genuine Irish hoods he had developed an independent faction on the city's West Side active in drug-pushing, loansharking, gambling and labour racketeering. He enhanced his reputation on the West Side by supporting homeless families. He paid for local children to attend private

Catholic schools. On Thanksgiving Day he had turkeys delivered to poor families. He was rewarded with a network of loyal look-outs who warned him of strangers or unfamiliar cars in the neighbourhood.

The Nardi-Greene alliance now sought to take over all organised crime in northern Ohio. One by one the rival Licavoli supporters were knocked off, many of them in car bomb hits, giving Cleveland the title of "the bomb capital of America". The Nardi-Greene forces scored their biggest blow on September 1 1976 when the Licavolis top enforcer, Leo "Lips" Moceri, was kidnapped in a hotel parking lot and subsequently murdered. A witness recalled seeing a stocky redheaded man getting out of Moceri's car. Moceri was a "made" man and in killing him Greene signed his own death warrant. Licavoli put out a contract on both him and John Nardi.

In May 1977 Nardi was killed using a new technique, the "Trojan Horse" method of murder. A car packed with dynamite and shrapnel was parked beside Nardi's Cadillac in the Teamsters office car park. A remote control device on the charge was triggered as Nardi unlocked his car. The blast stripped him naked and peppered his body with dozens of nuts and bolts. The loss of his top ally did nothing to Greene's ego. He was seen sitting bare-chested on the street beneath a big Irish flag. "If somebody wants to come after me," he told reporters. "I'm over here by the Celtic Club. I'm not hard to find." Greene, like many mobsters before, felt he was unkillable. His foes had made eight attempts to kill him and he had survived them all - giving the Cleveland Mafia the derisory title of "The gang that couldn't shoot straight." Greene denounced his Mafia foes as "yellow maggots". But his days were numbered.

The Mafia was making an all out attempt to get rid of their most feared enemy. Hitmen were imported from outside Cleveland, among them Jimmy Fratianno and Ray Ferrito. They began taping conversations at the apartment of Greene's girl-friend, Denise Schmidt. They learned that Danny had a dental appointment on October 6 and they set to work. A bomb was placed in the passenger door of a Chevy and parked beside Greene's Lincoln in the car park of the medical centre where Greene was getting a dental filling. Shortly after 3 o'clock, as Greene unlocked his car, the bomb was set off by remote control. Greene was killed instantly by the bomb. All his clothing except his boots and socks were blown off him by the blast. His severed left arm landed one-hundred feet away.

Though Greene was dead, he got the last laugh. A couple driving by when the explosion occurred followed the bomber's car and took its registration. The car was traced to Ray Ferrito and he was positively identified as an occupant by the couple. Ferrito was arrested and charged with murder. He turned state's evidence and implicated Jimmy Fratianno who also turned informer and for the first time in the history of racketbusting an entire leadership of a Mafia family, including Blackie Licavoli, were put behind bars. In destroying Danny Greene the Cleveland Mafia had destroyed itself.

CHAPTER 11

LABOUR WARS

The United States has one of the most violent labour histories in the world. The Irish immigrant contributed much to the early history of American labour unrest. The Irish tradition of labour organisation goes back to the secret societies of 17th and 18th century Ireland. They first surfaced on the blossoming canals and railways of America in the 1830s. In 1834 near Williamsport, Maryland, along the Chesapeake and Ohio Canal, where 1,800 Irish labourers were employed, labourers from County Cork had organised to establish job control along the canal. On January 16 a labourer from County Longford was beaten to death by Cork men. Work along the canal halted as both sides prepared for war. On January 24 700 Longford men routed 300 Cork men, killing at least five and wounding dozens. Order was restored by local militia reinforced by regular troops. Thirty-four arrests were made. Delegates from the two groups of labourers met and signed a truce, each pledging not to inter-fere with the others right to work.

It was not the end of disturbances along the line. In 1836 Irish groups fought among themselves and then attacked a group of "Dutch and country borns" (German immigrants and native-born Americans) who refused to join a strike. The following year Irish strikers drove off forty English immigrant workers who had been brought in by one of the contractors. In 1838 Irishmen burned the shanties of German labourers who were working for a cheaper wage and then armed with guns and clubs attacked the German workers. The militia again restored order shooting dead eight labourers and seizing 120 weapons.

The labour disturbances on the Chespeake and Ohio canal mirrored the unrest elsewhere on the blossoming canals and railways of America and was attributed to "a regularly organised society". Labour unrest was not confined to the canals and railways but reached every section of the American labour market. The Irish labourer organised themselves into gangs, clubs, unions and secret societies and fought with every nationality he came up against. The most serious disturbances were in the coalfields of Pennsylvania, where the Molly Maquires inflicted a reign of violence and terror in which several hundred died. New York City was the capital of labour unionism. By the 1850s the Irish were well on their way to establishing their prominence in the New York labour movement. They dominated all the major unions and of 229 labour leaders in the city at least 106 were Irish.

By the dawn of the new century America had become the leading industrial and manufacturing nation in the world. The new immigrants provided a mass of cheap labour for the necessities of urban growth. Conditions for workers were horrific. As well as adults of both sexes, children joined the ranks of the low paid, often working twelve hours a day, six days a week. Like labourers everywhere they struggled for better wages and working conditions. Unions were organised and strikes were staged to force the employers to raise wages and improve conditions. The employers reacted by hiring company spies, often from the Pinkerton Private Detective Agency, to identify union leaders, who were then fired. Strike-breakers were hired and if these proved inadequate the police and even the National Guard could be used. The unions organised their own protection to guard against management goons. However, in the first decade of the twentieth century a need arose for a more professional approach. The only ones with a steady supply of muscle were the organised criminal gangs.

Gangsters like Paul Kelly and Dopey Benny Fein became an integral part of the New York's labour movement. They were given union cards as pickets and they protected fellow pickets with their own gang members. Paul Kelly organised the ragpickers and became vice-president of the International Longshoreman's Association. Benny Fein became a power in the garment district, hiring thugs from such gangs as the Hudson Dusters, including Legs and Eddie Diamond. it soon became clear that it was easier to hire gangsters than to fire them. By gaining a toehold the hoods came to dominate many of the industries into which they were invited. By inviting in gangsters many local unions, and some internationals, were delivered into the hands of some of the most bloodthirsty criminals in American history.

According to the Permanent Subcommittee on Investigations in 1982 "at least four international unions ... and a majority of the locals in most major cities of the United States in the International Brotherhood of Teamsters, Hotel and Restaurant Employees Union, Labourers International Union of North America and the International Longshoreman's Association are completely dominated by organised crime."

In Chicago in the early part of the century gangsters gained control of some unions by terror tactics. During 1921 open warfare broke out between building employers and the unions. Housing was scarce and rents had rocketed. Federal Judge Kenesaw Mountain Landis, arbitrator in the dispute, pronounced that Chicago's building industry was rotten with corruption and decided against the unions, recommending wage-cuts. The mob replied with a campaign of bomb attacks. During the Building Trades War of 1922 fourteen buildings were blown up and two policemen shot down. Big Tim Murphy, Frenchy Mader, Con Shea and Dapper Dan McCarthy were named as the instigators. Mader had, at gun point, got himself elected as President of the Building Trades Council. Whenever disputes arose he sent in Big Tim Murphy and his bombers. When Andrew Kerr was arrested and charged with ordering the bombing of dozens of union offices not only did he admit to overseeing the bombings but boasted that he had the "best bombers in Chicago", naming Con Shea, Jim Sweeney and Soup Bartlett as his top bombers. Kerr and Sweeney were jailed while Shea became one of Chicago's most notorious labour racketeers, responsible for bringing many unions under the control of North Side boss Dion O'Bannion.

Con Shea was arrested, along with Mader, Murphy and McCarthy and all were released on bonds of $150,000. They stayed free. Shea, as secretary of the Theatrical and Building Janitors Union, had an impressive record. He had already served a term in Sing Sing for the attempted murder of a woman, was Teamsters strike leader when 21 men were killed and 416 injured and was tried and acquitted for the murder of Police Lieutenant Terence Lyons. President of the Theatrical and Building Janitors Union was another O'Bannion stalwart, Louis "Two-Gun" Alterie. To gain his presidency Alterie and several gunmen had pistol-whipped the officials into a quick election. Alterie had been told by O'Bannion to organise several unions and went about his orders with ferocious gusto battering union leaders to elect him and other mobsters as presidents for life. From his union rackets Alterie pocketed $50,000 a month after giving Deanie his cut. Alterie kept control of this and other unions until his murder in 1935.

Timothy "Big Tim" Murphy, born in 1886, was the first of the Chicago labour racketeers seizing control of the Street Sweepers Union. The one-time Illinois state legislator was allegedly the mastermind of the $385,000 mail train robbery at Chicago's Polk Street station in 1921. Convicted and sentenced to six years Murphy claimed he was framed by William Fahy, a postal inspector who was later convicted of being the inside man on the $2 million Rondout train robbery in 1924. On June 26 1928 Big Tim was machine-gunned to death outside his home at 2525 West Morse, probably on the orders of Al Capone, after attempting to take over the Cleaners and Dyers Union. Murphy's widow went on to marry another Chicago notable, Dingbat Oberta, and when he too was murdered she had her second husband buried beside her first husband in the Holy Sepulchre Cemetery. "They were both good men," she said.

Dapper Dan McCarthy was another O'Bannion union organiser. He was business agent for the Journeyman Plumbers Union. McCarthy dressed and behaved so elegantly the newspapers called him Dapper Dan, but he was a ruthless gunman. He shot a policeman who had come to arrest him for desertion from the army in 1918. He became O'Bannion's social companion and partner in one of his early breweries, Cragin Products. By the time O'Bannion was murdered in 1924 Dapper Dan was no longer a full time member of the North Siders, as he was too busy looting his unions and was not considered for the leadership position.

Most unions were owned by gangsters like Dapper Dan and Two-Gun Alterie who either had helped organise them or muscled in and took them over. The racketeer owners paid benefits, negotiated and called strikes for better wages and conditions. But they also bled off much of the dues, pilfered pension funds and extorted money from employers to avoid strikes and for lush contracts. The membership generally stayed quiet, preferring not to rock the boat. Membership dues were the same as taxes, just another deduction. As long as their wages rose, they were content. Those that did object were first offered executive positions. If that did not shut them up, violence did.

Simon J. Gorman, a veteran of Ragen's Colts, started his racketeering career as business agent of the Cook County Horseshoers Union and went on to dominate the Chicago laundry rackets. With his partner, Johnny Hand, he organised the Chicago Wet and Dry Laundry Owners Association, which netted them $1,000 a week. Gorman had powerful connections in City Hall and used them to keep recalcitrant laundrymen in line. On May 21 1929 Hand was machine gunned to death in a lot behind the Hawthorne Inn, Capone's headquarters. Gorman went on to dominate the Laundry Owners, Linen Supply, Hand Laundry and Laundry Service associations, imposing levies as high as ten per cent of the gross business.

Al Capone very early realised the potential of labour racketeering. He began muscling in on the city's unions in the late 1920s and with the end of Prohibition in sight he accelerated his infiltration. He targeted the building trades, of great importance with Chicago projecting a World's Fair in 1933. His chief labour plunderer, Red Barker, was gunned down in 1932 by the Touhy gang. Capone turned his attention to City Hall, sending in Danny Stanton to organise the municipal workers.

In 1928 the state's attorney of Cook County listed 91 Chicago unions and business associations under organised crime control. Most of these had been won over by violence and coercion. The Hotel Employees and Restaurant Employees International Union was established in Chicago in 1891 and today is the largest service union in the United States. Many of the 235 locals are reputed to be under mob control. In 1973 Edward Hanley, who began his career in Chicago Local 450 in 1957 as business agent, was elected to the HEREIU presidency.

Local 450 was dominated by one of the Outfit's top men, Joey Aiuppa. Local 54 in New Jersey was controlled by the Philadelphia crime family and has about 15,000 members, most of them employed in the Atlantic City casino business. As a result, the mob was able to force hotels in Atlantic City to buy supplies and provisions from companies they owned. In 1980 Big John McCullough, president of the Roofers Union in Philadelphia, began to organise independent locals among bar and restaurant workers and security guards in Atlantic City in competition with Local 54. Nicky Scarfo, the Philadelphia Family's man in Atlantic City, could not tolerate such rivalry.

Phil Testa, boss of the Philadelphia family, invited McCullough to a meeting and they met at the Testa's Bank Street restaurant. Testa and Scarfo suggested that the Roofers Union stop trying to extend its interests. They invited McCullough to another meeting but McCullough, fearing an ambush, refused and began carrying a gun. Testa gave the violent Scarfo the green light to deal with the matter in his own way. Scarfo knew of only one way to deal with a problem. In 1963 Scarfo had got into an argument in a South Philadelphia diner with an Irish longshore-man. The two men wanted to sit at the same table. Scarfo pulled a knife and stabbed the Irishman to death. He was sen-tenced to two years for involuntary manslaughter but served only two months.

On December 16 1980 a flower delivery van pulled up out-side the Philadelphia home of John McCullough. One of the two men inside got out and walked up to McCullough's door, carrying a box of flowers. Mrs. McCullough opened the door and took the flowers. The delivery man said he had a larger box for them in the van. John McCullough was in the living room talking on the telephone. He told his wife to give the man a big tip, since it was near Christmas. The delivery man returned car-rying the larger box. He stepped inside and pushed Mrs.

McCullough out of the way, pulled a .22 revolver from the box and shot Big John in the head. As McCullough fell to the floor the gunman shot him five more times. Mrs. McCullough, screaming tried to reach the door. The gunman threw her back, ran out and fled in the van.

In July 1982 Williard Moran Jnr. admitted that he had shot McCullough on the orders of Albert Daidone, another Atlantic City union boss, who became vice-president of Local 54 soon after the killing, and Ray Martorano, a Philadelphia Family man. Both were allies of Phil Testa and Nicky Scarfo. Moran, Daidone and Martorano were all convicted of McCullough's murder.

Corruption is rife in many other unions, none more so than the Teamsters Union. The International Brotherhood of Teamsters derived from a merger of two rival unions in 1903. It is now the largest labour union in the country representing more than two million workers involved in the transport business. In 1907 Dan Tobin became president of the union and served until 1952 when he was succeeded by Dave Beck. The power behind Beck was James R. Hoffa, head of the Teamsters in Detroit. When Beck was convicted of embezzling union funds and income-tax violations and sentenced to five years, Hoffa was elected president in his place.

Hoffa, born in 1913, had risen to a leadership position in Local 299 by 1941. Under pressure from the Congress of Industrial Organisation in their bid to represent the Detroit Teamsters, Hoffa turned to some friends in the Detroit underworld. The CIO goons were beaten off the streets in Detroit and Hoffa's relationship with organised crime was cemented. When he became president of the Teamsters, Hoffa helped his gangster friends in their money making schemes: extortion from employers, pension-fund frauds and loansharking. With Hoffa's help some mobsters were elected president of union locals. Barney Baker was Hoffa's country-wide organiser and ambassador of violence. The 325lb Baker was a former professional boxer, longshoreman, confident of hoodlums and bouncer before joining the Teamsters. He was jailed three times in the 1930s. In 1936 he was wounded in a gangland rub out near a 34th Street restaurant in Manhattan. Baker, his trainer-manager Farmer Sullivan, Joe Butler and John O'Rourke, who later became Hoffa's hand-picked Teamster vice president in New York, were fired on as they approached the New Yorker Hotel. Baker and O'Rourke were wounded, while Joe Butler was killed in the fusillade of shots.

The Teamsters is one of the most powerful institutions in the country and in many major metropolitan areas they control all transportation, from the delivery of foodstuffs, department store merchandise, newspapers, rail and freight to even ambulances and hearses. They touch every corner of American life. In 1957 Hoffa promised to clean up the union if he became president. Within two years he claimed the union was corruption free. The reality was that under Hoffa the Teamsters leadership was the most corrupt and dishonest the union had ever seen. On March 4 1964 Hoffa was convicted of jury tampering and sentenced to eight years in prison. He was replaced by Frank Fitzsimmons, who was content to let the mob run the union. In 1971 Hoffa was pardoned by President Nixon - the IBT had a huge voting bloc and supported Nixon's campaign for the presidency. Soon after his release, Hoffa began his attempt to regain control of the union. The mob was happy with Fitzsimmons and feared Hoffa's comeback would lose them their control of the Teamsters.

Hoffa plotted to murder Fitzsimmons and his mob sponsor Anthony "Tony Pro" Provenzano, a New Jersey racketeer. He confided in his adopted son, Charles "Chuckie" O'Brien, who smarting from Hoffa's refusal to allow him to run for a powerful union position, informed Provenzano. In the summer of 1975 Local 299 vice president Richard Fitzsimmons, son of Frank, narrowly escaped death when his car was blown up. Luckily Fitzsimmons had gone back to a restaurant to retrieve his jacket. On July 30 Hoffa went to a meeting with Salvatore Briguglio and Tony Jacks Giacalone. He was last seen in the parking lot of the Manchus Red Fox restaurant getting into a car. From there he disappeared without a trace. Several stories surfaced about what happened after his disappearance. One story was that Hoffa was driven to a house at Mount Clemens, in Detroit, and allegedly murdered by New York hitmen, Joe Sullivan and Tony Frankos. According to Frankos, who later turned state's evidence, Hoffa's body was dismembered and ended up in the foundation of the New York Giants Stadium in New Jersey, transported, ironically, by the truckers the union boss had fought all his life for. Charlie Allen, another mob hitman, said Hoffa was garrotted and his body ground up at a meat processing plant and dumped in the Gulf of Mexico. Whatever his end Hoffa was legally declared dead in 1982 and the case remains unsolved.

The Teamsters also provides, along with the Labourers International Union, most of the manpower in the construction industry. The construction industry is both lucrative and highly competitive and the Teamsters and the LIU are heavily involved with the mob giving mobsters control over many building sites. In New York City when a contractor wins a contract he is informed by a mob emissary or a union official who his suppliers will be, who his subcontractors will be, from whom he can purchase his materials and what price they will be bought at and which unions he can use. Such is the power of the mob in the construction industry.

The most powerful construction union in NYC is Teamster Local 282. Its membership is around 4,000 but they have control of the industry because they alone are permitted to drive trucks on and off the city's building sites. Local 282 was con-

trolled by John Cody as president, until 1982, when he was sentenced to five years for racketeering, extortion and evading
taxes on more than $160,000, which he had extorted from the
industry. Cody was born in 1919 on the Lower East Side and left
school at an early age. He spent most of his early years in
reform school and prison for crimes ranging from assault, robbery and burglary to possession of a gun. The big, heavily built
Cody was a natural for the rough politics of union unrest. His
men were proud of his tough leadership, but Cody's real
strength came from his connections to the Gambino Family
and with Big Paulie Castellano, successor to Carlo Gambino,
and the most powerful figure in the New York Mafia. Cody used
his power against non-mob companies and he controlled the
fate of every company bringing in concrete to Manhattan. His
power went as far as the quarry owners on Long Island. He
could destroy a cement manufacturer by telling the quarry
owners not to supply him. The quarry owners would not disobey
Cody in case their mining permits were withdrawn by the local
politicians he had under his thumb.

The prosecution of Cody shed a partial light on why building
costs in the city were increasing by twenty per cent a year.
Cody received a kickback on practically everything. If you
wanted your cement and steel delivered on time you paid. If
you didn't your crews sat idle costing you more money. One
contractor gave Cody's mistress a luxury apartment and two
free parking spaces - one of the most precious of Manhattan
commodities. Another contractor carried three Teamsters on
the payroll, to serve as Cody's bodyguards and chauffeurs. Big
Paulie Castellano, of course, took a cut of everything Cody
extorted from the contractors and suppliers.

As Cody went on trial in 1982 he showed his muscle by bringing New York construction, which was in the middle of a building boom, to a standstill. Fifty-thousand workers were laid off as

a result. The excuse for the strike was the building contractors refusal to hire hundreds of extra 282 men as security guards on building sites. Earlier there had been several "confrontations" at some building sites. These confrontations were staged fights by Cody supporters in order to justify the hiring of security guards, a move Cody knew the contractors could not agree to, hence a strike. Cody was convicted of racketeering, extortion and income-tax evasion. (It is a peculiarity of American law that taxes are accepted on illegal and criminal business.) The Teamster boss appealed his conviction, but lost it and ended up in prison. Bobby Sasso, a Gambino associate, was elected in his place. Sasso told law enforcement officials that the union had changed, but it was believed Cody was still giving orders from his prison cell.

CHAPTER 12

PARTNERS IN CRIME
THE COSA NOSTRA AND
THE 'KOSHER' NOSTRA

For several centuries the Mafia in Sicily was a patriotic clandestine society, a band of nationalists who conducted resistance to foreign invaders. Forged by blood and honour the Honoured Society created a hierarchy of dons (chiefs) who commanded separate Mafia Families in every village and town on the island. By the 19th century the Mafia, like the Camorra in southern Italy, were nothing more than glorified bandits. When the mass of Italian and Sicilian peasants emigrated to America they brought their "Honoured Society" with them. Mafia and Camorra criminal gangs first surfaced in the New World in the 1880s, especially in New Orleans where both groups fought for supremacy. By the turn of the century there were Mafia Families in every city where a sizeable Italian-Sicilian population had settled. They preyed mainly on their own people using Black Hand extortion tactics until other more lucrative rackets overshadowed this primitive extortion system.

When the Mafia sought to expand their rackets they were met by other criminal groups, like the Irish and Jews, who were not too willing to give up their hard earned rackets. Because of Old World values the Mafia chiefs were not prepared to co-operate with other ethnics and fought bloody wars among themselves and with other criminal groups. In 1931, after the Castellamarese War, Salvatore Maranzano founded the five family concept in New York and the twenty nation-wide family concept which survives to this day. Maranzano called this new organisation Cosa Nostra (Our Thing). The Mafia would be ruled by a Commission on which the strongest families had a representative, usually the five New York bosses, Chicago and one or two eastern cities – where half the Mafioso in the country is located.

Maranzano did not believe in co-operating with Jews, Irishers and other ethnics and made plans to knock off some of the emerging "Young Turks" like Lucky Luciano and Vito Genovese. However, the young Turks struck first and bumped off Maranzano. The new American Mafia came into existence with Maranzano's death and co-operated like never before with other ethnics in the pursuit of their main goal - to make money. Luciano did not believe in the old family structures but realised that many of the survivors of the earlier Mafia wars still clung to their upbringing as Mafioso and the need to belong to a powerful family structure. A family organisation was based on a boss, an underboss (second in command), a number of capos (lieutenants) in command of a group of soldiers (a crew). Maranzano was an avid reader of ancient history and based this structure on the Roman Legions. This was not an entire family but many more hoods were hangers on and associates of "made men" - a fully inducted member of the Mafia. The aspiration of all these hoods was to become a made man. Most made members had to "make their bones" - kill at least once in order to become "made". However, some hoods bought their membership - a clear breach of the rules. Jerry Anguilo, the Mafia boss of Boston, paid Raymond Patriarca $50,000 to become a made man.

Kosher Nostra.

Lucky Luciano's partner in his visionary concept of organised crime was the Jewish gangster Meyer Lansky. Between them they can be credited with forming the national crime Syndicate as a permanent and efficient part of American organised crime. At that time Jewish gangsters actually out-numbered their Italian and Irish counterparts. Typical of the Jewish-Italian co-operation was the composition of an enforce-ment arm of the national Syndicate. Over sixty per cent Jewish, Murder Inc. was a highly efficient enforcement arm. As a result of this Jewish-Italian co-operation in most eastern cities proba-bly more Irish gangsters were wiped out in the establishment of organised crime than any other ethnic group.

If there was ever a Godfather of American organised crime it was Meyer Lansky. He was the brains of the Syndicate and was always treated with the utmost respect. Born Maier Suchowljansky in Grodno, Poland, he arrived in America as a child and settled with his family in New York's teeming Lower East Side. At an early age he teamed up with the headstrong Bugsy Siegel and later Lucky Luciano. There is a myth that Lansky abhorred violence. Nevertheless, he and Siegel formed the Bug and Meyer Gang, a ruthless mob of young bootleggers and hijackers which went on to form the nucleus of Murder Inc., Lansky was well read and very intelligent and a master at organisational business. With Luciano he organised the 1929 Atlantic City convention, the forerunner to the national crime Syndicate. Luciano's advice to his fellow gangsters was, "Always listen to Meyer." Everyone listened to Lansky's advice because it paid. He was a shrewd money-maker and once boasted of the Syndicate that, "We're bigger than U.S. Steel."

While the Italians had their structural organisation the Jews showed no need for one. When Moe Dalitz, of Cleveland, and the Detroit Purple Gang saw their criminal revenues falling they switched their organisations to the gambling paradises of Nevada and Florida. As the leading Jewish mobsters of the 1930s and 1940s died off and the Jews climbed up the social ladder they left the way open for the Italians to fill the void. When Meyer Lansky died of natural causes in 1983 Jewish influence in Syndicate matters declined greatly. Many Jewish gangsters remained in lower levels and as a result the Mafia is the dominant force in organised crime. Most Jews are active in loansharking, gambling and drug pushing. The Italians despise the blacks and Hispanics and will not deal directly with them. Most Jews have no such problem and act as middlemen for Italian drug pushers.

The Godfather.

By 1972 Carlo Gambino had become the most powerful mob leader in America. The leaders of the other New York families were terrified of him and willing to do as he said. Gambino had survived the gang wars of the 1920s and 1930s and the upheavals of the 1950s to emerge as head of the nation's richest and most powerful crime family. He was the role model for Don Corleone in the 1972 *Godfather* movie. On July 11 1972 Tommy Eboli, joint boss with Jerry Catena of the Genovese Family, was shot dead in the Crown Heights section of Brooklyn. He was hit as he left his mistress's apartment, a sign of respect as his assassins could easily have killed him entering the place. His killers were "Zips", a name given to Sicilian born Mafioso, imported by Gambino to introduce new blood into the Mafia. Gambino replaced Eboli with Frank Tieri, thus cementing his hold on the Genovese Family. Gambino, as leader of the biggest and richest family in the country, became the Mafia's new *Capo di tutti Capi* (Boss of all Bosses), the first since Salvatore Maranzano to hold the title.

When Gambino died on October 15 1976 of a heart attack he was replaced by his cousin, and brother-in-law, Paul "Big Paulie" Castellano. Carlo had married his cousin Kathyrn Castellano, sister of Big Paulie. Gambino had decreed that Castellano would succeed him. Big Paulie, in turn, would name Carlo's son, Tommy, as family leader. Castellano was not a strong leader and faced opposition from inside the family from a group of Young Turks led by a violent capo, named John Gotti, who allied themselves with Aniello Dellacroce, who as underboss, was the natural successor to the dead Godfather. Gotti modelled himself on his idol, the kill-crazy Albert Anastasia, who incidentally, was murdered by the Gallo brothers on the orders of Vito Genovese and Carlo Gambino. John Gotti was a little known hood until an incident in 1972 catapulted him into the big time.

In May 1972 Emmanuel "Manny" Gambino, the 29 year old nephew of Don Carlo, was kidnapped by a reckless bunch of Irish gangsters from the West Side led by James McBratney. These wild men from Hell's Kitchen had a profitable sideline of abducting low-level bookmakers, loansharks and assorted associates of the Gambino and Genovese Families, and holding them for ransom. Usually the victims were released following negotiations in which some money was paid. The kidnappers demanded a $350,000 ransom for the safe return of Manny Gambino. Negotiations went on for some weeks and part of the money, believed to be $100,000 was handed over. The family waited for Manny to come home but he never did. After a tip-off to the FBI his body was found in a New Jersey swamp in January of the following year. McBratney had taken the money and for reasons unknown, had murdered him. The FBI arrested two suspects. Carlo Gambino put a contract on the third suspect, McBratney, and ordered that he was to die slowly and painfully.

James McBratney was from Staten Island and was married with two children. He had recently served a sentence for armed robbery. On May 22 1973 a three man hit team, consisting of John Gotti, Angelo Ruggerio and Ralph Galione, three up and coming Gambino button men, tracked McBratney to an Irish bar and restaurant on Staten Island called Snoope's. The plan was to kidnap McBratney and torture him before killing him. Snoope's was well lit and there were quite a few customers in the bar. The three hitmen, pretending to be plainclothes cops, flashed police badges and told McBratney he was under arrest. McBratney was not fooled and when one of the Italians tried to handcuff him, a furious struggle broke out. McBratney, a weightlifter, stood 6'3" and weighed 250 lbs, all of it muscle. He dragged the three Italians down the bar until Gotti and Ruggerio managed to pin him against the wall. Several customers came to his aid and Galione pulled a gun, warning them to keep back. One man attacked him and when Galione pushed him the gun went off accidentally. Galione panicked and fired three bullets at point blank range into McBratney's chest. The Irishman fell dying while the three Italian hoods quickly left the bar. It had been a sloppy job but it had served its purpose. The Godfather had avenged his nephew and sent a message to the rest of the underworld.

Armed with eyewitness descriptions the police went looking for the three hoods. McBratney's men got to Galione first. He was shot dead outside his apartment in Queens. Gotti and Ruggerio went into hiding but they were eventually arrested. They were told to plead guilty and take the rap by Gambino, after all the triggerman was already dead. Gotti was not impressed, but Gambino knew what he was doing. Gotti and Ruggerio were sentenced to seven years for attempted manslaughter. They were released in 1977 after serving just two years. Gotti was richly rewarded for his loyalty. He was advanced far up the ladder to capo and given his own crew.

Meanwhile the Gambinos were having trouble again on the West Side, this time by a more violent band of Irish thugs, known as the Westies. Paulie Castellano, ever the diplomat, met with the Westies leader, Jimmy Coonan, and offered them a working relationship. The Westies, who seemed to enjoy killing, would carry out contract killings for the Gambinos while the gang would share in some of the families rackets. John Gotti was to be liaison with the Westies. When tough guy Jimmy Coonan returned from his first meeting with Gotti he told his men, "I just met a greaseball tougher than we are."

On February 26 1985 after a long, searching investigation of the five New York crime families and the Mafia's ruling Commission the authorities struck. Nine of the cities most pow-erful mobsters: Paul Castellano, Gambino Family boss; Fat Tony Salerno, Genovese Family boss; Tony Ducks Corallo, Lucchese Family boss; Phil Rastelli, Bonanno Family boss; Jerry Catena, Colombo Family boss; Aniello Dellacroce, Gambino Family underboss; Sal Santoro, Lucchese Family underboss; Christopher Furnari, Lucchese *consigliere* and Ralph Scopo, Colombo Family member and president of the Concrete Workers District Council, Labourers International Union of North America, were arrested and eventually convicted, receiving lengthy prison sentences. The Commission was broken, and though it would be replaced, it would be a long time before it would be as efficient as the one it succeeded.

Castellano never made it to the trial. Expecting a long prison sentence he named Thomas Bilotti his underboss to succeed him. Dellacroce was dying of cancer and with Bilotti as boss this would leave Gotti out in the cold. Dellacroce died on December 2 1985. Gotti waited two weeks and then struck. On December 16 Castellano and his newly appointed underboss, Tommy Bilotti, stepped out of their car in front of Sparks Steak House, on East 46th Street, to be confronted by three men wearing fur hats and trenchcoats. The men pulled out semi-automatic handguns and shot Castellano and Bilotti repeatedly. As the two fell to the ground one of the assassins leaned over and fired the *coup de grace* into Castellano's head. The assassins fled on foot east to the corner of 2nd Avenue, one of them talking into a walkie-talkie as he ran. They got into a waiting car, sped south and disappeared. Within days John Gotti took over the reins of the Gambino Family becoming the youngest boss of the biggest and most powerful Mafia family in the country. Angelo Ruggerio took over as liaison with the Westies, who continued their enforcement work for the new Godfather.

In February 1986 John O'Connor, the vice-president and business manager of the Carpenters Union, appeared at the Bankers and Brokers restaurant that was under construction in Lower Manhattan. O'Connor was notoriously corrupt and shook down construction projects, threatening to place pickets which no other workers would cross unless he received a bribe. He informed the owners of the Bankers and Brokers that since the work crews were non-union there could be "a problem". The owners offered O'Connor $5,000 to solve this "problem". It was not enough. O'Connor wanted more and the owners threw him out. Several days later a team of crowbar-wielding thugs caused $30,000 worth of damage in an hour.

The restaurant, however, had a silent partner - John Gotti. Angelo Ruggerio reported the incident to his boss. "Bust him up! Put a rocket in his pocket!" Gotti ordered Ruggerio. This was overheard by the State Organised Crime Task Force bug at the

Bergin Hunt and Fish Club in Queens - hangout and headquarters for Gotti. Ruggerio gave the job to the Westies. Their orders were not to kill O'Connor but warn him not to mess with Gotti. Early on the morning of May 7 Kevin Kelly and Kenny Shannon drove to the offices of the Carpenter's Local 608 near 51st Street and Broadway and waited for O'Connor to arrive. Kelly followed O'Connor into the lobby and as he entered the elevator shot the union boss four times in the buttocks and legs. While recuperating in hospital O'Connor told police that he had been attacked by "four Puerto Rican gunmen". Why, he just did not know. After a month in hospital O'Connor was released and arrested and jailed on labour racketeering charges. Gotti's words spoken so incautiously would later come back to haunt him.

Meanwhile, the Godfather was under attack from an overzealous young female prosecutor. Diane Giacalone, an Assistant U.S. Attorney, prosecuted Gotti, in 1986, in an open and shut case, or so she thought. Born in Ozone Park - Gotti's home turf - of second-generation Italian parents, Giacalone hated everything Gotti and the Mafia stood for. She assembled an array of a half-dozen criminals who claimed they had knowledge of Gotti's rackets. Among them was Crazy Eddie Maloney, the last survivor of Jimmy McBratney's kidnap gang and James Cardinali, a violent thug whose record included the pistol-whipping of a priest and the murder of several drug dealers in New York and Florida. Another was Matthew Traynor, a bank robber serving 14 years for assault and robbery. Traynor was a former Ozone Park teenage gang member. As a ranking member of the Saints, a street gang of mixed Irish and Italian teenage hoods, he began working for the local Mafia unloading hi-jacked goods. Traynor, one of the gangs leaders, struck up a friendship with Gene and Richard Gotti, brothers of John. Later, Traynor became a bank robber and also a drugs courier for Gene Gotti. He knew John Gotti and claimed he was shaken down by him for $10,000 from a bank heist Traynor had pulled in the area. He resented Gotti for this and cited this as his reason to testify. In 1984, after a string of successful bank jobs, he accidentally shot a woman teller when he tried to jump a counter. Arrested and facing fourteen years he decided to testify against John and Gene Gotti, but later balked after a serious of confrontations with Giacalone. Traynor had committed perjury from the start. He claimed that he had been given narcotics, promised all charges against him were to be dropped and offered sexual release if he agreed to testify falsely about the Gotti's.

On March 6 1987 the case went to the jury. After a week of deliberations the jury acquitted Gotti and the other defendants. Traynor later admitted he committed perjury and was given a further five years to run concurrent with the 14 years he was already serving. However, Gotti's troubles were not over. The Westies had been broken by a full-scale police assault directed by the Manhattan District Attorney's office, which had converted several of them into prosecution witnesses. Chief among them was Mickey Featherstone, one of the gang's top killers, who not only provided evidence against other gang members, but also agreed to wear a concealed recorder in prison during conversations with several Westies, involved in the John O'Connor shooting. Kevin Kelly and Kenny Shannon freely spoke about the reasons for the shooting and how it was decided they should carry it out as a "favour for the greaseballs". John Gotti's name was prominently mentioned and another Westie, Studs McElroy, serving heavy time for federal racketeering convictions, then agreed to become a witness.

Gotti's recorded threats had come round full circle. He already had two felony convictions on his record. A third conviction meant he would be defined as a "predictable felon" under the law and would be liable to a sentence of 25 years in jail. His trial began on January 29 1990 and lasted until February 5 when the jury retired to consider a verdict. Four days later they returned a verdict of not guilty. When interviewed by reporters the jurors expressed mixed feelings about the hours of secretly recorded tapes. One said, "The Westies were undisciplined. They were wild. They didn't need anybody's permission to kill anybody." However, in 1991 Gotti was convicted, on the evidence of the FBI's taped conversations, of racketeering, loansharking, obstruction of justice, bribery and murder. He was sentenced to life and sent to the maximum security Federal Penitentiary in Marion, Illinois.

CHAPTER 13

RACKETS
AND LAW ENFORCEMENT

In 1986 the West Side Irish Mob, or as they were known in the press, the Westies, were decimated by a RICO prosecution. RICO, the 1970 Racketeer-Influenced and Corrupt Organisation Act was originally designed by Notre Dame University Law School professor Robert Blakely, to provide prosecutors with a weapon against organised crime infiltration of labour unions and business. He believed the Act could be used effectively to combat the entire structure of organised crime and was upset that federal prosecutors and the FBI had not understood RICO's potential as a prosecutorial weapon. In the 1970s juries were not convicting RICO cases, and appeals courts differed on the statute's proper use. In 1981 the Supreme Court resolved the disputes with a interpretation of federal power and instead of using it to attack the Act against individual mobsters the FBI began using it to attack the structure of organised crime. Now mobsters would get long prison sentences if the government could prove their connection to a "criminal enterprise" or a "criminal commission" that functioned as a criminal enterprise, i.e. the "Commission Trial".

With a utilised RICO the FBI reviewed their whole strategy and reorganised their war against the mob. Instead of individual FBI squads combating specific crimes, such as hijacking or gambling, nine elite squads were created in New York, five of them targeted against the five Mafia families, two against labour racketeering and the rest against organised crime on Long Island and the surrounding counties. The FBI campaign would be a joint one, operating with detectives of the New York City Police Department's elite Organised Crime Control Bureau.

The FBI's history of action against organised crime was a shameful blot on the Bureau's record. For years its director, J. Edgar Hoover, denied the existence of the Mafia and organised crime. Hoover refused to stalk mob gangsters preferring to target so called Public Enemies like John Dillinger (who was responsible for two deaths), Ma Barker (who was never charged with any crime) and Machine-Gun Kelly (who never fired a gun in anger at anyone) and lesser criminals. In the 1930s the full resources of the FBI were utilised against these relatively easy targets instead of large criminal enterprises run by big city gangsters. In the 1950s the FBI in New York only had four agents investigating organised crime while over 400 agents were assigned the job of probing the "Communist conspiracy" - a far lesser evil than the mob.

There are many theories why Hoover denied the existence of the mob. Some critics say he was too afraid to go after big time criminals. He was well aware of how corrupt Prohibition agents and ordinary police had become by their association with organised crime. Others said it was because of his fondness for gambling. Hoover's preoccupation with horse racing and betting was legendary. The mob soon found out and through Walter Winchell, the famous gossip columnist, passed on "sure things". Winchell got his tips from gambling kingpin, Frank Costello, who got them from Frank Erickson, the country's leading bookmaker. Whether this arraignment had any effect on Hoover's attitude is debatable but he once told Costello, in the Stork Club, to stay out of his bailiwick and that he in turn would stay out of Costello's.

The Hoover charade ended in 1957 when a state trooper stumbled upon a Mafia conference in Apalachin, New York. Over sixty Mafia figures were arrested in the biggest roundup of organised crime bosses in history. Now Hoover could no longer deny the Mafia's existence. He threw the FBI into a frenzy, demanding his agents to find out all they could on organised crime. The FBI were now three decades behind in the fight against the mob and had a lot of catching up to do. The appointment of Robert Kennedy as attorney general in 1961 kept Hoover on his toes. Unlike his predecessors Kennedy was not afraid of Hoover and urged him to crack down on organised crime. Kennedy was the first attorney general to make a serious attack on the Mafia and organised crime. Many former attorney generals would launch a campaign against the mob and when they realised how much time and effort it took, they would let the campaign run out of steam. Kennedy was different. He knew all the names of the big racketeers in any given district and in consultation with local law enforcement he would follow his investigations through.

Jimmy Hoffa, the corrupt leader of the Teamsters union, remained immune from prosecution until he became a target of Robert Kennedy's "Get Hoffa" campaign. Hoffa and Kennedy had first become enemies when Kennedy was chief counsel to the Senate Select Committee on Improper Activities in the Labour or Management Field (more popularly known as the McClellan Committee). When Kennedy became attorney general he named Hoffa his top priority. His efforts resulted in Hoffa's trial in 1962 for extorting illegal payments from a firm employing teamsters. The case ended in a hung jury, but Hoffa was then tried for trying to bribe one of the jurors. He was sentenced to 8 years and was then convicted of misappropriating $1.7 million in union funds. Hoffa fought off entering prison until 1967 and had his sentence commuted in 1971 by President Nixon with the agreement that he stay out of union politics for ten years. He didn't and wound up murdered.

Robert Kennedy resigned as attorney general in 1964 and the onslaught on organised crime fizzled out. It was not until Hoover's death in 1972 that the FBI war against the mob really began. Since then the two foes have been in persistent confrontation. The feds brought in new tactics to fight the mob, using teams of "techies" who specialised in electronic bugging operations. The teams included electronics technicians, locksmiths and expert burglars, who would penetrate high security at the homes and hangouts of top mobsters and plant sophisticated bugs. in the 1980s many big crime bosses were convicted on the strength of tapes resulting from bugs planted in their homes or workplaces.

Informants have always been a part of law enforcement's war against organised crime. One of the earliest and most successful was Ed O'Hare who helped topple Al Capone. Edward J. O'Hare was a lawyer from St. Louis who did a bit of bootlegging on the side. With Owen P. Smith, the inventor of the mechanical rabbit, as his partner O'Hare exercised national control of dog tracks. When Smith died in 1927 O'Hare became the top man in dog racing. He became involved with Al Capone, managing the Hawthorne Kennel Club, and using Capone's connections to branch out further across the country. O'Hare was cultured and well read and did not consider himself a gangster. He felt he could use gangsters in business without becoming one. By 1930 he wanted to change sides hoping his co-operation with the law would pave the way for his adored son Edward, known as Butch, to attend Annapolis.

O'Hare was once called "the best stool pigeon the government ever had." Co-operating with the IRS he informed agents where they could seize books that would show Capone's income. By 1931 Elmer L. Irey, chief of the IRS's Enforcement Branch, and his team of agents had established Capone's income for 1924 to be in excess of $120,000 and that taxes for this amount, about $32,000, had never been paid. Furthermore, they established that Capone had earned more than $1 million from 1925 to 1929 and had paid no taxes on this income either. Irey and everyone else knew this income was only the tip of the iceberg, but it was income that could be proven on paper.

Just before he went on trial Capone offered the government $400,000 to drop the case. His offer was refused. He then went after the jury. Ed O'Hare informed Irey's agents that Capone had obtained a list of the jurors. Judge James H. Wikerson had the jury switched with a jury hearing another case only minutes before Capone's trial began. Capone was convicted of income tax evasion and sentenced to 11 years. By 1938 it had become common knowledge that O'Hare had played a major part in helping to convict Capone. It had even been printed in the papers. On the afternoon of November 8 1939 O'Hare left his office at Sportsman's Park - formerly Capone's Hawthorne Kennel Club. Driving up Ogden towards the Loop his car was overtaken and two shotgun blasts were fired from a passing sedan, ripping into his head and neck. His car slewed across the road and crashed into a pole. O'Hare was killed instantly. (Edward "Butch" O'Hare went to Annapolis and was shot down in the South Pacific. He was posthumously awarded the Congressional Medal of Honour. Chicago named its airport in his honour.)

Organised crimes most famous law enforcement adversary would undoubtedly be Eliot Ness. A university of Chicago graduate, Ness was appointed head of a special group of men, drawn from the ranks of the Chicago Police Department and other law enforcement agencies, who were deemed incorruptible, or as Ness and the press dubbed them "Untouchable". This special group of ten were all under thirty years of age and their specific task was to harass the Capone mob. Television, films and books - including one by Ness himself - have created a myth that the Untouchables put Capone out of the bootleg business and brought down his empire. Nothing could be further from the truth. The Untouchables received considerable publicity but did little damage to the Capone mob. They cost Capone a lot of money but they did not contribute directly to his downfall. Capone tried to bribe these new adversarys but found they were indeed "untouchable".

In the years from 1929 to 1935 the Untouchables racked up an entirely praiseworthy record of effectiveness and incorruptibility, however it was in Cleveland that Ness achieved more success. Here he smashed widespread corruption in the police department and among local politicians and destroyed the operations of the powerful Mayfield Road Mob. The ruthless Mayfield Road Mob had emerged from the bloody gang wars of the 1920s with control of Cleveland's lucrative bootleg booze racket. During the Roaring Twenties the city was as violent as Chicago in that same period, with Italian, Jewish and Irish gangs battling for supremacy. With the repeal of Prohibition the emerging Syndicate had to move into new areas of business like the policy and clearing house rackets. (Clearing house is a racket in which players bet on a series of numbers found in the daily stock market listings while policy are bets based on numbers drawn from a bag or a spinning wheel.) Policy was largely in the hands of small-time black criminals, who were brutally beaten or murdered by the Syndicate in their bid to control the racket. Once again killings became commonplace on

Cleveland's streets. In 1935 Harold Burton was elected mayor on a promise to purge America's fifth largest city of crime and corruption. He needed help and Eliot Ness was recommended. Ness accepted on one condition. He demanded complete freedom from political interference. He got it and became Cleveland's youngest Safety Director in command of 2,400 men in the city's police and fire departments.

Ness organised a new group of Untouchables to fight the power of the mob. They were known as "The Unknowns" and were financed by a group of Cleveland businessmen, as there was no official knowledge of their undercover campaign. Organised crime cannot flourish without police and political protection and the police department became one of the Unknowns first targets. Cleveland's police force was one of the most corrupt in the country with some policemen actually working for the mob as enforcers, while others ran their own rackets. Within a month of taking command Ness transferred 28 lieutenants, 126 sergeants and 400 patrolmen to new assignments. He gained convictions against two captains, a deputy inspector, two lieutenants and three patrolmen. He set up Cleveland's first police academy and introduced red, white and blue patrol cars to the city believing that this would make the public and the criminals more aware of a police presence on the streets.

Ness's first major move against the mob was against the city's organised gambling rackets. By 1938 Ness and the Unknowns were ready to strike. Supported by informers within the mob and armed with mounting evidence gathered by his intelligence man Ness and a squad of trusted detectives raided every known gambling den in the city. The raids took the mob completely by surprise. Cleveland's mob bosses went underground. Moe Dalitz, Tommy McGinty, Morris Kleinman and Sammy Tucker left the city after their gambling operations were closed down, switching their ventures to surrounding county areas. Years later they would surface in Las Vegas as backers of the Desert Inn casino. Dalitz and McGinty would go on to be powers in nation-wide gambling. Ness gained convictions against 23 members of the Mayfield Road Mob, including its leader Big Angelo Lonardo.

Ness was also credited with smashing Cleveland's labour rackets. In 1936 a violent labour war broke out in the city when Sam Salupo, who ran a lucrative window cleaning racket, was blown apart by a bomb planted in his car. Labour leader Arthur Whitlock died after he was shot in his home and union official Frank Convere was wounded. Behind the unrest was Don Campbell, president of the Painters District Council, and John McGee, business agent for the Glaziers Union. They had risen to power after a campaign of window-smashing that produced huge profits for the building trade. The two labour racketeers had been in constant conflict with the law.

Cleveland's new hero launched a crackdown against the two racketeers and both were indicted on extortion charges. Ness had evidence that they had held up the installations of windows in a new restaurant until the owner paid them $1,200. After death threats and a drive by shooting attack Ness had to have two detectives assigned to guard him around the clock. He moved to a secret address and send his wife Edna out of the city. The constant strain and fear was too much for her and she filed for divorce. Ness found his Cleveland posting far more dangerous than Chicago. Both Campbell and McGee were convicted and each of them were sentenced to one to five years for extortion.

While investigating the labour rackets Ness had also come upon the activities of Harry Barrington and Albert Ruddy of the Carpenters Union. Barrington and Ruddy visited construction sites and finding technical violations informed site bosses that carpenters would be taken off the job unless they were given a bribe. Contractors and builders had to pay up or they would be fined for breach of contract. Ness compiled enough evidence to bring Barrington to trial but failed to indict Ruddy. Barrington fled to California but was captured by the Unknowns and returned to Cleveland for trial. On advice from Ruddy and other labour leaders Barrington pleaded guilty, expecting to be out when the "fix" was put in. He was sentenced to 3 to 15 years for extortion and racketeering. Abandoned by Ruddy and his pals, Barrington got in contact with Ness, who obtained his release and put him in protective custody. He testified against Ruddy, who was sentenced to 5 to 10 years for extortion and labour racketeering.

Despite his success against organised crime and corruption Eliot Ness soon fell from grace. He failed to solve a series of mutilation murders and resigned. During the war he became director of the Division of Social Protection for the Office of Defence, fighting prostitution near U.S. military installations. He did not achieve fame until his book, *The Untouchables,* exaggerated his part in the downfall of the Capone mob. Ness died in 1957, aged 54, the year his book was published.

RACKETS.

The word racket came from the Tammany Hall run balls, dances and fundraisers that produced much noise and racket from drunken revellers. Tammany politicians doled out gambling and liquor licences and contracts for city work at these affairs and the word racket became synonymous with Tammany Hall. It was later adopted by hoodlums to describe their activities.

Bootlegging.

The first major racket of modern organised crime was the

sale of bootleg liquor during Prohibition. Bootlegging made millionaires out of otherwise petty criminals and revived the dying breed of Irish gangsters. Irish success in politics - which provided the most readily available road to upward social mobility - coincided with a decrease in the crime rate among Irish immigrants until Prohibition suddenly offered a new fast track to economic success.

When Prohibition became law many of America's criminals had made preparations for the continued supply of alcohol. Many saloons continued to do business as if nothing had changed. Customers wanted beer and spirits and there were many willing to supply the demand. Illegal breweries flourished and home-made alky was organised into an industry, though mainly among Italian and Sicilian immigrants. Federal law permitted the manufacture of alcohol for medicinal purposes, to be sold only to pharmacies and physicians. Breweries sold this legal alcohol who "cut" it with caramel colouring or plain water. Some unscrupulous bootleggers cut good alcohol with chemicals, which resulted in blinding or killing unwary drinkers.

Canada banned the direct export of alcohol to the U.S. but many breweries sold it to bootleggers who trucked it across the border or brought it by speedboat across the lakes to waiting wagons or trucks. In time booze was brought across the Atlantic and unloaded along the east coast. The Coast Guard sought to prevent this but the opportunities for corruption were widespread and when Big Bill Dwyer's smuggling operation was smashed, Coast Guard officers were among those convicted of rum-running.

The profits from bootlegging were enormous. Most bootleggers paid $25 for a case of Scotch off the boat (this included the cost of bribery) and sold it for $30 a bottle. Cut whiskey could make $1,000 a case. The illegal liquor business generated much needed income and employment to thousands of slum-dwellers. Drivers, mechanics and loaders were needed to move and distribute bootleg. Warehouses, trucks and boats were required to transport and store booze while armed guards were needed to protect shipments. Hijacking of booze shipments became commonplace and gang wars broke out over distribution rights. Syndication of criminals arose out of the need to transport and distribute bootleg and to settle disputes and to divide local and regional markets. Some meetings consisted of just one ethnic group while others consisted of a variety of ethnic gangs. By 1929 and the Atlantic City conference, syndication was practically nation-wide. All this would not have happened had it not been for Prohibition. "The Great Experiment" provided organised crime the opportunity to blossom into an important force in American society.

Prohibition led to a general wave of lawlessness across the country and a massive increase in gangland murders as well as deaths among the civilian population. Over 200 civilians were killed by Prohibition Bureau agents, who were notoriously inept and corrupt. When Prohibition ended in 1933 many bootleggers dropped out of organised crime and continued in the now legitimate liquor trade. Joseph Reinfeld, a partner of New Jersey kingpin Longy Zwillman, became Reinfeld Importers, Ltd., and later received a knighthood, while Joseph P. Kennedy of Boston, father of a president and two senators, moved from bootlegging to head Somerset Importers and became Ambassador to the Court of St. James.

Protection.

Protection rackets began with sidewalk peddlers who paid protection to stand at their stalls unmolested. Others paid for the rights to operate in certain neighbourhoods, i.e. Jewish peddlers operating in Irish areas. From there protection spread to shopkeepers and restaurants, mainly in poor immigrant neighbourhoods. Owney Madden, who dreamed of taking over all the rackets in New York, raked in $200 a day from his criminal ventures. Dozens of store owners in Hell's Kitchen were forced to pay protection money or have their stores fire-bombed. Restaurants paid, too. A favourite tactic of Madden's was to bombard reluctant restaurants with stink bombs at peak business hours.

The Whyos, prominent in New York after the Civil War, introduced the shakedown racket. "Big Josh" Hines would drop by the faro dens and dice parlours each night and demand a cut of the take. Two pistols tucked into his waistband deterred anyone from arguing. This cut of the action made sure that no one else interfered with the players and dealers. These techniques were adopted by gangs of all creed. Illegal gamblers and thieves paid a percentage to operate in the area dominated by a gang such as the Whyos. This practise continues to the present day. Today, gamblers, thieves and drug-pushers pay "street taxes" to operate in a particular area. The New England Mafia is small but ruthless and non-Mafia allies hold "licences" to be bookies, loansharks or fences. The Mafia takes 25 to 40 per cent of receipts. Some Mafia allies have licences for whole territories. The ageing town of Somerville, Mass., was the haven of Howard Winter. A 1967 FBI report stated: "Winter pays tribute regularly to Anguilo's men."

Hijacking and robbery.

In the late 1950s Idlewild Airport - later renamed Kennedy Airport - became the chief entry point for imports into the U.S., replacing to what had then been the mobs most lucrative field, the waterfront. By the 1960s nearly $30 billion worth of goods moved each year through a network of airline shipping companies. Hijacking became the mobs new and most profitable racket. Losses from hijacking ran to $2 billion a year. Valuable information to the hijack crews came from cargo handlers and other employees around the airport. Some of these employees were in debt to mob gamblers or loansharks. A cargo supervisor in debt to a connected gambler, provided information that led to the largest robbery in American history - the $8 million Lufthansa Heist. The man worked out all the details; how many men would be needed, the best time for the robbery and how to bypass the security and alarm system.

The mastermind of the Lufthansa heist was Jimmy "The Gent" Burke. He was a polite, assertive stone killer, who loved to steal. Born in Brooklyn in 1926 Burke was first jailed at the tender age of eleven. He allegedly performed his first murder when he was sixteen. He mainly worked with Mafia hoods, especially Paulie Vario, a Lucchese Family captain, and was sometimes referred to as "the Irish guinea". When Burke hijacked a truck he would take the drivers licence. If the driver testified against him, he knew Burke had his licence and home address. While paroled to the Hotel Bryant, on Manhattan's West 54th Street (a halfway house for paroled criminals) Burke left in the dead of night and was picked up by an accomplice and driven to Queens, where he met his hand-picked crew. From there they proceeded to Kennedy Airport where they pulled off the Lufthansa heist. By the time the story broke Burke was back in the Hotel Bryant, thereby establishing a perfect alibi.

While not usually engaging directly in robbery or burglary the mob has an extensive network and can provide professional criminals with invaluable information and assistance, transport and weapons. They will also assist in helping professional criminals carry out more complex crimes like payroll robberies, hijackings, large-scale commercial burglaries and the theft of stocks and bonds. They will help finance frauds, swindles and move stolen securities and goods and market stolen credit cards, securities and checks. Joe McGinnis, a convicted drug dealer and robber, and Carlton O'Brien, a former bootlegger, were thought to have masterminded the $2.8 million Brinks heist, which at the time was the biggest robbery in American history.

Joseph McGinnis was born the son of a policeman in Providence, Rhode Island. As a youth in South Boston he joined the Kneeland Street Gang, who controlled the area around South Street Station. When he was 17 he was shot by a policeman and sent to the reformatory. He later married a brothel keeper from South Boston and was convicted of narcotics possession. On his release he bought a saloon and formed a gang of professional robbers committing several big robberies, including a Revere factory heist which netted them $108,000 in 1947. Carlton O'Brien was a former Providence bootlegger who had moved into gambling operations in competition with the New England Mafia.

On January 17 1950 several men wearing Halloween masks held up the guards at Brinks on Prince Street and escaped with nearly $2.8 million in cash and securities. The more wiser of the gang wanted to lie low and let the heat die down but within weeks the gang began to fall out when the money was not immediately shared out. Two of the gang, Joseph "Specs" O'Keefe and Stanley "Gus" Gusciora, were arrested. Carlton O'Brien was murdered on May 17, either by members of the robbery gang or by the Mafia with whom he was in competition. McGinnis was arrested but released when his alibi - he was with a high ranking policeman on the day - held up. O'Keefe was released on bail and three attempts were made to kill him. He was convinced McGinnis was behind the murder attempts and spilled the beans on the Brinks robbery. With O'Keefe as prosecution witness indictments followed and McGinnis received a life sentence.

Thieves, robbers and swindlers all need the mob to move their goods. A fence with mob connections can raise large amounts of cash on short notice to offer a jewel thief or stock swindler the best deal. Dealing with such a fence guarantees the thief that he will not be ripped off by other criminals. If a mobster hears of a job pulled in his turf by professional criminals he will look for his "tax". Bank-robber Matthew Traynor had to pay Gene Gotti, brother of Godfather John Gotti, $10,000 from the proceeds of a heist he had recently undertaken. Gotti claimed he was short of cash at the time and Traynor had to pay for the privilege of robbing in the Gotti's area of operations.

Willie Sutton was a bank-robber from Brooklyn's Irishtown, noted for using trickery rather than violence. He was thought to have stolen over $2 million in his long criminal career. In 1952 Arnold Schuster, a 24 year old Brooklyn clothing salesman, became a short-lived-hero after he spotted the highly publicised Sutton, while riding on a New York City subway train. Sutton had escaped from prison in 1947 with some mob guys and had been placed on the FBI's "Ten Most Wanted" list. He was respected and well liked in the underworld. Arnold Schuster followed Sutton and contacted the police. Sutton was arrested. On March 9 1952 Schuster was found shot dead on the street where he lived. He had been shot four times, twice in the groin and once in each eye.

Schuster's death had been ordered by Albert Anastasia, the boss of the Brooklyn Mafia. He had been watching Schuster being interviewed on television bragging about his role in Sutton's capture, when he flew into one of his murderous rages. "I can't stand squealers!" he screamed. "Hit that guy!" The murder was carried out by Fred Tenuto, who had escaped with Sutton in 1947. The Schuster murder generated intense heat from the police and from Anastasia's enemies. He made amends by having Tenuto murdered, but the Schuster killing led indirectly to Anastasia's downfall. Willie Sutton was released from Attica in 1969 and died in 1980, aged 79.

Loansharking.

Next to gambling, loansharking is the mob's primary source of steady income. Also called shylocking, the loanshark racket can generally produce a profit of up to 20 per cent a week. For every $5 borrowed the borrower must return $6 at the end of the week. The borrower can pay the $1 interest and keep the $5 loan in force for another week. Months later he could have paid back $20 and still have the $5 debt. A crime boss usually finances the operations himself, making money available to his underlings for about one per cent weekly interest. The boss's net comes to 52 per cent a year and his men have accepted full responsibility for his money. If they fail to keep up the interest payments or return the entire capital required they are in big trouble.

Jimmy Coonan, the West Side mob boss, was heavily involved in loansharking. His viciousness can be summarised in the case of one member of his gang, Paddy Dugan. Despite warnings from Coonan, Dugan continued his non-sanctioned shakedowns of loansharks and in defiance of his boss, murdered one of Coonan's friends. Coonan murdered Dugan and chopped up his body with a machete. Dugan's severed fingers went into a bag Coonan allegedly kept for frightening reluctant payers to pay up. However, violence is seldom needed. Loansharks are not in the muscle business, they are in the credit business. They lend money and expect it to be paid off and for the customer to return for another loan. Sometimes a little muscle is needed. Loansharks employ enforcers to see that the interest, or "vigorish" or "juice", is paid on time. Debtors are rarely murdered, a corpse cannot repay a loan, whereas a debtor with a few broken limbs can. Occasionally, a welsher might be murdered, as an example and usually he owed very little, so the lender has lost nothing.

Contract Killing.

A mob killing is known as a contract. It is a business term. After all, contracts are strictly business. There are many reasons for a contract but the formula is still the same as that set out in the 1930s by the infamous Murder Inc. the mob's enforcement arm. The method of the orders given tend to insulate the man who gives them. The boss gives the contract to a second party. He picks the hitmen, who are given the victim's identity and background on his habits and a place where he can most likely be found. Sometimes a spotter or a fingerman points out the victim. When the killing is finished the assassin or assassins vanish, contacting the person who had given the specific orders. This information is passed on to whoever had issued the contract in the first place. The police are left with a killing, no clues and no suspects because the killers more than likely do not even know the victim. If a hitman is arrested and charged, which is highly unlikely, he most often would not know who ordered the contract in the first place.

John Sullivan, a West Side Irish mobster, was a contract killer for Fat Tony Salerno, boss of the Genovese Family. Sullivan handled contracts for Salerno, doing them himself or farming them out - for a fee - to other killers like Joe "Mad Dog" Sullivan and Donald "Tony the Greek" Frankos. In 1975 Sullivan allegedly acquired his most prestigious hit - the contract on Teamsters leader Jimmy Hoffa. On July 30 1975 Hoffa was waiting in the car park of Machus Red Fox restaurant in Detroit's suburbs for a meeting with Tony Jacks Giacalone, a Detroit Mafioso. Hoffa disappeared from the car park and his body has never been found. Tony Frankos, who turned state's evidence, said he and Joe Sullivan murdered Hoffa in a house at Mount Clemens in Detroit, while John Sullivan looked on. (Frankos also claimed Jimmy Coonan was there, so his version of events might not be the truth. However, Joe Sullivan had being going around for years saying he killed Jimmy Hoffa.) Hoffa, according to Frankos, was buried in the foundation of the Meadowlands arena - the home of the New York Giants football team. Sullivan was working on the construction of the stadium and dumped a 10 gallon drum, which contained Hoffa's body, into a ditch and poured concrete over it.

Freelance killers handle contract killings the Mafia consider too risky or killings they do not want their men to do for whatever reason. There are no demands on freelance killers. They do not have to pay protection or split their profits with mob bosses. Joe Sullivan was such a killer. He was born in Queens, the son of a violent alcoholic police officer, who wanted him to join the force. By the time he was twelve young Joe Sullivan was carrying out armed robberies and proving himself to be a violent and unstoppable street fighter, whose favourite tactic was eye gouging. He was polite, soft-spoken and well read, yet he possessed a fierce anger and a terrible temper. He acquired his nickname "Mad Dog" because he foamed at the mouth during conversation and especially during murders. Of course, nobody ever called him Mad Dog to his face, his friends called him "Sully". Tony Frankos revealed many of the stories of Sullivan's criminal career and behaviour and claimed the two worked on many contract killings together.

Sullivan committed many of his murders between 1975 and 1981. He carried out contracts for John Sullivan, Junior Persico, boss of the Colombo Family, Fat Tony Salerno and Carmine Tramunti, boss of the Luchese Family. He became the most prolific killer in American criminal history. He carried out many of the underworld's most famous murders: West Side mobsters Eddie "The Butcher" Cummiskey and Mickey Spillane; Angelo Bruno, the Philadelphia Mafia boss, murdered in 1980 and Gino Gallina, a former Manhattan D.A. who became a top mob lawyer. Sullivan was reputed to have killed 110 people, including strangers in bars and a Texas policeman, and was described by law enforcement officials as "the most dangerous man in America". (He was not the first Irishman to be labelled "America's biggest mass murderer". In 1906 Al Horsley, a fugitive from the law in Ontario, Canada, confessed to murdering 38 people, including ex-Governor of Idaho, Frank Steunenberg, while in the employ of the Western Federation of Miners, at the behest of its corrupt officials. Horsley turned state's evidence and had his death sentence commuted to life.)

Sullivan was believed to be the only man to escape from Attica. In 1971, a month before the famous riot, he hid under 100 sacks of flour and was driven through the gates by an unsuspecting truck driver. He was eventually recaptured and paroled in 1976. On February 23 1982 acting on a tip-off eight FBI agents captured the fugitive Sullivan, who had been on the run for several months, outside the Denonville Motel in Rochester. In September he was convicted of the murder of John Fiorino, a Rochester Teamsters leader shot dead on December 17 1981. Fiorino was believed to be closely involved with the mob and Sullivan was hired by an insurgent Mafia faction during the bloody Rochester wars of the late 1970s and early 1980s. Sullivan was sentenced to 75 years with no recommendation of parole.

Narcotics.

Morphine, a derivative of opium, became popular during the Civil War when the intravenous use of the drug was used indiscriminately to treat battlefield casualties. After the war morphine was sold by pharmacies and general stores as a treatment for every ailment from toothaches to consumption. Addiction or abuse was not wildely known or realised until the late 1870s. At the turn of the century heroin, another derivative of opium, was introduced as a non-habit-forming analgesic to replace morphine. It turned out to be more popular and more addictive. The Harrison Act of 1914 made it illegal to sell or give away opium, or opium derivatives, without registering with the commissioner of revenue. Only medical professionals could register and they had to maintain records of the drugs they dispensed. Heroin had by now become popular among prostitutes and inhabitants of pool halls and bowling alleys, usual haunts of the underworld.

As the illegal use of drugs increased criminal gangs added drug trafficking to their business ventures. After the repeal of Prohibition and the disappearance of bootleg profits, drug trafficking became an important source of revenue for gangsters. Most organised crime groups trafficked in this enormously profitable business and after WW2 the Mafia emerged as the dominant group in the trade. They imported most of the narcotics from refineries controlled by Mafia gangs in Italy and Sicily and from Corsican gangs in the French port of Marseilles.

The organisers who arrange for the importation of narcotics rarely ever see the drug. The distribution is done through the lower echelons, the street hoods. After importation heroin is first sold to wholesalers who "cut" the heroin (dilute it with quinine, lactose and dextrose). It is then sold to dealers, who might cut it again, and then on to the street retailers who push it on the addicts. At each step the value of the heroin increases making a $90,000 kilo of almost pure heroin worth $1.5 million on the streets. The drugs trade is enormously profitable and of low risk to the importer. It is also a very violent trade. Jack "Legs" Diamond was one of the first key importers of heroin. Diamond, one of the underworld's most vicious gangsters, learned the trade from the Mr. Big of organised crime, Arnold Rothstein. Diamond eventually fell out with Rothstein over a drug deal, leading Rothstein to try and kill Legs' brother Eddie. When the murder attempt failed Legs hunted down all five hitmen involved in the attack and killed them. Rothstein was also murdered and Legs was one of the suspects. Diamond also quarrelled with Charlie "Lucky" Luciano, another importer of heroin. The two travelled to Europe to set up a narcotics route to America. Diamond was deported back to America and Luciano travelled on without him, setting up his own drugs route. In October 1929 henchmen of Diamond's hijacked a shipment of heroin at the Brooklyn docks and brought Luciano, who was waiting for the heroin, along for a ride. The Diamond hoods tortured and beat Luciano, slashing his face with a knife and leaving him for dead on Staten Island. Luciano lived and earned his sobriquet "Lucky" from this encounter. When Diamond was murdered in 1931 Luciano had the pleasure of taking over Legs' drug trade.

Mickey Spillane was boss of Manhattan's West Side when drugs, especially heroin. exploded on the streets in the late 1960s and early 1970s. Spillane, an old time gangster, had no interest in the narcotics trade. He thought it was bad for his image and was against the sale of drugs, even marijuana, on principle. He believed it was a lowly trade fit only for the dregs of the underworld. He forbid his men to push drugs and was content to let other hoods from the Westies and the Mafia do the dealing.

Street level drug-pushing is an easy entry business, requiring only a source and funds. In many of the poor urban areas street gangs deal heroin to the addicts. In the 1950s and 1960s heroin decimated the street gangs. After the Vietnam war the street gangs were back on the streets with a vengeance. Today street gang members are much more intelligent. They are typical users of marijuana and maybe a little cocaine, but not of heroin. Their older mob contacts come to trust them and they can advance in the trade and join the Syndicate ranks.

Gambling.

Illegal gambling is the principal source of revenue for organised crime. The numbers racket is without doubt the biggest and most profitable of all, with at least 20 million people a day engaged in this lucrative pastime. Numbers, or policy, is a mode of gambling especially congenial to the poor. The bets are small, as little as a nickel, while the odds are high. The odds against winning are 999 to 1, but if a bettor's three numbers come up he receives a payout of 600 to 1. The numbers are priced from the daily reports of the New York City Clearing House printed in the financial pages of newspapers. The winning numbers have to be legitimate and cannot be fixed - originally they were taken from Treasury Department figures, released daily by telegraph.

Numbers have been played in America since 1880. (The numbers game in various forms has been known to the world since at least 1530 when the Italian national lottery began.) Policy shops first appeared in the 1880s in New York and soon caught on in other cities. Eventually every poor neighbourhood had its policy makers and bankers, each assisted by runners and collectors. Numbers became vastly profitable and it was not long before bankers began paying off politicians and police for protection. Al Adams, a New York operator, had about 1,000 policy shops and was one of the biggest bribe payers to the Tammany machine. Reform and raids signalled the end of policy around 1905, and it became defunct in 1915. With the coming of Prohibition the game was reborn around 1923, particularly in Harlem, where it was known as numbers.

While each ethnic neighbourhood had its own bankers and makers and ran their own shops they all eventually came under the thumb of the Syndicate. Independents who did not toe the line were simply rubbed out. Franchises were given to other ethnics, who paid for the protection the Syndicate gave them from police raids and stick-up men. Carlton O' Brien, a former boot-legger, ran a bookie network in Providence, Rhode Island independent of Mafia boss Raymond Patriarca. He also obtained control of the valuable racing-wire service. O'Brien's bookies were held up, his bookie parlours wrecked and his employees beaten up and robbed. Finally in 1950 O'Brien was killed by a shotgun blast. (Others say he was killed in the fall-out over the Brinks heist but it is more probable O' Brien was murdered by the Mafia, who took over his gambling operations on his death.)

With the repeal of Prohibition gambling had become the principal source of income for organised crime. In the late 1920s Moe Annenberg had formed the Nation-Wide News Service, supplying information from race tracks to thousands of pool-rooms and bookie joints across the country. Annenberg had come up the hard way starting out as circulation agent for William Randolph Hearst in the Chicago circulation wars. With the co-operation of the mob he made millions with his wire service but ended up in jail on income tax evasion, leaving the racing-wire business in disarray. James Ragen stepped into the vacuum with his Continental Press Service, outmanoeuvring the Syndicate and becoming the most powerful figure in nation-wide gambling. Ragen had started out as a slugger in the newspaper wars and as an operative of his brother Mike's outfit, Ragen's Colts. The mob coveted Ragen's service and offered him a sell-out price but he was around long enough to know that he would never collect his pay-off. The Syndicate set up their own service, Trans-American Publishing, under Bugsy Siegel, forcibly taking over the California market. Ragen, however, maintained a tight rein on the rest of the country.

On June 24 1946 Ragen was blasted by a shotgun as he drove his car along State Street. Wounded in the arms and legs Ragen survived and was rushed to hospital, where he was put under 24-hour police guard. From his hospital bed Jim Ragen named his would-be killers. It was an unwise move. He died on August 15, supposedly of his wounds. However, his autopsy revealed he died of mercury poisoning. Three of the Chicago Outfit's top killers, Dave Yaras, Lenny Patrick and William Block were indicted for Ragen's murder. Charges were soon dropped after one witness was murdered, one fled and two others changed their stories. With the Continental Press Service under their control the Syndicate now dominated illegal gambling from coast to coast.

CHAPTER 14

THE BOSTON STORY

In 1845 the population of Boston was 114,366. In that same year over 12,000 Irish emigrants landed in Boston followed in 1846 by another 12,000. In 1847 another 37,000 Irish emigrants arrived, many of them in a poor and wretched condition. Geographically, at this period Boston was not suited to receive large numbers of immigrants. To leave the city for the suburbs, it was necessary to cross bridges and pay tolls of twenty cents a day, which in effect confined the poor immigrants within the city. The Irish flooded into Ward 8, Fort Hill and the North End. Overcrowding was on a huge scale. The gardens and grounds of fine old houses were covered with shacks; backyards and alleyways were built over; rooms were divided and sub-divided; cellars without light, air or drainage were packed out with occupants. Drinking, fighting and crime flourished.

A return from the Clerk of the Boston Police Court for 1848 demonstrates the effect the new emigrants, three-quarters of them Irish, had on the city. Capital offences had increased 266 per cent; attempts to kill 1,700 per cent; assaults on police 400 per cent; aggravated assault committed with knives, dirks, pistols, slingshots, razors, pokers, hot irons, clubs, iron weights, flat irons, bricks and stones, 465 percent.

The Irish in their Boston slums expressed their clannishness in street gangs, volunteer fire companies (the wooden shanties which housed the immigrants were notorious fire hazards), political clubs centred in grog shops and mob action against other ethnic competitors and nativist opponents. St. Patrick's Day, March 17, became a day to celebrate interclass solidarity, political strength and Irish achievement. Making inroads into American political life the Irish ward bosses employed street gangs to distribute literature, hang posters and canvas for votes. The gangs were also useful as repeaters and sluggers intimidating opposing voters with violence and thuggery. By the 1880s, despite nativist opposition, the Irish had gained a level of acceptance. The city's Democratic Party, the police force and the fire department were predominantly Irish. In 1885 the Massachusetts legislature stripped Boston's police force from city control when Hugh O'Brien became the city's first Irish Catholic mayor.

The Boston political machine grew to be one of the most powerful in the country and would pave the way for the election of America's first Irish Catholic President, John Fitzgerald Kennedy.

Gang violence first surfaced in Boston in the late 1820s as nativist gangs clashed with Irish immigrants. Nativists regularly invaded Irish sections of Boston looting shops and in 1834 burning down the Ursuline Convent in Charlestown. On June 11 1837 a company of firemen, returning from a call, clashed with an Irish funeral along Broad Street. The resulting fistfight, when neither side would give way, escalated into a full-scale riot involving some 10,000 people. Eight-hundred militia with fixed bayonets and headed by a mounted force of lancers eventually ended the Broad Street Riot. Trouble broke out again in Irish neighbourhoods during the Civil War in Boston's Draft Riots which resulted in the deaths of six people.

Rioting again marred the city during the Police Strike of 1919. With wage increases and working conditions lagging behind those of ordinary workers Boston's policemen had, in desperation, attempted to join the American Federation of Labour. Nineteen policemen were dismissed. On September 9 1919 the police force went on strike. Once word of the strike got around, groups of people gathered at police stations throughout the city. Some were sympathetic friends and relatives but most were there to vent their anger and resentment against policemen who no longer had the protection of their uniform. Near the corner of East 4th Street and K Street in South Boston over 1,000 people gathered in front of Station 12. Among them were the Gustin Gang, who came up from their hangouts on Lower Dorchester Street between 8th and 9th Streets. Deriving its name from its leaders, Steve and Frank Gustin, this gang was reputed to be the toughest street gang in Boston. As soon as the striking policemen appeared in the doorway of the station house and began walking down the flight of steps they were pelted with stones, bottles and rotten vegetables. It was the same at every station as the policemen had to run the gauntlet.

Later in the evening and into the night rampaging mobs indulged in vandalism, destruction and looting. At the height of the disturbances 10,000 people reportedly milled up and down Broadway. The trouble continued the next day and the National Guard were called out. Three youths were shot dead and ten injured in rioting in South Boston effectively ending the disturbances. The strike left a lasting bitterness among the Irish of Boston as all the striking policemen were laid off and a new force recruited. The Boston Yankees pointed to the police strike as evidence of Irish Catholics unstable nature and untrustworthy character and likened the strike and riots to the Draft Riots of 1863.

South Boston and its port was controlled by huge gangs of

undisciplined Irish thugs who constantly fought among themselves. They dominated Boston's organised crime until the
arrival in the 1880s of large scale Italian and Sicilian immigrants.
The Italians and Sicilians settled in Boston's West End and North
End and like most criminal groups were content to exploit their
own people. Prohibition changed that. Small time gangsters
were hurtled into the big time with the enormous profits from
peddling bootleg booze. When the Italians sought to expand
their influence outside their own ghettos they found the bootleg business in the hands of Irish and to a lesser extent Jewish
mobsters. The Gustin Gang had evolved from being just a street
gang to become one of the most powerful bootleg gangs in
the city.

Frank and Steve Gustin were two red-haired brothers from
South Boston who had quit their boxing careers to become full-
time bootleggers with the coming of Prohibition. Frank was the
brains of the gang and was arrested 25 times in his criminal
career. He was indicted for the *Detroit News* payroll robbery in
which one man was killed and two others wounded. He
claimed he was in South Boston at the time and had several
other boxers to back up his alibi. Eventually the charges were
dismissed. He was known for his apparent good nature when
arrested and his willingness to help the police. The Gustins had
several confrontations with their Italian rivals, the Buccola Mob.
In 1931 things came to a head when the Gustins hijacked a
quantity of Buccola owned liquor in Nantucket. The Italians
played the Gustins at their own game and informed the
Federal authorities where they could find the hijacked booze.
The Gustins were not pleased.

On December 22 1931 Frank Gustin, accompanied by
Barney Walsh and Tim Coffey, went to Joe Lombardi's offices at
C.F. Importers in the North End - Boston's answer to Little Italy.
They had been asked there to discuss a peace treaty. Waiting
for them was Buccola's partner Joe Lombardi and two of his

henchmen, Salvatore Congemi and Frank Cucchiara. As soon as the Irishmen walked in the Italians started shooting. Frank Gustin staggered down the corridor to the office of lawyer Julius H. Wolfson and fell into a chair, took a few last gasps of air and died. Barney Walsh ran up a staircase, turned around and was shot down. Tim Coffey also made it in to Wolfson's office. He was found cowering behind a screen. Coffey upheld the code of the underworld and refused to identify Lombardi, Congemi and Cucchiara as Gustin and Walsh's killers and the trio were released.

After this double killing the Gustin Gang were effectively broken as a serious rival to the Mafia. On January 24 1933 Charles "King" Solomon, Jewish ally of Phil Buccola, was shot dead at his Cotton Club in Boston by James "Skeets" Coyne. The murder was linked to Daniel Carroll, a South Boston mobster who was making a move to regain the Gustins' empire. In May 1933 another prominent member of the Gustins, Red Curran, who was also making threats against the Italians, was shot dead and his body dumped in 120 feet of water in a quarry at West Quincey. From then on the Irish grip on Boston began to wane and the Mafia became the dominant force in organised crime.

Crime and bootlegging, in particular, was one profession which allowed social and financial advancement from poverty. Joseph P. Kennedy was a young tavern owner from East Boston, the son of emigrants from County Wexford. To provide for his young family and to make a quick profit he became a bootlegger. Kennedy, later ambassador to Britain and father of a president and two senators, eventually controlled the importation of all whiskey from Haig and Haig in Scotland during Prohibition, however, he was lucky to survive the bootleg wars of the Roaring Twenties. In 1927 a convoy of whiskey, imported from Ireland, was hijacked outside Brockton, Mass., by Jewish hoods working for King Solomon. It was the biggest hijacking of a bootleg shipment during the Prohibition era. With the loss of the shipment Kennedy's operation was virtually destroyed. In an effort to recoup his losses he fell foul of Detroit's Purple Gang by running bootleg booze through their territory, without the Purples' consent. The Purple Gang put out a contract on Kennedy. Fearing for his life he turned to friends in the Chicago Outfit. The contract was rescinded through influence from Chicago's Diamond Joe Esposito and the Outfit's political fixer, the Welshman Murray Humphreys. With the repeal of Prohibition many bootleggers went legitimate. Joe Kennedy was one of them. He built an impressive fortune fuelled by legitimately imported Scotch whiskey and during WW2 became America's ambassador to Britain. Like many other bootleggers who went legit, he created a dynasty bankrolled in the early days by running illegal alcohol.

During the 1930s when the national Syndicate was emerging the criminal gangs of Boston realised there was more money to be made by co-operation rather than rivalry and though each grouping had their own territory they could combine operations whenever needed. This arrangement still stands to this day. Since Prohibition, apart from the Irish Gang War in the 1960s, there has never been a major falling out between the Mafia and the Irish Mob. Unlike many Mafia families the New England Office was quite prepared to forge alliances with non-Italians.

In May 1961 a gang war broke out between two of Boston's most powerful Irish mobs, Bernard McLaughlin's Charlestown mob and Buddy McLean's Winter Hill mob. Bernie McLaughlin was shot dead in October and the war escalated with gangsters from aligning gangs, Irish and Italian, taking sides. When the McLaughlins began shaking down Mafia operations to fund their war Raymond Patriarca, the Mafia boss of Boston, tried to broker a peace deal. It failed and Patriarca gave his men the go ahead to team up with the McLeans. Patriarca's ruthlessness was legend. He claimed all of New England as his territory. He had a working relationship with the Winter Hill Mob and was well connected to Boston's police and politicians. With the power of the Office behind the McLeans the outcome of the Irish War was inevitable; the McLaughlins were wiped out.

Throughout 1981 the FBI maintained a court approved bug at Jerry Anguilo's office in Boston's North End. Mob informer Vinnie Teresa claimed that the Office controlled 300 of Boston's 365 detectives and when some of their names were mentioned on the tapes 40 of them were transferred. Reminiscing about the Irish War Anguilo was taped boasting how he and his brothers "buried twenty Irishmen to take this town over, we can't begin to dig up half we got rid of. And, I'm not bragging either." However, Anguilo was doing just that. It was his predecessor, Raymond Patriarca, who had handled the killing. Anguilo would never have been strong enough to handle the McLaughlins and their allies, the fearsome Hughes brothers, Steve and Connie. Traditionally, the Mafia required that a made man had to commit at least one murder before he joined the Honoured Society. There were few exceptions. Anguilo was one. He bought his way into the Mafia by giving Patriarca a $50,000 pay-off. When Patriarca died Anguilo became boss, but his reign was short lived. Patriarca's son, Raymond Junior, took over and demoted Anguilo to a mere soldier.

After the Irish war the Office continued their working relationships with the Irish mobs. In 1976 an arms depot in Danvers, Mass., was broken into by a joint Irish-Italian mob operation. Security at the depot was lax and the hoods encountered no problems. The depot was cleared of its weapons - which included a large quantity of M16 rifles and seven M60s, the standard general purpose machine gun of the U.S. Army. The gang, believed to be members of the Winter Hill Mob and the Flemmi Mob, sold the weapons to an Irish Republican Army support unit. Howard T. Winter was at the time leader of the Winter Hill Mob, while Steve "The Rifleman" Flemmi, who served as a paratrooper in the Korean war, had his own gang of Mafia associates, who preferred the relative independence of working with the Irish mob rather than the more structured format of the Office. The Winter Hill Mob controls the docks and Local 25 of the International Brotherhood of Teamsters. All trucks that service the waterfront must pay protection money to the Winter Mob; stores, restaurants and other dockside business also pay protection money. Permission to operate a criminal enterprise in these territories comes from Winter, Flemmi and James Bulger. It is estimated, by law officials, that independent drug dealers pay a "street-tax" of 25 per cent to the Irish leaders to operate in their turf.

The M60 was a prestige weapon for the IRA (who wanted it to shoot down British Army helicopters) and contacts were kept up with Irish criminal gangs with regard to purchasing more of these weapons and surface to air missiles. Several fundraisers and supporters for the IRA were killed in suspicious circumstances – one, a security guard, was shot dead in a robbery in New York; another NORAID (Northern Irish Aid) fundraiser, who was also a union organiser, was shot dead in Philadelphia in 1976 and a Boston based fundraiser for NORAID was shot dead in a Mafia related dispute in 1977. Many Irish Republicans and their supporters believe that there are more sinister motives to these killings and point to the hidden hand of British and American intelligence who wanted to disrupt the arms pipeline. The truth, of course, may never be known.

In 1981 five associates of the Winter Hill mob were charged with transporting a shipload of arms to the IRA and on April 16 1986 seven indictments were handed down on six Massachusetts men and a former U.S. Marine who was an Irish citizen and was already serving 10 years in Ireland on a gun-running charge. Only one of the men indicted was in custody in the U.S. at the time. Another was reported to have been murdered by the IRA, or the Winter Hill Mob acting on their behalf, though his body was never found. The IRA suspected him of co-operating with the police. The weapons, a huge arms shipment seized by the authorities and destined for the IRA was said by the Alcohol, Tobacco and Firearms Agency to have either been stolen from military bases or purchased legally.

On August 22 1979 Howie Winter was jailed for 10 years for leading a multi-million dollar, five-state horse-race-fixing scam from 1973 to 1975. Informer Anthony Ciulla, a self-proclaimed master fixer, revealed that the scam involved owners, jockeys, Las Vegas bookmakers and Boston mobsters. Tickets would be bought for those horses whose jockeys had not been bribed. Ciulla would call Winter from the track and give him the names of the "live" horses. Winter would then call the Vegas bookmakers who would lay off the bets to independent bookmakers who were the ultimate losers. Even when these independents learned the races were fixed they still paid up such was the fear Winter and his associates dispelled. Winter and five associates, mobster James Martorano, Las Vegas casino executives Elliot Price and Melvin Goldenberg, and North Reading horse owners Charles and James Demetri were jailed while Ciulla was given immunity and entered the Witness Protection Program.

With Howie Winter in jail leadership of the Winter Hill Mob passed to James Bulger, brother of Senate President William Bulger. James J. "Whitey" Bulger was born in South Boston in 1929 and served 10 years for armed robbery in the late 1950s. Bulger joined the Winter Hill Mob in 1965 when he was released from prison. His older brother William had risen to the powerful and prestigious post of President of the Massachusetts Senate. William Bulger served in the Massachusetts House of Representatives from 1961 to 1970 and advanced a variety of social and environmental issues, including parole reform and child protection laws. He was a prominent opponent of court-enforced bussing and a defender of the residents of South Boston.

On January 4 1980 Salvatore Sperlinga, the right-hand man

of Howard Winter, was shot dead in a private club at Somerville's Magoun Square. Fifty-two year old Sperlinga was out on bail awaiting appeal of an extortion conviction when he was slain. Daniel Moran, of Somerville, was identified as the killer and was quickly arrested. On October 11 Moran was found guilty of the murder of Sperlinga and sentenced to life imprisonment. Police speculated that the killing was a matter of pride and personal insult rather than a power struggle within the Winter Hill Mob.

Consolidating his position as boss James Bulger continued the working relationship with the Flemmi Mob and other Mafia criminals, surviving until the 1990s because he was doubling as a top FBI informant for over twenty years. As early as 1980 Bulger was called to boot by the FBI to see whether he would be retained as an informant. In November 1980 top agents from the Boston FBI office summoned Bulger to a secret meeting at the Hilton Hotel at Logan Airport to decide whether he could continue his moonlighting job or would be cut loose because he had become more trouble than he was worth. Bulger had learned that a police state bug had been placed in the garage he was using as headquarters and then never uttered another word there. Obviously, Bulger convinced the FBI that he was still of use to them as an informant and he would clean up his act. However, he was regarded as a master in the evasion of electronic surveillance as he learned that the FBI had planted a bug in his car leaving agents no choice but to retrieve it in 1984. Three years later he was still going strong and fled from a surveillance checkpoint at Logan Airport after security guards spotted $100,000 in his baggage.

In 1990 fifty-one people were arrested as being part of a South Boston-based narcotics ring. All those arrested pleaded guilty and two turned state's evidence. Eddie McKenzie, a kickboxer who ran Connolly's Corner Cafe, was first to spill the beans, revealing the Boston links to a Los Angeles based drugs gang, while his boss Timothy Connolly revealed he had been making regular payments to a Bulger associate and when he fell behind was threatened and fined $50,000. However Bulger's troubles seemed to be over the following year when he won $14 million on the Mass Millions lottery. Now he had a legitimate income and with the help of a European Union passport - thanks to an Irish grandparent - he began to travel extensively. The US Attorney's office claimed the lottery win was a scam and that Bulger had offered the real winner $2 million to name him and two others as joint winners. In 1995 the FBI seized Bulger's annual cheque saying it was money involved in a money-laundering conspiracy. Bulger kept one step ahead of the authorities, something he had perfected while doubling as an FBI agent.

An avid reader with an interest in history, Bulger has been seen frequenting libraries and historic sites while travelling extensively to Canada, Ireland and Italy. He is known to have a violent temper and possesses a knife at all times. He maintaines his physical fitness by working out at health clubs and walking.

In 1998 he was tried, in absence, along with Steve Flemmi and Frank Salemme, now leader of the New England Mafia. It was revealed in the trial that Bulger as head of the Irish Mob in the 1980s was the equal of Mafia boss Jerry Anguilo. He is still on the FBI Ten Most Wanted List with a reward of $250,000 for information leading directly to his arrest. If he ever turns up, his trial will be an embarrassing one for the authorities as it is thought his defence will be the same as that used by Jackie Presser, Teamsters leader and FBI informant, that his illegal activities were sanctioned by the FBI.

CHAPTER 15

STATE OF GRACE

Philadelphia.

Philadelphia was home to dozens of Irish gangs during the latter half of the 19th century, the Killers and the Bloody Tubs being the biggest and most influential. Irish immigrants to the City of Brotherly Love settled heavily in South Philadelphia. By the mid 1840s the Irish were the most solid voting bloc (except for the free Negroes, who cast their votes in the opposite direction from the Irish) and it was widely believed that the Irish vote provided James K. Polk's margin of victory in 1844 sparking off battles between nativists - mainly Ulster Presbyterians - and Irish immigrants. The militia were called in to separate the two factions and in a three way battle 16 people were killed, scores injured and dozens of buildings, including two churches, were burnt down. Race riots were also quite common in Philadelphia, the first being the Flying Horse Riot of 1834. Most of the rioters were poor and working-class with many Irish in their ranks. Irish gangs figured prominently in these riots and in driving blacks from the waterfront and labour marketplace. In 1842 a riot was provoked by a black temperance parade on the anniversary of the emancipation of slaves in the

British West Indies. The combination of temperance - in a suburb that boasted 450 liquor dealers, most of them Irish - and praise for Britain, was too much for the local Irish who attacked the black parade.

Like their counterparts in New York and Chicago the Irish gangs worked as sluggers for the Democrats during elections and as muscle in labour disputes. South Philadelphia boasted many gangs: the Bouncers, Rats, Buffers, Bleeders, Pluckers, Deathfetchers, Bloody Tubs and Killers. The Bloody Tubs, sometimes known as the Blood Tubs, were an offshoot of Baltimore's Bloody Tubs while the Killers, who were originally nativist, were the biggest and most violent of Philadelphia gangs. The most prominent Irish gangster-politician in Philadelphia was William McMullen. Born in the suburb of Moyamensing in 1824 of Irish immigrant parents McMullen worked in his father's grocery store before joining the U.S. Navy. When he returned to Philadelphia he joined the Moyamensing Hose and its allied street gang, the Killers. (Fire companies were allied with, and in some cases were indistinguishable from, one or another street gang.) McMullen was known as "Bull" and was prominent in the Nativist Riots of 1844 where he shot dead a nativist and stood guard outside Catholic churches. He was invaluable to the Democratic Party who employed him and his gang to keep opposition voters away from the polls. In 1846 McMullen was convicted of stabbing one policeman and injuring another. He joined the army when the Mexican War broke out to keep out of jail and on his return to Philadelphia he resumed his activities with the Moyamensing Hose and the Killers.

In 1850 Bull McMullen was elected president of the Democratic Party Keystone Club. His support was instrumental in the 1856 election and in return six members of the Moyamensing Hose Company were named police officers. McMullen was rewarded with an appointment to the Board of

Inspectors to Moyamensing Prison where he immediately secured the release of many of his friends and followers who had been jailed for various offences. The following year McMullen became known as "The Squire" when he was elected alderman. When the Civil War broke out McMullen, along with 84 members of the Moyamensing Hose joined the Union Army. After his three month tour was over he returned to city politics and remained a political force in Philadelphia until his death in 1901 in spite of many scandals, brawls and two attempts on his life. McMullen was expelled several times from the Democrats after forming alliances with Republican candidates - who were every bit as corrupt as their opponents - but always managed to preserve his political base in the Fourth Ward. Despite his unsavoury background McMullen got what counted the most - votes for the Democrats and jobs and services for his constituents. Unlike the other major cities, which had corrupt Democratic boss rule, Philadelphia was controlled for decades by corrupt Republican boss rule, until it was ousted by Democratic reformers in 1950. The reason why, was the ability of the Republicans to work out a satisfactory arrangement with the Irish after the white-supremacist riot of 1871.

By 1920 the big Irish street gangs were a thing of the past and organised crime in Philadelphia was dominated by Jewish mobsters like Max "Boo-Boo" Hoff and Harry Stromberg. Their major Irish rivals were William and Mickey Duffy, two brothers from South Philadelphia. William Duffy was killed on February 25 1927 in Philadelphia's first machine gun murder by the Boo-Boo Hoff gang while Mickey Duffy was shot dead in Atlantic City by Frankie Carbo, a New York hitman. With the repeal of Prohibition the Jewish elements began to lose their grip and by the mid-1940s the Mafia stepped in extending their influence to Atlantic City and New Jersey. Angelo Bruno emerged as boss of the Philadelphia Family and had little tolerance for drugs and violence. In his 22 years as boss murder was uncommon and he exiled his most violent subordinate, Nicky Scarfo, to Atlantic City after he killed an Irish longshoreman, Willie Duggan, in an argument over who was in turn to sit at a restaurant table. In Atlantic City, Scarfo bided his time and plotted the take-over of the Philadelphia Mafia.

During the 1950s and 1960s Atlantic City had been in decline, but the 1976 Casino Referendum changed that. The construction industry and Local 54, the union of restaurant workers, bartenders and hotel workers, had been penetrated by the Mafia under Scarfo. By late 1977 casino construction was under way in earnest. A construction boom hit South Jersey and as hotels and condominiums flew up the mob with control of construction was making a fortune. On the evening of March 21 1980 Angelo Bruno, "The Gentle Don", was returning home after dining at a South Philadelphia restaurant. He stopped briefly to buy a newspaper, then had his driver bodyguard pull up in front of his narrow row house on Synder Street. Before he could get out of the car a man, alleged to be New York hitman Joe "Mad Dog" Sullivan, walked up to the open window and shot Bruno once behind the ear, killing him instantly. The hitman then shot Bruno's bodyguard wounding him. Frank "Funzi" Tieri, boss of the Genovese Family, had ordered the hit. It was followed by the deaths of Bruno's *consigliere* and two capos - allegedly part of the conspiracy to kill Bruno, but rather a power ploy by the New Yorkers and Phil Testa, who became boss with the blessing of the New York families, who wanted to control the lucrative Atlantic City rackets.

By 1980 casino construction was winding down, which meant the lucrative construction contracts were gone. Exiled mobster Nicky Scarfo had to deepen his penetration of the casinos in order to retain his control. However his influence over the service unions was being challenged by Atlantic City union figure Big John McCullough, head of the Roofers Union. McCullough was organising independent locals among bar and restaurant workers and security guards. Scarfo had asked Bruno to intercede and force McCullough out, but the old boss had refused. Now with Bruno gone Scarfo appealed to Phil Testa, who invited McCullough to a meeting. McCullough met Testa but did not appear for a second meeting. Angry at the rebuff Testa gave Scarfo free rein to handle the matter his own way. Several days before Christmas 1980 McCullough was shot dead by Williard Moran, posing as a flower delivery man. Three months later, Phil Testa returned to his house in South Philadelphia and as he reached for the knob of the screen door a remote-controlled bomb exploded, destroying the front of the house and shattering windows for blocks around. Bits of Testa's body was scattered around the street. His flesh and debris from the house were riddled with thousands of finishing nails. It was not a typical mob hit and police theorised that the Roofers Union had rigged the bomb in retaliation for McCullough's murder.

St. Louis.

St. Louis as a port of entry for newly arrived emigrants was a rough and boisterous city with a polyglot collection of criminal gangs, mainly centred around the waterfront. One of the most prominent gangs was Egan's Rats founded in East St. Louis around the turn of the century by gangster-politician Jack "Jellyroll" Egan, a big lumbering thug, who used his gang as muscle for businessmen trying to prevent unionisation. The Rats specialised as labour sluggers in the city's union wars but by WW1 this racket had virtually ceased. Had it not been for Prohibition the Rats would have faded away. Prohibition gave the Rats and other criminal gangs a new lease of life. Originally Irish, the Rats adapted to the changing times and by 1920 its membership had become a melting-pot of Irish, Jews and Italians. Jack Egan was particularly fond of one of these new-comers, Maxwell "Big Maxey" Greenberg. He thought so much of Big Maxey that through the St. Louis Democratic machine he persuaded President Woodrow Wilson to pardon Greenberg after he served two years of a 10 year sentence for larceny.

In 1920 Greenberg left St. Louis and went to New York, learn-ing the bootlegging trade from none other than Arnold Rothstein. In 1925 Greenberg fell out with his one time mentor. Egan paid Greenberg to transport 4,000 cases of whiskey up the Mississippi River, but the consignment never reached its des-tination. Greenberg claimed it was hi-jacked, while Egan accused him of being the hijacker. War broke out between the two friends and Egan wound up murdered. Greenberg, fearing for his life, fled St. Louis. William "Dinty" Colbeck took over the gang but went down shortly after for mail robbery. Throughout the early 1920s the Rats fought with the emerging bootleg gangs to corner the market in St. Louis and it was said that the Chief of Police held a conference in the Rats hangout and told them if they did not declare a truce with the Hogan Gang he was going to call out the militia. A truce was declared but did not last too long.

During Prohibition there were five major gangs in the city; Egan's Rats; the Hogan Gang; the Syrian Cuckoo Gang and two Mafia groups, the Green Dagos and the Young Turks. The Rats were the most important and hired out their members to other mobs looking for out of town talent. There is considerable speculation that the Rats supplied the gunmen for the St. Valentine's Day Massacre. Dinty Colbeck had considerable political protection from the city's politicians and worked closely with Al Capone in running booze into Chicago. When Capone needed out of town talent he sent for the Rats as trig-germen. Fred "Killer" Burke got his start with the Rats and was recruited by Capone to help wipe out Bugs Moran and his North Side Irish mob. Though never formally charged with the murder of seven of Moran's men in the St. Valentine's Day Massacre, all the evidence points in his direction. A tommy gun found in his home when police were searching for Burke provided bullets that were identical to the ones extracted from the bodies of the seven slain Moran hoods. Police believed that the machine gun was also used in the 1928 murder of Frankie Yale, president of the *Unione Siciliana,* killed on Capone's orders in Brooklyn, after hijacking Outfit booze trucks en route to Chicago. Between 1924 and 1931 Burke was accused of at least a dozen murders, including that of a patrolman killed after a routine traffic accident.

Arrested in March 1931 both Chicago and Michigan State applied for his extradition. Burke elected to go to Michigan, where he was sentenced to life for the murder of Patrolman Charles Skelly. Killer Burke died in prison in 1940 of a heart attack, never revealing whether he had participated in gangland's most infamous killing.

The Rats also provided the gunman in another infamous Chicago killing, the murder of Jake Lingle, star crime reporter for the *Chicago Tribune.* As a $65 a week newsman Lingle had a sterling reputation with his editors, yet in reality he led a double life working for Al Capone, funnelling information on impending police raids and the activities of Capone's rivals. Lingle was so confident of his importance, he was protected by Al Capone on one side and Police Commissioner William P. Russell, a boyhood friend, on the other, that he boasted that he was the real power behind Capone saying, "I fix the price of beer in this town!" To recoup his losses at gambling - he was a hopeless gambler and by 1930 he was supposed to be in debt to the tune of $100,000 to various gamblers - he began supplying the same information to Bugs Moran that he was passing to

Capone along with demanding large kickbacks from Capone for influencing his police contacts to allow Capone's speakeasies, brothels and gambling dens operate without grief. Capone decided Lingle had outlived his usefulness and sent to St. Louis for and out of town specialist that Lingle, who knew every gunman in Chicago, would never recognise.

Leo Vincent Brothers was born in St. Louis in 1909 and went to work for Egan's Rats as a gunman, bomber and labour terrorist. He was an expert assassin and was hired out to gangs as far away as New York, where he performed several murders of leading Mafia figures in the 1930-31 Castellammarese War. Brothers was an expert at disguise and in the murder of Lingle he dressed as a priest. Jake Lingle was shot dead on June 9 1930 as he walked towards the train station that would bring him to Washington Park racetrack in Homewood.

A suspicious priest was seen nearby and there were at least two other suspicious characters in the vicinity of the killing. A $50,000 reward was posted for the capture of Lingle's killer. Brothers was finally unearthed when a private detective, ex-con John Hagen, went underground and actually joined the Moran gang and Egan's Rats to find the killer. Brothers was convicted of first-degree murder but was only sentenced to 14 years. The press claimed the jury was bribed, but there was no evidence of this and the sentence was upheld. Brothers was released after serving 8 years and went back to the St. Louis rackets, which by now had undergone considerable change.

With the repeal of Prohibition the Rats lost their influence to the unified Mafia gangs. The last of the Rats moved into other criminal enterprises which within a few years were swallowed up by the emerging Syndicate. Dinty Colbeck was paroled in 1941 but was killed two years later for trying to muscle in on Mafia gambling rackets. The Hogans and Cuckoos were also victims of the emerging Syndicate who became the dominant force in the city. After WW2 the Kansas City Mafia took control of St. Louis.

San Francisco.

When gold was discovered in California in 1848 the West Coast of America incurred a massive influx of immigrants. San Francisco was the main port of entry and within a year more than half the population were foreign born. The majority of the new immigrants were Irish and they settled heavily on Telegraph Hill and the North Beach area. The notorious Barbary Coast was spawned in the Gold Rush to cater to the lusts of a huge city of males drained of hope and with no passage home. The main thoroughfare was Pacific Street, a string of saloons, grog shops, gambling dens, dance halls and brothels, stretching some half-a-dozen blocks west from the waterfront. Rough sections of the Barbary Coast acquired names like Murderers Corner, Battle Row, Bull Run, Devil's Acre and Dead Man's Alley, while murder and violence were commonplace in grog shops with names like the Morgue and Devil's Kitchen.

Prostitution (there were ten men to every one woman), violence and drunkenness were commonplace and the Coast was a sanctuary for gangs of hoodlums - a word said to have been coined there - who terrorised Chinatown and other non-white areas. The two main gangs were the Sydney Ducks, an Australian gang of ex-cons, many of them of Irish extraction, and the Hounds, a gang from New York. These gangs robbed, extorted, looted and terrorised other foreign communities like the Chinese, Mexicans and Chileans. The law was slow to react but the citizens were not. As a warning several of the Hounds were expelled from the city limits. The next time there was no warning, several Hounds were lynched. The citizens of San Francisco regularly made torchlight processions into the Barbary Coast and lynched criminals who had escaped the law. In 1856 James Casey, a city councilman of dubious character, shot dead the editor of the *Evening Bulletin* after he had printed an article charging Casey of corruption. Casey met the same fate as ordinary criminals. he was lynched along with a cohort, a gambler named Charles Cora.

James P. Casey, a former inmate of Sing Sing, became a county supervisor in San Francisco; a reward for having imported the ingeniously false ballot box. The mechanical genius of eastern politicians had made its way west in the form of a ballot box with false sides and bottom, prestuffed with conveniently marked ballots. In one election in San Mateo the political machine achieved the miracle of counting 1,900 marked ballots in a community of 500 citizens. When James King, editor of the *Evening Bulletin,* printed the fact that Casey had served a sentence in Sing Sing, Casey ambushed him and shot him dead as he left his office. Casey rushed to the police station which was controlled by his friends but it did not save him. The citizens of San Francisco were outraged. A huge crowd of vigilantes marched to the police station, seized Casey and Charles Cora, who had recently got off a murder charge on the grounds of self defence, and lynched both of them.

The Irish in San Francisco made their first inroads into acceptance through politics and hard work. The Democratic Party as usual was the Irish choice and it was not long before city politics was dominated by the Irish Democratic machine. Christopher Buckley controlled City Hall from his Den of Thieves saloon over on the Barbary Coast. However, there were prices to pay for acceptance and the Coast's days were numbered. Reformers were pushing for a clean up and it was not long before the people who had come from the Barbary Coast were leading the campaign to close down the vice and gambling dens. By the 1880s the Barbary Coast was in sharp decline.

During Prohibition the West Coast suffered much the same

lawlessness as the rest of the country. There were gangland shootings and killings though not on the scale of Chicago, New York and other eastern cities. San Francisco and Los Angeles endured the same corruption and vice as other big American cities but it never seemed to be as efficient as the east. When Bugsy Siegel arrived from the east to develop Syndicate rackets in Southern California he found little organisation and virtually no opposition. Siegel met movie moguls Jack Warner, Harry Cohn and Louis B. Meyer and extorted millions from them with threats to close theatres nation-wide by calling their mob controlled projectionist unions to strike unless payoffs were met. In Hollywood Siegel met an old friend from the West Side of New York, a local boy made good, George Raft, a rising star in gangster movies. Raft had once worked for Owney Madden as a driver of bootleg beer trucks and as a hanger-on in his outfit before heading west to make his fortune.

When Bugsy Siegel was murdered in 1947 his empire fell to Frankie Carbo, Jack Dragna and Mickey Cohen. The diminutive Cohen was a brash and loud-mouthed gangster who fell foul of practically every mobster on the West Coast. Carbo, Dragna and Irish mobster Jack Whalen marked Cohen for dead. His home was bombed twice and there were several attempts on his life. In 1959 Cohen, who boasted he liked to do his own killing, shot dead Whalen. Within months he was jailed for income tax evasion. With Cohen out of the way the Mafia forces consolidated their hold on the West Coast.

CHAPTER 16

PUBLIC ENEMIES
IRISH GANGSTERS IN THE MOVIES

Jimmy Burke and Henry Hill were two Irish hoods portrayed in the hit Academy Award winning movie *Goodfellas*, by top Hollywood stars Robert DeNiro and Ray Liotta. Henry Hill, born of an Irish father and a Sicilian mother, was a Mafia runner from his early teens. Hill's greatest ambition, from the time he was twelve, was to be a "wiseguy" a made Mafia man. But he and Jimmy Burke could never be - they had Irish blood and while they worked hand in glove with the Mafia they would never be "goodfellas". Jimmy "The Gent" Burke was one of New York's top hijackers. He loved stealing and named his two sons, Jesse James Burke and Frank James Burke after the Wild West bankrobbers. Burke masterminded the 1978 Lufthansa terminal hi-jack at Kennedy airport which netted his gang $8 million. Relations between the gang soured when the police found the getaway truck and retrieved finger prints off the spare wheel. The wheelman was the first to go. Burke began cutting every link between him and the robbery and began a purge of his accomplices. Months after the robbery bodies were still turning up. All told 14 men died in the aftermath of the hijack.

Burke, Henry Hill and Tommy DeSimone (portrayed by Joe Pesci in the movie) hung around together and occasionally worked for Paulie Vario, a Lucchese Family captain. The Vario crew handled most of the strong-arm work for the Lucchese crime family. The three hoods were elated when Tommy DeSimone got word that he was to be "made". It was as good as the three of them becoming wiseguys - fully fledged members of the Honoured Society. DeSimone got dressed up for the occasion and went off in a car with some of the boys, who promply murdered him. DeSimone was knocked off by the Gambinos for murdering one of their made men, an act that could not be forgiven. Burke and Hill were lucky not to have met the same fate for their part in the killing.

After long surveillance Henry Hill was arrested in 1980 on a serious drug charge. Facing a long prison sentence Hill turned state's evidence. As a result of his testimony Jimmy Burke, Paulie Vario and several other mobsters were arrested and received lengthy convictions. Burke was given 20 years for the murder of a drug dealer who owed him $250,000. Though never formally charged with the Lufthansa heist, Burke was widely identified in published reports as the mastermind of the robbery. He died in prison in 1996. Hill was put in the Witness Protection Programme and given a new identity. While living a new life Hill resorted back to his old ways. He was arrested for narcotics possession but was lucky not to be jailed. Fortunately, for him the authorities released him on a suspended sentence.

The portrayal of gangsters in the movies is as old as Hollywood itself. In the 1930s three noteworthy crime movies were released based on Chicago's warring gangs. They were *Public Enemy, Little Caesar* and *Scarface.*

Public Enemy was produced in 1931 and starred James Cagney, himself a product of an Irish slum, as Tom Powers, an Irish gang boss. It was based on the exploits of the North Side

O'Bannion mob. In 1923 when O'Bannion stalwart Nails Morton was thrown by his horse while out horse-riding and kicked to death his friends and fellow gang members, Two-Gun Alterie, Bugs Moran, Hymie Weiss and Schemer Drucci hired out the same horse and shot it dead. This scene was re-enacted in *Public Enemy*, in which Cagney shot dead a horse which had kicked to death his fellow gangster Nails Nathan. *Public Enemy* made James Cagney a star. As the wisecracking, cocky Tom Powers Cagney created a tough guy image that real gangsters tried to imitate. Jean Harlow - who had an affair with New Jersey crime lord Longy Zwillman - played gangster moll Gwen Allen. A major theme of the movie was the tension between bootlegger Tom and his law-abiding brother Mike (Donald Cook). The movie ends with the delivery of Tom's dead body to the family home - the consequence of his anti-social behaviour and a message that crime does not pay. The establishment of early Hollywood tried to squeeze out the ethnically distinct elements of early cinema and by the time of the release of *Public Enemy* the Irishness was only coded at the level of accent, gesture and context. There was no overt reference to Irishness in it. Only those viewers with an Irish background would recognise the trace. Crime was one profession which allowed Irish immigrants rapid social and financial advancement from poverty. This fact was not tackled by *Public Enemy* or any of the movies that followed it.

Little Caesar was released six months before *Public Enemy* and was based on the exploits of Chicago's Cardinalli Mob, with Edward G. Robinson playing the part of the Little Caesar.

In early 1924 Chicago's Democratic Party threw a banquet for North Side mobster Dion O'Bannion for "services rendered". O'Bannion sat at the head of a great table flanked by his top labour racketeers and killers; Hymie Weiss, Bugs Moran, Two-Gun Alterie, Con Shea, Frank Gusenberg and Maxie Eisen. Dozens of local politicians and public figures also attended. The guest of honour, O'Bannion was given a $1,500 platinum watch for his electioneering contributions. The best of food and drink was on hand for the many guests. this was during Prohibition yet there was no shortage of alcohol, all provided by O'Bannion. The evening was topped off by a gun wielding display from Two-Gun Alterie, O'Bannion's flaky Colorado born sidekick.

Alterie had noticed a waiter passing a plate for tips, a custom at the hotel. Alterie pulled out his famed two revolvers and pointed them at the terrified waiter. "Hey, you!" he shouted. "None of that racket stuff goes here!" As the startled dignitaries looked on, Alterie turned to O'Bannion and asked sincerely, "Should I kill him, boss?"

O'Bannion tilted his chair back against the wall. Laughing loudly he pondered Alterie's question and then said, "Naw, let the bird suffer a little and then send him on his way."

The outraged press and clergy dubbed this notorious banquet "The Balshazzar Feast", while Hollywood was impressed enough to depict it in *Little Caesar*.

While the public flocked to see *Public Enemy* and *Little Caesar* it was the 1932 movie *Scarface* that made the greatest impact on the cinema-going public. It was based on Chicago crime lord, Al Capone, and that was what gave the movie its notoriety. Paul Muni played Tony Camonte, who had come to Chicago in 1920 from Five Points in New York to work for crime boss Johnny Lovo. Camonte took over Lovo's organisation and fought a gang war with his North Side rival O'Hara. The scar Camonte had was an X on his cheek, which he claimed he got in WW1 - something Capone also did. Capone could see the similarities and sent some of his boys around to have a chat with the writer of the screenplay, Ben Hecht, who had worked in Chicago as a reporter in the early 1920s.

"Is this stuff about Al Capone?" one hood asked Hecht, producing a copy of the script.

"God, no. I don't even know Al Capone." Hecht assured them. He explained that he knew Dion O'Bannion, Hymie Weiss, Bugs Moran and Big Jim Colosimo in his early reporting days.

"Then why 'Scarface'. Everybody will think it's him", the hood said.

"That's the reason," Hecht said. "Al Capone is one of the most fascinating men of our time. If we call the movie 'Scarface', everybody will want to see it, figuring its about Al. That's part of the racket we call showmanship."

This the Capone hoods could understand. Assured, they left. The city of Chicago was not so easily placated and they banned the movie until the end of the decade.

Throughout the 1930s and 1940s Hollywood produced dozens of gangster movies. Many of the gangsters portrayed had Irish sounding names, a fact that did not seem to bother Irish immigrants. James Cagney had become the gangster's gangster. Cagney was born in New York, the son of an Irish saloon keeper. Some of his friends and neighbours ended up hoods and criminals. Cagney could have ended up like them but went to Hollywood and played out the part on the silver screen, immortalising some of his characters like Rocky Sullivan and Cody Jarret.

In *Angels With Dirty Faces* (1938) Rocky Sullivan returns to his New York roots and meets up with his childhood sweetheart Laury (Ann Sheridan) and his old friend Father Jerry Connolly. (Pat O'Brien) Rocky befriends a group of street kids (shortly to be known as The Dead End Kids in their own series of movies) and tries unsuccessfully to take over the rackets. Captured after a shoot out with police Rocky is unrepentant. Fr. Connolly convinces Rocky to turn "yellow" and die begging and crying in the electric chair so as to appear a coward and deflate his image in the eyes of the street kids who adore Rocky's defiance and cockiness. Hollywood loved this type of story, a film with a social message.

In real life the hoods loved Cagney, many of them imitating his aggression, vitality and fast-talking bully-boy tactics. Trigger Burke, a West Side killer, tried in every way to mimic his idol. He would stand at a bar, knocking back shots of whiskey, wrinkling his face and shrugging his shoulders. Woe betide anyone who thought it was funny. Burke was unpredictable and deadly dangerous. It was believed he killed over 100 people before he was sent to Sing Sing's electric chair. Unlike Rocky Sullivan he did not go crying and screaming but swaggering and unrepentant. Westies leader Jimmy Coonan was another big fan of Cagney and constantly mimicked his idol.

In 1952 Malcolm Johnson, writing in the *New York Sun,* revealed the wholesale corruption and racketeering on New York's waterfront. A campaign of reform was begun by the cities of New York and New Jersey - which owned many of the large piers - and by many of the longshoremen themselves, tired of being at the mercy of the racketeers. Leading the reformist longshoremen was Father John Corridan, "The Waterfront Priest". Two years later, Hollywood produced their version of the story. *On The Waterfront* vividly portrayed the "shape-up" and corruption and racketeering on New York's docks. The award winning film directed by Elia Kazan depicted the degradation of the shape-up and the intimidation and violence of life on the waterfront. Marlon Brando played Terry Malloy ("I coulda been a contender") brother of Charlie "The Gent" (Rod Steiger), right-hand man of hiring boss Michael T. Skelly a.k.a. Johnny Friendly (Lee J. Cobb) who doles out jobs and money at his waterfront bar.

Terry Malloy, boxer turned thug, lures his friend to death for local mobsters. He falls for the dead man's sister and is befriended by Father Barry (Karl Malden) who sees the corruption on the docks and tries to do something about it. Terry Malloy joins Fr. Barry's campaign and when he is subpoenaed to appear before the Waterfront Commission he testifies against Johnny Friendly. *On The Waterfront* stands as one of the most realistic early Hollywood films on organised crime.

There were several movies about real life Irish gangsters, including *The Rise and Fall of Legs Diamond* (1960) and the 1984 Francis Ford Coppola movie *The Cotton Club,* which had Vincent Coll and Owney Madden as a major theme. Richard Gere played the lead character, Michael "Dixie" Dwyer, a trumpet player who becomes a movie star. It is a colourful tale set in Harlem's famous Cotton Club in the 1930s. The Cotton Club was owned by Owney Madden and Big Frenchy DeMange. It was a mecca for struggling black entertainers, including Duke Ellington and Cab Calloway. In a club where all the entertainers were black, no blacks were allowed socialise there. The gangsters of the era were the main stars and the wealthy and famous like James Cagney, Charlie Chaplin and Gloria Swanson rubbed shoulders with the infamous like Lucky Luciano and Dutch Schultz.

In *The Cotton Club* Dixie Dwyer saves Dutch Schultz' life and the Dutchman gives him a job escorting his mistress about town. Owney Madden (played by English actor Bob Hoskins) arranges a truce between Schultz and the Flynn brothers but Schultz stabs Joe Flynn after the Irish gangster makes a racist remark. Dixie decides to get away from the mad mobster (Dutch Schultz has appeared in several movies and his character is always the most unsavoury) while his younger brother, Vince (Nicholas Cage), goes to work as a gunman for the Dutchman. While Dixie heads to Hollywood, with Owney Madden's backing, Vince helps Schultz take over the Harlem numbers rackets. He asks for a cut but the notoriously mean Schultz says no and the pair fall out. A gang war between Vince

Dwyer and his young cohorts erupts and in an ensuing gunbattle Vince earns the nickname "Mad Dog" after a youngster is killed in the crossfire. Vince, strapped for cash, kidnaps Frenchy DeMange (Fred Gwynne) and eventually meets his end in a telephone booth, while he is talking to Madden.

In the 1970s and 1980s the American gangster was redefined by the *Godfather* movies and in the process positioned the Italian gangster at the centre of the genre. In the 1990s three films *State of Grace*, *Goodfellas* and *Miller's Crossing* broke the mould by positioning Irish gangsters at the centre of the action.

In State of Grace (1990), based on the real life Westies, Terry Noonan (Sean Penn) returns to New York's Hell's Kitchen after been away for a number of years. He meets an old friend Jackie Flannery (Gary Oldman) brother of the Kitchen's most powerful mobster Frankie Flannery (Ed Harris). The psychotic Jackie tells Terry that the traditional Irish neighbourhood has been redeveloped for "yuppies" and "renamed Clinton. It sounds like a fuckin' steamboat." The gang does not know that Terry is a cop who has been sent to sabotage an alliance being negotiated between the Flannerys and the Barelli Family. Noonan is led deep into a dark underworld of deceit, corruption, betrayal and murder. His old flame Kathleen Flannery (Robin Wright) complicates things further. Racked by guilt Noonan begs to be taken off the case. ("These guys don't even know what century it is.") When Frankie kills his brother Jackie to appease the Barellis, Noonan exacts revenge in a bar room shoot-out on St. Patrick's Day.

The Flannery-Barelli alliance was based on the real life alliance between Jimmy Coonan's Irish Mob and the Castellano crime family, the most powerful mob in the country. As depicted in the movie Jimmy Coonan and Mickey Featherstone went to Brooklyn to meet Paul Castellano. The Mafia boss had called "the Irish kids" to a meeting. Coonan told the rest of the Westies that if he and Featherstone did not call back in two hours they were to come in shooting. Back in Hell's Kitchen the rescue team, led by Jackie Coonan, were pacing back and forth. "We'll give them another five minutes," Jackie said several times. These five minutes stretched into a half-an-hour until finally Mickey Featherstone rang. "Where the fuck were you?" he shouted. "We coulda been dead." Later it was a source of great amusement but it only revealed the unorganised state of the Irish Mob.

Miller's Crossing was written by brothers Joel and Ethan Coen with Jewish gangsters in mind. However, Gabriel Byrne convinced the producers to change the main character to an Irish mobster. The movie is set during the Roaring Twenties in an eastern city run by Leo (Albert Finney). The power behind Leo is Tom Reagan (Gabriel Byrne). Their friendship is severed when they both fall in love with the same girl (Marcia Gay Harden) and a bloody gang war erupts. The most memorable scene in the movie is when rival gangsters try to kill Leo who turns the tables on them. To the strains of Frank Patterson singing *'Danny Boy'*, Leo slaughters his would-be assassins with a tommy gun. Tom ends up switching sides working for Johnny Casper, Leo's Mafia rival, and eventually ends up on top of the pile. Achieving cult status *Miller's Crossing* portrays the time as it was - gangsters, molls, corrupt cops and crooked politicians.

CHAPTER 17

WEST SIDE STORY

There is a dark side to Manhattan known for its crime, hard drinking and brawling. It is an area on the Lower West Side, known as Hell's Kitchen, a descriptive name for one of New York's poorest and most violent areas. Impoverished Irish immigrants settled here, followed by Greeks, Italians and Hispanics. By the turn of the century the tenements were the most overcrowded in the Western world and disease and infant mortality were rife. The Kitchen was a breeding ground for crime and dozens of gangs roamed the streets fighting and killing to control the rackets and dominate the Hudson River waterfront. In the 1970s Hell's Kitchen was renamed Clinton in a bid to shake off the neighbourhoods bloody and unsavoury past and became home to yuppies and warehouse apartment blocks.

The first gang of importance in Hell's Kitchen were the Gophers, who controlled the area from the 1890s to the 1910s. More than 500 thugs paid allegiance to the gang, making it a formidable force that even Monk Eastman's powerful mob avoided. The gang even had a juvenile section, the Baby Gophers, and a woman's branch, the Lady Gophers. Many other West Side gangs, like the Parlour Mob and the Rhodes

Gang acted as satellites of the Gophers and were on hand when needed to repel invasions from other gangs. The Gophers spawned some of New York's most notorious gangsters like One-Lung Curran, Goo-Goo Knox, Biff Ellison and Owney Madden.

Goo-Goo Knox was one of the leading members of the Gophers, but left to form his own gang, the Hudson Dusters, after trying unsuccessfully to wrest control of the gang from Marty Brennan. Knox was so highly thought of, that Brennan did not exact revenge. Later, the Dusters became allies of the Gophers and shared in the spoils of pilfering from the Hudson River waterfront. The Hudson Dusters went on to control the West Side below 13th Street and east to Broadway, bordering Paul Kelly's Five Points territory. The Dusters used the Golden Swan Bar, on the corner of 6th Avenue and 4th Street, as their headquarters. Variously called The Hell Hole, Bucket of Blood and other enticing nicknames, the saloons past stretched back as far as the first street gangs. Not far away was the Mousetrap - a wide and hazardous meeting of several busy streets - Waverly Place, West 4th Street and 7th Avenue, where in 1863, during the Draft Riots, a marauding mob assembled there and attacked the black community. Only for the protest of a large force of local people the mob would have strung some of them up. Around the turn of the century the Dusters became election specialists, earning the political protection of Tammany Hall. The gang disintegrated shortly before WW1, due to police arrests and drug addiction, leaving the way open for Tanner Smith's Marginals to take over the area.

Owen Vincent Madden graduated from the Gophers to become one of New York's most feared gangsters. Madden dreamed of becoming overlord of all of the city's rackets. Orphaned at an early age he came to New York from his native Liverpool in 1903 to live with an aunt in Hell's Kitchen. At the age of 11 he joined the Gophers and by the time he was 19 he had become the nominal leader of the gang. The Gophers aided Jimmy Hines to victory in the 1907 election for the Eleventh Assembly district. Between 1911 and 1914 the Gophers grew in size and influence, becoming election specialists and labour and protection racketeers. They began to move into the area controlled by the Hudson Dusters who forgot their alliance with the old Gophers and tried to kill the ambitious Madden. Eleven Dusters followed him to the Arbor Dance Hall on November 6 1912. Several Dusters surrounded him but Madden was unafraid, "C'mon youse guys!" he yelled. "Youse wouldn't shoot nobody! Who did youse ever bump off!" Undeterred the Dusters pumped eight bullets into Madden, leaving him for dead. While in hospital recovering from his wounds the Gophers knocked off six of the Dusters involved in the attack. Two years later Madden was jailed for 10 years after luring Little Patsy Doyle to a saloon on 8th Avenue and shooting him dead, for boasting that he was taking over the Gophers. By the time Madden was released in 1923 the Gophers were gone; its members were either dead, in jail or had joined the various bootlegging gangs battling for control of the illicit booze distribution racket.

The game had changed since Madden had gone to prison. Bootleg booze was the new racket, making more money for gangsters than all the other rackets combined. Throughout the Roaring Twenties Madden and other mobsters like Dutch Schultz, Legs Diamond, Mad Dog Coll and Waxey Gordon waged war for the control of distribution rights on the West Side. However, Owney Madden became the dominant force in the area and supplied much of the beer consumed in New York from his brewery, the Phoenix Cereal Beverage Company, located on 10th Avenue. Originally, Prohibition agents had pad-locked the brewery, but a tunnel had been drilled under the street to a warehouse where the beer-brewing continued.

Madden's police and political protection thwarted all attempts to raid the brewery. If strangers parked in the vicinity of the brewery they were immediately moved on by policemen, who appeared out of nowhere. There was a huge demand for Owney's high-quality beer, known as Madden's Number One and he supplied it to other gang leaders like Vannie Higgins and Dutch Schultz.

In 1932 Vincent Coll decided to cut himself into Madden's rackets. He informed "The Duke of the West Side" that he was becoming a partner in the Phoenix Brewery and proposed to bring Jack Marron, Owney's brother-in-law, for a one-way ride unless he received $100,000. (Coll had previously pocketed $35,000 after kidnapping Madden's partner Big Frenchy DeMange.) Marron, a local bail bondsman and Tammanyite, was terrified and appealed to Madden for protection. Owney contacted Coll and said he needed time to get the money together. The Mad Dog gave him two weeks but Coll was cornered in a phone booth in a drugstore on West 23rd Street, allegedly making a threatening phone call to Madden, when two men walked in and riddled him to death. A few months after Coll's demise Madden was arrested on a parole violation and imprisoned. He remained in jail for a year, despite newspaper reports that he offered a $1 million bribe to the state parole board. When Lucky Luciano and Meyer Lansky were forming the Syndicate Madden was included as a personal friend of Luciano's. Now Owney was sick of New York. He quit his rackets in the Big Apple and headed to Hot Springs, Arkansas, opening a health spa.

With the repeal of Prohibition in 1933 the mob needed replacement money making rackets and the New York waterfront became the mob's most profitable racket. Nothing moved in or out of the port without the mob getting their "dues". Infiltration of the docks and its workforce had been going on since the 1890s and throughout the 1930s and 40s the mob increased its stranglehold. They were so powerful the U.S. Navy even had to appeal to the mobsters sense of patriotism to stop sabotage and labour disputes hampering the war effort. Ruthless thugs like Johnny Dunn, Jeremiah Sullivan and Albert Anastasia threw themselves wholeheartedly into the war effort using mob tactics - including murder - to deal with the "problem". By the end of 1942 there were no acts of sabotage, no union disputes and no delays to Allied shipping. The waterfront was secure.

In that period the West Side's crowded tenements were still home to dozens of Irish gangsters. The chief mobsters were Eddie McGrath, Johnny "Cockeye" Dunn, Hughie Mulligan, Tough Willie McCabe and Elmer "Trigger" Burke. The most powerful racketeer was Eddie McGrath, a big red-haired thug who had started his criminal career as a beer truck driver for Owney Madden. He had a record of twelve arrests for crimes ranging from larceny to murder. He had ties to the Luciano crime family, the most powerful group in the country, and was closely connected to the West Side's most important Tammany politicians. McGrath was an ILA organiser for 15 years having been appointed an "organiser at large" by Joe Ryan, the union's president. Ryan owed his position and his control of the union to McGrath and Cockeye Dunn. McGrath's main muscle was his brother-in-law Cockeye Dunn and Andrew "Squint" Sheridan, a former gunman for Dutch Schultz. McGrath controlled the numbers racket throughout the West Side and was on intimate terms with Luciano, Meyer Lansky, Joe Adonis and Moe Dalitz. When Cockeye Dunn was on the lam for murder he hid out in Meyer Lansky's house in Miami. John Dunn was business agent for Local 21510. In 1948 he was convicted, along with Squint Sheridan and Daniel Gentile, of the 1947 murder of Boss Stevedore Anthony Hintz, who was slain in the hallway of his home in Greenwich Village. In court the widow testified that before he died Hintz said, "Maisie, I'm dying. Johnny Dunn shot me." Sheridan and Gentile were sentenced to life while Dunn, who was believed to have murdered 30 people, went swaggering and unrepentant to the electric chair in Sing Sing the following year for the murder.

With Hell's Kitchen as its base one of the most powerful locals was Local 824 of the ILA. Local 824 was known as the "Pistol Local" because its membership was made up of so many convicted thugs and leg-breakers. Harry Bowers was the local's boss, but the real power behind Local 824 was his cousin, Mickey Bowers, a McGrath hood. Bowers police record showed thirteen arrests between 1920 and 1940. He was believed to be behind the deaths of several rivals, including Tommy Gleason, gunned down in a 10th Avenue funeral parlour, a convenient place for a hit.

The West Side was always a violent place and few neighbourhoods have contributed more to the saga of New York gang history. Of all the gangs and gangsters the West Siders were always the most audacious. Elmer "Trigger" Burke was born in Hell's Kitchen in 1925 and orphaned at an early age. He was trained in crime by his older brother, Charlie. They operated as petty thieves on the mean streets of the West Side. Elmer, by the tender age of 10 was an incorrigible truant and he was sent to Elmira Reformatory three times by 1941. When America declared war on the Axis powers, Burke, in an effort to escape the reformatory, volunteered for duty with the U.S. Army. He did not like the army's discipline but he proved to be an aggressive soldier who loved handling weapons, especially the Thompson submachine gun. Sent overseas, Burke performed many heroic deeds in combat killing dozens of enemy soldiers, a job he seemed to enjoy. On one occasion he stormed a machine gun nest and killed 8 German soldiers. An officer had to restrain him later when he was still pumping bullets into the dead soldiers.

After the war, Burke went back to Hell's Kitchen and his criminal pursuits, robbing local stores and hiring himself out as a freelance killer, using his favourite weapon, the tommy gun, on rival gangsters and earning the sobriquet of "Trigger". Badly scarred by teenage acne the young killer was quick to fly off the handle. He would often stand at a bar in the West Side saloons knocking back shots of whiskey and making Jimmy Cagney faces. He was not possessed of great intelligence. One day in 1946 Burke held up a liquor store, pausing on the sidewalk so long to count his loot that the police arrived before he could make his getaway. He was sentenced to two years in Sing Sing for armed robbery.

While Elmer was in prison, his brother Charlie was killed by rival gangsters and Elmer vowed to avenge him. When he was released Elmer began hunting for his brother's killers. He killed several local hoods before deciding, without any real evidence, that his brother's killer was gangster rival, George Goll, who had been arrested and released after Charlie's murder. On February 24 1953 Trigger Burke caught Goll on a West Side street and shot him twice in the head. Burke was one of the most reliable freelance contract killers on the East Coast and the next year took on a contract to murder Brinks robber Specs O'Keefe in Boston. However, Burke was arrested in Boston in June 1954 after an unsuccessful gun attack on O'Keefe. Burke had an automatic in his pocket when arrested and police later found a machine gun, five revolvers and another automatic at his Boston address. Burke was wanted in New York for the February 1951 slaying of a truck driver. Three months later, on August 24, in one of the great jail escapes of the decade Joseph Connelly and Allen Locke broke into the prison and freed him. Burke was quickly recaptured in the Back Bay area and taken back to New York to stand trial for the murder of Edward "Poochy" Walsh.

On July 23 1952, in a West Side saloon, in front of several witnesses, Burke had shot Walsh in a fit of pique because he no longer wished to be called "Trigger", prefering the name "Killer". Trigger Burke was convicted of the murder of Poochy Walsh and was sentenced to die in the electric chair in Sing Sing. It was believed that he was responsible for the deaths of over 100 men, including those he killed in combat. On January 9 1958 Burke was executed after a steak meal followed by six cigars. He spent his last evening alive perusing his newspaper cuttings, including his war ones, which he wanted preserved for posterity.

Most West Side racketeers paid tribute to Eddie McGrath, as lord of Hell's Kitchen. He got his cut from all the rackets; hijacking, extortion, loansharking, numbers and the waterfront rackets. In the bustling post-war period the New York waterfront was extremely profitable for West Side gangsters. Hughie Mulligan, a short jowly man with thick-rimmed spectacles, served as a bookmaker for Eddie McGrath and a go-between for the neighbourhoods various ethnic factions. At the time the largely Irish police force did not like dealing with Italian gangsters so Mulligan ensured the Irish cops still got their bribes. Once during an investigation of police corruption, detectives hid a recording device in his car as he made the rounds from pier to pier making his collections. "Look at that bunch over there," he said sadly. "There ain't a white man in the bunch. Not a single fuckin' white man." The men he was referring to were a crew of Italians.

Profits from the waterfront rackets; pilfering, hijacking, payroll padding, no-show jobs, kick-backs, gambling and loansharking were enormous, the most prosperous period since the Prohibition era. However, like Prohibition it would have to end. In 1951 the Kefauver Committee first declared that racketeers were "firmly entrenched along New York City's waterfront". A year later governor Tom Dewey's New York Crime Commission Hearing began an investigation of ILA activities. By the end of the decade two-thirds of all transatlantic passengers arrived in New York by airplane and the waterfront began to decline. Idlewild airport replaced the waterfront as the main freight entrance. The decline in employment led to a decline in the Hell's Kitchen neighbourhood. Housing deteriorated and the middle-class occupants began to leave. Even the gangsters began to depart. Eddie McGrath retired to Florida in 1959, while his sidekick, Hughie Mulligan, retired to a respectable life in Queens village. He died in 1974.

The West Side rackets were left in the capable hands of Michael John "Mickey" Spillane, a one-time runner for Hughie Mulligan. Spillane had risen through the ranks to become king of the West Side. He was first arrested at 16, when he was shot and wounded by a patrolman while robbing a movie theatre. His arrest sheet would eventually grow and would include burglary, assault, gun possession, criminal contempt, kidnapping and illegal gambling. In 1960 the handsome, black-haired Spillane married Maureen McManus, daughter of Eugene McManus, Democratic Party district leader and nephew of Thomas J. "The" McManus, leader of the Midtown Democratic Club and an avid practitioner of Tammany Hall politics. Spillane continued his predecessors' relationship with the Mafia and the West Side rackets were evenly divided between the Hell's Kitchen Irish Mob and the Genovese and Gambino Families. The mobs divided the labour force and the unions at Madison Square Garden, the city's premier sports arena, located at 50th Street and 8th Avenue, between them. However, there was always a level of resentment and mistrust between the Irish and the Italian. The Irish, once the power in organised crime, never liked playing second fiddle to the Italians.

To show his independence and to keep his men placated Spillane kidnapped local merchants and Italian hoods, usually numbers men or loansharks. The Italians tolerated this once the ransom never exceeded the $10,000 range. (In 1970 Spillane was questioned in an inquiry into police corruption. He refused to answer questions until asked was he related to the Brooklyn-born writer of cops-and-robbers books, Mickey Spillane. "No," he replied. "But I'd be happy to change places with him at this moment." He got a laugh from his audience and 6 months for contempt from the judge.) Spillane liked to think he was a cut above the average gangster. He dressed sharply, helped people out with their financial problems and tried to look respectable, yet he was still a hood.

One night his men kidnapped a local accountant, John Coonan, who ran a tax service at West 50th Street. Coonan was taken to Spillane's White House Bar at 45th and 10th Avenue where he was slapped around by Spillane and a few cohorts until a ransom was paid. Coonan was released and chose to forget about the affair. Coonan's two sons, Jimmy and Jackie were different. They were not willing to let the insult go. For young Jimmy Coonan the humiliation would not go away. Jimmy knew he was too young and inexperienced to take over Spillane's rackets, so he began to make a name for himself, confronting Spillane wherever he could.

Coonan formed his own mob with Eddie Sullivan, a small-time burglar and bank robber from the East Side. Sullivan was fifteen years older than Coonan and an enemy of Spillane's, who with his twin brother Marty had given Sullivan a hiding in the White House Bar. On hearing that Sullivan was gunning for him Spillane put a contract out on Coonan's new partner, but Coonan and Sullivan got to the hitman, Little Bobby Lagville, first and shot him dead in Long Island City on March 23 1966. (They also drove over Little Bobby to make sure he was dead.) Several days later Jimmy Coonan opened up on Spillane and several of his top aides, including Tommy Collins, with a machine gun at West 46th Street.

The excited Coonan opened fire too soon with the grease gun and missed his targets. In the ensuing gun-battle Jackie Coonan, Jimmy's older brother, was shot in the leg, the only casualty in the shoot-out.

On April 3 1966 Jimmy Coonan, Sullivan and two accomplices picked up two innocent bar-hoppers, believing them to be out of town hitmen hired by Spillane, drove them to Queens and pumped bullets into them. One miraculously lived to tell the tale and Coonan and his pals were picked up. Sullivan was identified as the shooter and was given a life sentence while Coonan plea bargained and wound up getting five to ten for felonious assault. For the time being the Spillane-Coonan War was put on hold. When Coonan was released in 1970 he formed his own mob with a younger breed of criminals. These young toughs would eventually form the nucleus of the "Westies", what prosecutors called "the most savage organisation in the long history of New York City gangs."

In the bicentennial year of 1976 New York City was bankrupt. For months the mayor, Abraham Beame, had been cutting back on all city services. Working class and poor areas of the city were hardest hit. The streets were not swept and police patrols became fewer. Crime rose and Hell's Kitchen began to look like the South Bronx, New York's most notorious and crime-ridden ghetto. Fat Tony Salerno, boss of the Genovese Family began to look towards the Kitchen and a take-over of its rackets. On July 20 1976 Tom Devanney, one of Spillane's top aides, was shot dead in a bar-and-grill on Lexington Avenue. Exactly a month later on August 20 Eddie Cummiskey was drinking in the Sunbrite Bar on 10th Avenue, when a car pulled up outside and double-parked. A lone man got out, walked into the bar and fired one shot into the back of Cummiskey's head. The hitman was Joseph "Mad Dog" Sullivan, a free-lance killer. Sullivan was famous as the only one to escape from maximum security

Attica prison, the only one to do so in its forty year history. Sullivan had hidden in the back of a truck that left the prison in broad daylight. He was recaptured five weeks later strolling through Greenwich Village.

Eddie Cummiskey was Spillane's top muscle, and his killing was a mystery. He had lately become associated with the Coonan mob, rivals of Spillane. Like the Devanney hit there was no clear motive. On January 27 1977 another Spillane stalwart, Tom "The Greek" Kapatos was gunned down on West 34th Street. Spillane began to get the picture. Fat Tony Salerno was looking to establish control over the planned Jacob Javits Convention Centre, on 11th Avenue. The construction of one of the largest convention centres in the country promised to be a big money venture. Since Spillane controlled the neighbour-hood and the local unions he believed the convention centre was his and he told Salerno so. Fat Tony had other ideas. Spillane, fearing he was next on the hit list, moved his family from the West Side to Woodside, a working class Irish district in Queens.

On May 13 1977 a black Cadillac pulled up to an apartment building on 59th Street in Woodside, home of the now semi-retired Mickey Spillane. The driver got out, buzzed and spoke into the apartment block's intercom. He returned to the car. Several minutes later Mickey Spillane appeared from the build-ing and walked over to the car. As he bent down to talk to a passenger in the back of the car he was shot five times in the face, neck, chest, stomach and arm. The car sped away leav-ing Spillane dead on the street.

Spillane's funeral was the last big Irish mobster funeral on the West Side attended by thousands of mourners, including dozens of politicians. Fat Tony Salerno got what he wanted, control of the new convention centre. Mad Dog Sullivan, who had performed the killings of Devanney, Cummiskey and

Kapatos with the belief that he would get a slice of the action was double-crossed. A bitter Sullivan tried to join the Westies and planned to kill Salerno but it all turned to nothing. Coonan did not trust the Mad Dog and Sullivan was not strong enough to go after Salerno alone. Spillane's demise left the West Side the domain of Jimmy Coonan and his crew.

CHAPTER 18

THE WESTIES

The Westies were an Irish gang from Hell's Kitchen, best known for their tendency to dismember murder victims before disposing of them. The group had ties to the powerful Gambino Family and performed dozens of murders on their behalf.

The leader of the Westies, blond blue-eyed James Coonan, born in 1946, came from a middle-class family. His father was a certified public accountant who ran a tax service at West 50th Street. At the age of 17 Jimmy Coonan dropped out of school and began hanging around with local criminals engaging in petty acts of crime and violence. He ended up in Elmira Reformatory where the strong, hulking youngster brushed up on his boxing skills. In 1966 the ambitious nineteen year old attempted to wrest control of the West Side rackets from Mickey Spillane - the politically connected boss of Hell's Kitchen

Coonan had a grudge against Spillane, who had kidnapped Coonan's father and pistol-whipped him until a ransom was paid. Coonan invited Spillane to a meeting at West

46th Street, intending to kill Spillane and his top aides in one stroke. The murder attempt failed when the excited Coonan opened fire too soon and missed his targets.

Spillane swore revenge. He had a lot of power. He had a partnership with Fat Tony Salerno, boss of the Genovese Family and delivered the vote for the Democrats. Coonan formed his own gang with his older brother Jackie, two years his senior, Eddie Sullivan, a small time hood from the East Side, Bobby Huggard, an up-town con man and thief and several other young thugs from the West Side. On April 3 1966 Jimmy Coonan, Eddie Sullivan and two acquaintances, Billy Murtha and Jimmy Gallagher, picked up two innocent bar-hoppers, Charles Canelstein and Jerry Morales, at a bar on 46th Street and believing them to be out of town hitmen looking for Coonan and Sullivan, drove them to Queens where Sullivan shot both of them three times. Morales died but Canalstein, badly wounded and left for dead, survived. Canalstein identified Sullivan as the shooter and Jimmy Coonan, Billy Murtha and Jimmy Gallagher as his accomplices. All four were indicted. Sullivan was convicted and given a life sentence. Coonan plea bargained and wound up getting 5 to 10 for felonious assault. He served his time at an assortment of penal facilities, including Sing Sing where he was reunited with his brother Jackie - who was serving a manslaughter term for the shooting dead of a Brooklyn bartender killed in an attempted robbery.

Jimmy Coonan was released in 1970 and after a few months going straight restarted his criminal career as a hijacker, stick-up man and kidnapper. In 1973 he bought the 596 Club, a typical Hell's Kitchen saloon, on 10th Avenue. In the early 1970s a younger breed of West Side criminals began hanging out at the 596 Club. These young toughs would eventually form the nucleus of the Hell's Kitchen Irish Mob, or Coonan's Crew as they were known in the underworld, or as the police and press labelled them, the Westies.

Coonan became friends with Mickey Spillane's top muscle, Eddie "The Butcher" Cummiskey. The small bantam like Cummiskey, looked and acted like a gangster from the Roaring Twenties. He had once fled to Brazil on an ILA freighter to avoid a murder rap. He was widely feared on the West Side and rumoured to have killed at least a dozen rivals. Once, the small slight terror had got in a fight with a burly bartender and socked him one. "You hit like a little girl," the bartender taunted. Cummiskey produced a .38 and fired three bullets into the barman. "Oh, yeah?" he retorted. "Well, do I shoot like a little girl." The bartender was in no position to reply. He was dead. It was Cummiskey who showed Jimmy Coonan the art of dismembering a corpse. He had trained as a butcher in Attica, while serving 7 years on an assault and robbery conviction and was there during the infamous riot of 1971. He also showed Coonan where to dump his victims. He told Coonan that the underwater currents swirling around Wards Island, an outcrop in the East River, were so swift that if a corpse was punctured in the stomach and lungs it would sink and sail past the southern tip of Manhattan and then on out to sea without ever popping to the surface.

Coonan cemented his friendship with Cummiskey with the killing in 1975 of Paddy Dugan, a fellow Westie. Several months earlier Dugan had killed Dennis Curley after a drunken argument. Curley was a mutual friend of Coonan's and Cummiskey's. He was also Paddy Dugan's best friend. Cummiskey was waiting for a chance to get even. Coonan wanted to woo Cummiskey away from Spillane and what better way to do this than to do Cummiskey a favour. Dugan was also continuing his non-sanctioned shakedowns of loan sharks despite several warnings from Jimmy Coonan. It was further a good hit for business with drugs tearing the neighbourhood apart. (Dugan and Dennis Curley were also heroin users.) Coonan murdered Dugan and cut up the body with a machete. The severed fingers were added to a bag full of the fingers of other murder victims that Coonan carried around to frighten various people into being more co-operative. Coonan phoned Cummiskey and told him he was bringing Dugan to the 596 Club for a drink and to meet him. Dugan's severed head was brought to the tavern where Coonan propped it up on the bar and for the next few hours, Coonan, Cummiskey and members of the Westies toasted his memory, at one point lighting one of Dugan's favourite brand of cigarette and putting it in the head's mouth. The murder of Dugan was an example of Jimmy Coonan's savagery and a warning to others not to cross him. Dugan's body was never found. This tactic was called "doing the Houdini" by the Westies. Murder victims were dissected and ended up in the Hudson River or in a foundation on a mob connected building site.

The Westies were like something out of the Roaring Twenties, unlike their counterparts in the Mafia who were more sophisticated. Once top Westie Mickey Featherstone played Russian roulette for $1,000 a turn of a loaded pistol chamber. They were afraid of no one, murdering or maiming even Mafia hoods who were foolish enough to invade their territory. When Fat Tony Salerno began to cast his eyes on the West Side rackets by ordering the deaths of Eddie Cummiskey, Tom Devanney and Tom Kapatos the Westies struck back at the Mafia incursions with the murder of Charles "Ruby" Stein. Lured to the 596 Club, on May 5 1977, by Jimmy Coonan in a proposed business deal, the nervous Stein found several Westies waiting in the dimly lit tavern. He was no sooner sitting down when Danny Grillo, a Gambino hitman, came out of the kitchen and shot him six times. With the club's bartender, Tommy Hess, standing guard

Coonan told two other Westies to put a bullet into Stein. Billy Beattie shot Stein with a silenced .22 pistol and passed it to Richie Ryan who put another slug in the out of luck gangster. Stein's body was dismembered and dumped off Ward's Island - Cummiskey's old dumping grounds - where the currents were exceptionally strong. But Coonan neglected to puncture the lungs and Stein's torso washed up in Brooklyn. The Stein murder was the start of police investigations into the Westies. Previous investigations had been hampered by lack of corpses. This was the first time that a corpse had actually turned up.

Ruby Stein's murder was a signal to the Genovese Family that Jimmy Coonan and the Westies were a force to be reckoned with and their incursions into Hell's Kitchen would not he taken lightly. Ruby Stein was a big money maker for the New York families. He was a loanshark and a gambler and connected to James "Jimmy Nap" Napoli, the Mr. Big of New York gambling. Coonan was also in debt to Stein, to the tune of $70,000, as was Danny Grillo and a lot of other West Siders, including Mickey Spillane and Tommy Collins. Stein's death wiped out everyone's debts, which also made the hit good for business. Stein's boss, Napoli, was a made man with the Genoveses and had considerable influence working with all the New York families in their gambling rackets. Eight days later Mickey Spillane was shot dead in Queens and Fat Tony put John Sullivan in control of Spillane's rackets. Salerno believed Spillane was responsible for Stein's murder. The Gambinos thought otherwise.

When Carlo Gambino died in 1976 his brother-in-law Paul Castellano succeeded him. The diplomatic Castellano was increasingly agitated over the continued assaults, kidnappings and murders of Mafioso on the West Side. He summoned Jimmy Coonan and Mickey Featherstone - "the Irish kids", as he referred to them - to a meeting in Brooklyn. Coonan and Featherstone arrived at Tommaso's, a restaurant in the Bay

Ridge section of Brooklyn. Tommaso's was in Gambino turf and next door to a Gambino social club known as the Veterans and Friends. (Back in Hell's Kitchen Jackie Coonan and a hit squad of Westies awaited their chiefs return, with orders that if they were not back at an agreed hour they were to go to Tommaso's and kill everyone in the restaurant. Luckily, Jackie let the agreed hour pass.) Awaiting them was Big Paulie Castellano, his underboss Aniello Dellacroce, his *consigliere* Joe N. Gallo and two of his most powerful capos, Carmine Lombardozzi and Nino Gaggi. Also present was Gambino car-theft chief Roy DeMeo and a representative of the Genovese Family, underboss Funzi Tieri, an ally of Big Paulie.

Coonan denied any knowledge of Stein's murder and of the whereabouts of the old shylock's little black book, which had all the details of money owed. Castellano told Coonan from now on his men were to stop acting "like cowboys" and if he wanted anyone "removed" they had to get permission from Roy DeMeo or Nino Gaggi. The Westies could use the Gambino name on the West Side in return for which the gang would give the Family ten per cent of all money made.

The Westies who seemed to enjoy killing, would carry out contract murders for the Gambinos and in return for Westie influence on the docks and in the convention centers, Castellano gave the Irish Mob access to Gambino money at one per cent interest a week - the same rate charged family members. Castellano ordered his underboss, Aniello Dellacroce to set up a liaison. This turned out to be the deadly Roy DeMeo, Danny Grillo's boss. (DeMeo was aware of Grillo's part in the Stein murder, so it was in his best interests to convince Castellano that the Westies had nothing to do with the Stein hit.)

Another rising mob star, John Gotti, later replaced DeMeo as the liasion. A subsequent meeting between Coonan and Gotti resulted in a remarkable affinity between the two. Coonan was later to say admiringly to his men, "I just met a greaseball tougher than we are," while Gotti said of Coonan, "He's pretty good, a good kid, a good ballsy kid."

There was a sigh of relief from Mafia quarters. The Westies would continue killing but at least they were killing for the Mafia. For Coonan it was what he had worked for. Coonan had always admired the Mafia's organisational structure. He liked their ideas of respect. His crew did not and when the Irish Italophile tried to mix business and pleasure together by socialising with Mafiosi it usually ended up in a brawl between the two groups. Coonan's crew contemptuously referred to Mafia hoods as "Al Colognes". They found it hard to trust the Italians who they said were always plotting against each other.

With Coonan's new found friends the Westies soared to new heights. They began dressing in the *Saturday Night Fever* style popular in the Veterans and Friends social club. (Later the Westies adopted their own colours - black leather jackets, black shirts and pants and black woollen mittens and longshoreman's caps.) The gang - which had a hard core of about two dozen members - were involved in dozens of murders on behalf of the Gambinos. The Westies were so efficient their hitmen were over extended. First rate killers are never short of work. Many bodies were never found. Jimmy Coonan bought a mansion in Hazlet, New Jersey for his wife and their two children and lived like a king from his loansharking, labour racketeering and contract killings. In early 1981 Jimmy Coonan and Mickey Featherstone, his right hand man, were both jailed. Coonan for four years on a weapons possession charge and Featherstone on a counterfeit charge. Both had recently beaten a murder rap for the savage killing of small time hood, Harold "Whitey" Whitehead in a West Side bar, after Whitey had implied that Jackie Coonan was a "rat". The case had collapsed after two of the witnesses had "done the right thing" - killed themselves rather than testify.

With the jailing of Coonan and Featherstone the police thought they had broken the Westies. They were wrong. Even in Coonan and Featherstone's absence the Westies flourished. From prison Jimmy Coonan still controlled the gang. Given that he would be out in a few years it would be foolish for anyone to try and take over his position. His wife, Edna, made the rounds in Hell's Kitchen collecting his weekly payments on loansharking and waterfront kickbacks. Jimmy McElroy and Richie Ryan, his two most trusted men, sometimes accompanied her. In Jimmy's absence one of the Westies most lucrative rackets continued to stem from their relationship with the Mafia, through Vinnie Leone, a Gambino Family capo and business manager of ILA Local 1909. Leone helped lead the Westies into new areas of extortion, like the outdoor concerts on Pier 82, sponsored by the Miller Brewing Company and featuring such popular international superstars as Elton John and Diana Ross. Any stagehand and carpenter working the concerts kick-backed a portion of their wages to the local, which was split between the Westies and Leone. They also co-operated in infiltrating unions that represented personal working aboard the *U.S.S. Intrepid,* which was docked directly across from Local 1909 offices at West 48th Street. The massive aircraft carrier was opened as a floating museum in 1982. The *Intrepid* had seen action in WW2 and Vietnam and had survived Japanese kamikaze attacks but was nearly sunk by a sophisticated skimming scheme. The ILA controlled around thirty jobs on board, including ticket takers, engineers and general maintenance. These were doled out to Westie members and their spouses. Between the no-show highly paid jobs and the siphoning off of ticket receipts the museum was nearly driven into bankruptcy. Additionally, and perhaps the most lucrative of rackets, was the infiltration of Local 817, the theatrical truckers union that delivered props and cameras to and from movie locations. Many Westies held union cards but never showed up for work only to collect their wages. Because of the increase in movies and commercials being filmed in New York, Local 817 became among the highest paid of any Teamster local in the city; a field boss could earn $2,000 a week, a driver $1,800 and a helper $1,600. An ex-boxer James Patrick "Studs" McElroy, born in 1945 the son of an Irish longshoreman, was a top enforcer with the Westies, a suspect in at least six murders. "I killed a number of men for Coonan," he once said, "without pay, to show that Jimmy Coonan had men who would kill." McElroy's presentencing report stated that he had once threatened "to kill one member per week of Teamsters Union Local 817 unless he received a no-show job."

The Westies also moved into narcotics, a racket Jimmy Coonan had always frowned on. Mickey Spillane's old acquaintance, Tommy Collins, his wife Flo and their son Michael and several other Westies became major cocaine dealers. Not only were the Westies becoming dealers, they were also becoming users. Jackie Coonan was shooting coke into his veins, as was Richie Ryan, who was becoming totally out of control. On the night of February 26 1982 Ryan barged into the 596 Club and pistol whipped the bartender, Tommy Hess, for the crime of slapping one of his girlfriends. Then, in front of numerous witnesses, Ryan pulled Hess's trousers down around his ankles, stuck a gun up his rectum and squeezed the trigger. When the police arrived, Hess was dead and the bar empty. The 596 Club (Coonan had sold it in 1979) was closed down and reopened as a "respectable" bar for the newer yuppie residents of "Clinton". The Hess murder was a particular act of savagery that belied the slow disintegration of the Westies. Jealousy and deceit was tearing the gang apart. Many of the gang resented Edna Coonan and her interference in gang matters. Drink and drugs played its part, too. On September 20

1983 Richie Ryan was found dead at the bottom of a flight of stairs in a tenement building at West 48th Street. The twenty-nine year old had died of an alcohol and drugs overdose.

Mickey Featherstone was released from jail in 1983 and ended up running the waterfront rackets with Jimmy McElroy and Kevin Kelly, a twenty-eight year old ambitious thug, who was married to a niece of Jimmy Mac's and now the man most likely to succeed Jimmy Coonan. On February 11 1984 Kelly and McElroy murdered Vinnie Leone on the orders of John Gotti. Leone was suspected of skimming loansharking profits from Paulie Castellano. After a bout of drinking McElroy was driving Leone to his home in New Jersey while Kelly sat in the back seat. McElroy pulled the car off the expressway in Guttenberg, New Jersey, and suggested they do some cocaine. Without warning Kelly leaned forward and fired six shots into the back of Leone's head. "Nobody steals from us," McElroy was reported as saying.

In December 1984 Jimmy Coonan was released from jail and took over the reins of his crumbling empire. The sophisti-cated gang that Coonan had strived to build (as a prelude to an alliance between the Boston and New York Irish Mafia, Jimmy and Jackie Coonan and Mickey Featherstone had once flew to Boston to help Michael "Pete" Wilson, a fellow Irish gang leader who had served time with Jimmy C. in Sing Sing, to rob a pharmaceutical warehouse) was beginning to self destruct in deceit, petty jealousy and resentment against Coonan and particularly his wife Edna. Coonan and his once right hand man, Featherstone were now plotting to get rid of each other. On March 29 1986 Featherstone was convicted of the 1985 murder of Michael Holly, a former bar owner who the Westies held responsible for the murder of one of their members, John Bokun, in 1977. Featherstone denied he had murdered Holly and it was common knowledge on the West Side that Billy

Bokun had finally avenged his brother's death. However, several witnesses picked Featherstone from a police line-up and he was convicted of the killing. Featherstone believed he was set up by Coonan and the Westies and faced with a life sentence he turned state's evidence and with his wife Sissy began taping conversation's with several Westies. (With this evidence Featherstones conviction was eventually overturned. Billy Bokun later admitted killing Holly and was convicted of his murder.)

Meanwhile, John Gotti had become leader of the Gambino Family by ordering the murder of his boss Paul Castellano, who was shot dead along with his underboss, Thomas Bilotti, outside Sparks Steak House on East 46th Street on December 16 1985. Within days Gotti assumed the mantle of boss of the family. Gotti was a tougher and more ruthless leader than Castellano, who thought of himself more of a businessman than a hood and who was despised by his men and the other New York Mafia bosses. The change of leadership of the Gambino Family changed nothing for the Westies. They continued killing for the Gambinos. In June 1986 they murdered Robert DiBernardo, a Gambino capo who was skimming money earned from the concrete-industry bid-rigging scheme which he was to invest in legitimate enterprises. There were rumours that DiBernardo could turn informant and that he had also forged links with the Genoveses.

John Gotti became known as the "Teflon Don" because the authorities could not convict him on any of the numerous charges he was arrested on. Gotti was targeted with all the resources available to law enforcement, including a bug, secreted by the State Organised Crime Task Force, at the Bergin Hunt and Fish Club in Queens - hang-out and headquarters for Gotti's crew. In February 1986 John O'Connor, the business agent of the United Brotherhood of Carpenters and Joiners of

America Local 608, paid a call to the new Bankers and Brokers restaurant that was under construction at Battery Park City. O'Connor was one of New York's most powerful labour leaders, a notoriously corrupt and imposing figure who was capable of shutting down any construction project unless union men were on the job. He informed the owners of the new restaurant that since the work crews were non-union there could be "a problem". The owners offered O'Connor $5,000 to overlook this "problem". O'Connor took the $5,000 then came back for more. He was rebuked and thrown out of the restaurant. Several days later a gang of labour union thugs wielding crowbars caused $30,000 worth of damage in one hour. The restaurant, however, had a silent partner - John Gotti. Angelo Ruggerio reported the incident to Gotti. "We're gonna, bust him up." Gotti ordered. (This was overheard on the FBI bug at the Bergin.)

Ruggerio, who had replaced Gotti as liaison with the Westies, when Gotti had become boss, gave the job to the Westies. Early on the morning of May 7 Kevin Kelly and Kenny Shannon drove to the offices of Carpenters Local 608 near 51st Street and Broadway. Kelly followed O'Connor into the lobby and shot him four times below the waist, in the buttocks and the legs, as he entered the elevator. They had orders not to kill him, only to warn him. Kelly later said he shot O'Connor in the buttocks because "he was a pain in the ass," and said "O'Connor has a new asshole." While recuperating in hospital, O'Connor told police that he had been waylaid by "Puerto Rican gunmen." Why, he insisted? he just did not know. O'Connor later claimed his shooting had nothing to do with Gotti but was part of inter-union rivalry between himself and the union's president Pascal McGuinness. After a month in hospital he was released and arrested on127 charges of bribery, extortion, coercion and grand larceny in connection with his union activities. Mob informer Mickey Featherstone wore a concealed microphone in prison and secretly taped conversations with Kevin Kelly and Kenny Shannon when they came to visit him. They freely discussed the O'Connor shooting saying "We did it for the greaseballs."

Armed with Featherstone's evidence the police began a large scale crackdown on the Westies. (Gentrification had probably done more to force the Westies out of Hell's Kitchen rather than law enforcement. Many of the old tenements were torn down and replaced by condos and apartment buildings. The Irish and Italian population were replaced by an upwardly mobile population. The gangsters were going too. John Sullivan retired to Florida and Jimmy Coonan had gone practically legit, investing in Marine Construction, a large contracting firm based north of the city in Tarrytown. In Coonan's absence the remains of the West Side rackets were taken over by Kevin Kelly and Kenny Shannon.) Federal agents raided the offices of Teamster Local 817 and ILA Local 1909 and seized files. Another Westie, Billy Beattie, arrested on a murder charge, turned state's evidence while several others connected to the gang also went into the witness protection programme.

In late November and December 1986, after months of surveillance and a build-up of tons of evidence, the police struck. Jimmy Coonan, who had gone underground, was captured at his hideaway in Jersey, while his wife was arrested at their family home in Hazlet. Others like Jimmy McElroy, Billy Bokun, Mugsy Ritter, Johnny Halo and Flo Collins (Tommy Collins was already in jail on a narcotics charge) were quickly rounded up. Kevin Kelly and Kenny Shannon could not be found. Rumour had it that they were hiding out in Ireland.

Of all the evidence amassed against the Westies, Mickey Featherstone's was the most damning. Featherstone had been part of the gang from the start. Born in Hell's Kitchen in 1949 Featherstone came from a troubled background. His father left home when Mickey was six, leaving his mother to raise him and his two brothers and three sisters. When he was 17 he enlisted in the army as an escape from poverty and violence. His mother had remarried and Mickey was one of four brothers in the service. He was sent to Vietnam in 1966 and assigned to an ordnance supply unit attached to the Green Berets. When he returned from overseas he had a drink and drug problem. After been involved in several violent incidents in the neighbourhood - including one in which a youth died of head injuries - Featherstone, diagnosed as having a nervous condition brought on by his Vietnam experience, was discharged from the army. Within months of being diagnosed a "paranoid schizophrenic" by a V.A. hospital he had killed two people in drunken brawls. He was found not guilty of murder due to a "mental defect." In 1976 he joined the Westies, eventually becoming Jimmy Coonan's right hand man and one of his most trusted friends. He was suspected of murdering at least a dozen people, including Mickey Spillane. However, he claimed he never dismembered corpses, because it made him sick. Featherstone revealed many secrets of the gangs activities to the FBI. he told how Coonan had chopped the hands off a victim and kept them in a freezer for false fingerprints in a future crime. The murders of Paddy Dugan, Ruby Stein, Whitey Whitehead and dozens more were revealed in grim fashion. The residents of Hell's Kitchen were shocked at the scale of violence.

Mickey Featherstone was sentenced to five years probation (a lenient sentence after admitting to fourteen charges of racketeering, including four murders, five conspiracies to murder, loansharking, extortion, numbers, counterfeiting and distribution of drugs) and was released into the Witness Protection Programme - he had already served three-and-a-half years on the Holly murder. On March 26 1988 Rudolph Guiliani, U.S. Attorney for the Southern District of New York, announced that ten people were been charged on fourteen counts with having taken part in a "racketeering conspiracy". The charges dated back to 1966 and included sixteen murders, attempted murders and conspiracies to commit murder. These charges, assured Guiliani, would finally bring an end to "the most savage organisation in the long history of New York City gangs." The trial lasted four months. Except for Johnny Halo, who was acquitted of all charges, the rest of the defendants, including Tommy Collins, who was not a member of the Westies, were found guilty on all fourteen counts.

Jimmy Coonan was sentenced to seventy-five years without parole and fined $1 million. He was sent to the harshest prison in the federal system, maximum security U.S. penitentiary in Marion, Illinois. Jimmy McElroy received sixty years, Billy Bokun fifty years; Mugsy Ritter forty years; Tommy Collins forty years - all with a recommendation of no parole. Flo Collins was given six months on a narcotics charge. The last to be sentenced was Edna Coonan, who stood before the judge holding her husband's hand. Jimmy Coonan had read a statement claiming that she was guilty of nothing other than been his wife. The judge, and the evidence, thought otherwise. He sentenced her to fifteen years plus $200,000 in fines.

In August 1988 Kevin Kelly and Kenny Shannon turned themselves in after nearly two years on the run. The reason, their attorney said, "It's tough being on the run. They wanted to see their families." They were convicted on murder and racketeering charges in their absence and were sent to serve their sentences. Shannon had been convicted of murder and racketeering and Kelly of racketeering.

Jackie Coonan, a cocaine user, contacted AIDS from a contaminated needle and died at the age of forty-four on April 24 1988 just two weeks before the Westies were sentenced. Eddie Coonan was given a three year suspended sentence for tampering with a government witness - Billy Beattie. The Westies were broken. The last of the New York's Irish mobs was no more. The Hell's Kitchen Irish Mob was the last vestige of a culture and a community that would never be seen again.

EPILOGUE

Following WW2 and through the 1950s Irish-Americans began moving form working-class to middle-class neighbourhoods. The old inner city neighbourhoods were abandoned for the suburbs. The new stable and more conservative middle-class communities were in considerable contrast to the vicious slums which had nourished the likes of Mad Dog Coll and Cockeye Dunn. As the communities that had bred organised crime changed, organised crime itself changed. Except for small pockets, the Irish were becoming less and less involved. The Jews, like the Irish, were making the best of the American education system and climbing the social ladder making the pool of available candidates smaller. Only in Italian communities membership remained adequate enough to fill the vacuum. Drugs became the new craze, akin to liquor in Prohibition times. The Mafia became the dominant force in organised crime and has remained so to this day.

Irish-American working-class neighbourhoods still exist in New York, Boston, Philadelphia and San Francisco and while their are underprivileged Irish-Americans there will always be recruits for criminal gangs. Besides it's a tradition spanning one-and-a-half centuries. In New York the old West Side bars which had housed the Westies and their predecessors are home to yuppies and the leather brigade. There are very few Irish gangsters left in the city. In Boston there are three predominantly Irish gangs, all of them working closely with the New England Mafia, while in Philadelphia there are several dozen Irish gangsters tied to the dominant Mafia crime family.

Irish gangsters may be alive and kicking but they are no longer a major influence in organised crime. That is the monopoly of the new breed of ghetto criminals.

INDEX